Luminos is the Open Access monograph publishing program from UC Press. Luminos provides a framework for preserving and reinvigorating monograph publishing for the future and increases the reach and visibility of important scholarly work. Titles published in the UC Press Luminos model are published with the same high standards for selection, peer review, production, and marketing as those in our traditional program. www.luminosoa.org

Possible Histories

AMERICAN CROSSROADS

Edited by Earl Lewis, George Lipsitz, George Sánchez, Dana Takagi, Laura Briggs, and Nikhil Pal Singh

Possible Histories

Arab Americans and the Queer Ecology of Peddling

Charlotte Karem Albrecht

UNIVERSITY OF CALIFORNIA PRESS

University of California Press
Oakland, California

Suggested citation: Karem Albrecht, C. *Possible Histories: Arab Americans and the Queer Ecology of Peddling*. Oakland: University of California Press, 2023. DOI: https://doi.org/10.1525/luminos.140

Library of Congress Cataloging-in-Publication Data

Names: Karem Albrecht, Charlotte, author.
Title: Possible histories : Arab Americans and the queer ecology of
    peddling / Charlotte Karem Albrecht.
Other titles: American crossroads ; vol 70.
Description: Oakland, California : University of California Press, [2023] |
    Series: American crossroads ; vol 70 | Includes bibliographical references
    and index.
Identifiers: LCCN 2022026740 (print) | LCCN 2022026741 (ebook) |
    ISBN 9780520391727 (paperback) | ISBN 9780520391741 (ebook)
Subjects: LCSH: Syrian Americans—Social conditions. | Syrian
    Americans—Economic conditions. | Peddlers—Social networks—
    United States. | Sexual orientation—United States.
Classification: LCC E184.S98 A43 2023 (print) | LCC E184.S98 (ebook) |
    DDC 305.892/75691073—dc23/eng/20220902

LC record available at https://lccn.loc.gov/2022026740
LC ebook record available at https://lccn.loc.gov/2022026741

Manufactured in the United States of America

32 31 30 29 28 27 26 25 24 23
10 9 8 7 6 5 4 3 2 1

To my father, who always supported and loved me

To my mother, who graciously answers my probing questions about her life

To the Karem and Abboud women who came before me

CONTENTS

I first heard about my great-grandfather Nicholas Karem as a young adult in my early twenties. My mother told me about him a few months after I came out to my parents. Living in Kentucky in the early twentieth century, he had married another young Syrian immigrant, named Mary, and the two went on to have nine children together. He was known for being a demanding employer, a strict father, and a sweetheart to his grandchildren. All of his boys worked in the family's twenty-four-hour restaurant, with the oldest son running the night shift on his own.

My great-grandfather, working alongside his wife and sister, owned and operated this business in Louisville, a racially segregated southern city. Their customers consisted largely of white truck drivers and Black laborers from Louisville's Haymarket area, where the restaurant was situated. The eatery, named Trucker's Restaurant, was specifically marketed toward a white clientele. While white customers ate inside the restaurant, Black customers could order inside—but, by the Karems' mandate, and in accordance with white supremacist norms, Black customers were then required to leave the restaurant to eat their food. This restaurant remained financially successful for my family until the construction of a freeway closed the original site of the Haymarket in 1962.

But my great-grandfather was also up to things that made people talk, according to my mother. His sexual encounters were not confined to his marriage. The evidence that my family—and the larger Syrian community in Louisville—offered to back up this claim was that he was assaulted on more than one occasion related to his sexual behavior. I have no way of knowing what was actually said or speculated during his lifetime; but by the time the rumor got to my generation, after I came out to my mother, I was told that he was bisexual and that he had been "beaten up for cruising." How these assaults that my great-grandfather experienced happened is unclear. Did rumor of his sexual desire incur such attacks, or did his attempts at sexual encounters with men result in violence? Was it, perhaps, the race of the men he might have engaged with sexually that led to this violence? Or was it his own liminal racial status? Did he have sexual encounters with other men in the Syrian community? Did he frequent a particular locale that may have been associated with nonnormative sexuality or that was heavily policed?

I have attempted to find arrest records to corroborate this story but to no avail. My mother suggested that there are no records because her own mother (Nicholas's daughter-in-law) was friends with the wife of a police officer who intervened on her behalf and prevented my great-grandfather's arrest. White supremacy structures a critical juncture in my family's history through this possible protection from police arrest. Just as our family-owned restaurant abided by southern racist customs, white supremacy provided my family with a layer of protection, insulating it from the racist and heteropatriarchal purview of law enforcement.

While my great-grandfather's potential encounter with the police is not archived, whatever did happen to spur this rumor had lasting consequences for him and our family among other Syrian (and later, Lebanese) locals. I have been told that sometime in the past two decades, a younger family member approached someone at a Louisville gathering whom he recognized as a Lebanese elder. He identified himself and told the man that my great-grandfather was his relative. The elder replied sharply, "Nick Karem? Nick Karem was a queer." And several years ago, an undergraduate student of a colleague contacted me after having read my dissertation, which formed the early research for this book. They described themselves as a young queer Arab American who was also descended from early Syrian immigrants. As it turned out, we were related through marriage, and both our ancestors had settled in Louisville. This young student's maternal relatives knew all about the rumors surrounding Nick Karem's life.

The rumor of his sexuality continued long after one imagines it would have. It functioned to ostracize my ancestor and his family from the local Syrian community. The gossip presumed that Nick and his family should feel shame for his desire, his actions, and the violence done to him. The rumor continues to circulate as a source of shame, communicating that his violation of sexual and gendered norms points to an intractable difference that ought to be minimized. Compounded by the already racialized difference of being Arab in the United States, the rumor teaches lessons about sexual and gendered expectations for Lebanese Americans in my family. Despite this legacy of shame, the rumor about my great-grandfather has taken on a second life, as it seems also to provide evidence to queer family members that our existence as queer Lebanese Americans is nothing new.

I have been told by family members that to continue circulating this rumor, as I am doing now, is unfair to my ancestor, as he is not able to defend himself against the accusation. This concern assumes, of course, that his deviation from heterosexuality and the punishing assaults he experienced possibly as a result are blights upon his memory. To either circulate or deny the rumor would inscribe his life and memory within forms of violence. Circulating the rumor relegates his desires to their outcome, that is, violent physical punishment; denying it disciplines his sexual desires into a heteronormativity forged through white supremacy. But can we imagine other ways in which he may have experienced desire and pleasure in his life, outside this evidence of his sexual existence? This rumor, with its focus on violence as evidence of sexuality-as-shame, leaves no room to imagine desire and pleasure as part of Arab American history and existence. It obscures the fuller dimensions of how my great-grandfather (and other queer Arab ancestors) loved, desired, and experienced a range of erotic intimacies during their lives.

I share this story because it was one of the early sites of inquiry that framed my entry into the historicist study of Arab Americans, sexuality, and race. This story was compelling for multiple reasons. It circulated as a kind of evidence of queerness in the Arab American past (especially among members of my family who were not heterosexual). It suggested the power of sexuality as a lasting rubric for self-policing in Arab American communities. And it called into question how we produce knowledge about the Arab American past. If the only evidence of historical queerness in a particular community comes through rumor, what can we say we truly know about sexuality and its imbrication with race in the early Syrian American diaspora? In the pages that follow, these questions of method unfold alongside an examination of the inextricability of sexuality from race in Arab American history.

ACKNOWLEDGMENTS

The research and writing of this book has spanned more than fifteen years, across multiple jobs and institutions, through illness and loss, and through a global pandemic. Producing a work like this is far from a solitary practice, and there are many people to whom I am grateful. While I would like to say that I have kept diligent records of every person along the way who has helped or supported me in some way, the past several years especially have tested my capacity for memory and organization. Please forgive any omissions.

I am grateful for several forms of institutional support that allowed me time and resources to work on this manuscript. These include the Francis Maria Fellowship in Arab American studies at the University of Minnesota's Immigration History Research Center, a postdoctoral fellowship at Denison University through the Consortium for Faculty Diversity, a fellowship at the University of Michigan's Institute for the Humanities, and an ADVANCE Summer Writing Grant from the University of Michigan.

This book began as doctoral research at the University of Minnesota. I am thankful for the guidance and support I received from so many people in the Twin Cities. I was incredibly lucky to have a wonderful advisor and doctoral committee: Jigna Desai, Sarah Gualtieri, Regina Kunzel, Erika Lee, and Shaden Tageldin. I am forever grateful for your support and collective interdisciplinary wisdom. Many graduate school and Twin Cities friends have nurtured me and this project, including Cathryn Merla-Watson, Elizabeth Ault, Emily Smith Beitiks, Jasmine Kar Tang, Jessica Giusti, Juliana Hu Pegues, Karissa White, Kelly Condit-Shrethsa, Myrl Beam, Rushaan Kumar, Ryan Cartwright, Simi Kang, Anne Jin Soo Preston, Bao Phi, Darren Lee, Ethan Laubach, Jna Shelomith, Reema Bazzy, Charissa Blue, Charissa Uemura, Marie Michael, Sharon Goens, Sun Yung Shin, Thea Lee, Kathy

Haddad, Lana Barkawi, and the whole Mizna family. David Chang enthusiastically talked with me about my project and offered suggestions when I walked into his office as a graduate student. Other faculty offered sources, encouragement, and affirmation throughout the dissertation process, including Lisa Albrecht, Joe Kadi, J. Kehaulani Kauanui, and Trica Keaton.

I have been humbled by the generosity of many people who have read parts or all of the manuscript at different stages and given me feedback. Jocelyn Stitt was a godsend for preparing fellowship application narratives, which also helped me to better conceptualize my project for a wider audience. Umayyah Cable and Nadine Naber generously offered to read and comment on my introduction and both provided key insights into framing the project's interventions. Phil Deloria helpfully read and suggested developments on an early version of chapter 1. The fellows of the Institute for the Humanities at the University of Michigan were generous and attentive readers of a later version of chapter 1, and they were also an amazing group of people who helped me to find enthusiasm for my book after a difficult period. Many thanks to those folks: Alena Aniskiewicz, Sahin Acikgoz, Marlyse Baptista, Joel Batterman, Megan Berhend, Nick Caverly, Sara Ensor, Zehra Hashmi, Kyle Frisina, Dan Kim, Heidi Kumao, Petra Kuppers, Ashley Lucas, Peggy McCracken, Sara McDougall, Diana Ng, Tiffany Ng, Shira Schwartz, Scott Stonington, and Elizabeth Tacke. Tracey Deutsch, Sally Howell, and an anonymous reader offered much guidance and feedback on an early version of chapter 2 that was submitted as an article to *Gender and History*. Retika Adhikari, Manan Desai, Allan Lumba, and Balbir Singh gave me excellent suggestions on an earlier version of chapter 4. Thank you to Evelyn Alsultany, Greg Dowd, Leela Fernandes, and Dean Hubbs, each of whom carefully read and offered feedback on an early version of this manuscript. Carol Fadda also offered insightful comments and helped affirm the direction of the book at a crucial moment in its trajectory. I am very appreciative of the work that Sarah Gualtieri, Anthony Mora, Nadine Naber, and Valerie Traub put into my manuscript workshop as readers. Your comments were instrumental in moving my manuscript out of the dissertation framework and into a compelling book. I am equally appreciative of all of my colleagues who participated in my manuscript workshop or supported me at other points in the manuscript writing process: Stephen Berrey, Rosie Ceballo, Matthew Countryman, Greg Dowd, Sandra Gunning, Jesse Hoffnung-Garskoff, Jennifer Jones, Leila Kawar, Su'ad Abdul Khabeer, Larry LaFountain-Stokes, Diana Louis, Sarah Murray, Ava Purkiss, Alex Stern, and Ruby Tapia. Finally, I am indebted to the three readers who gave their time to review my manuscript for the University of California Press, including Amira Jarmakani and Nayan Shah. Your comments were very generous, and I cannot understate how much they helped me to see more clearly what this manuscript was doing and where I could press further. Many of the suggestions I did not take were due to the limited time I had left in which to complete the manuscript.

I am fortunate to have a supportive intellectual community across several institutions and associations and, in particular, through the Arab American Studies Association, many of whom have already been named here. Thank you to my colleagues in the Women's Studies program at Denison University and in the departments of American Culture and Women's and Gender Studies at the University of Michigan. Thank you as well to Tahereh Aghdasifar, Leila Ben Nasr, Louise Cainkar, Meiver de la Cruz, Stacy Fahrenthold, Suad Joseph, Nadeen Kharputly, Neda Maghbouleh, Rachel Norman, Isis Nusair, Dana Olwan, Shaista Patel, Therí Pickens, Therese Saliba, Kristin Shamas, Mejdulene Shomali, Matt Stiffler, Randa Tawil, Stan Thangaraj, Pauline Homsi Vinson, and many others. I am also grateful to the generation of Arab American studies scholars who created paths when there were none, especially Alixa Naff.

Without the labor of a bevy of research assistants, librarians, archivists, editors, and other staff, this work would not have been possible. First, thank you to all of the staff of the American Culture and Women's and Gender Studies departments, especially Donna Ainsworth, Sarah Ellerholz, Mary Freiman, Judy Gray, Patti Mackmiller, Marlene Moore, Kevin O'Neill, Kate Sechler, and the late Tammy Zill. Thank you to Iman Ali, Haleemah Aqel, Ryah Aqel, Sena Duran, Belquis Elhadi, Yahya Hafez, Irene Inatty, Alice Mishkin, Raya Naamneh, Will O'Neal, and Dahlia Petrus, for the research assistance, translation and transliteration work, conversation, and enthusiasm for my work. Thank you to Meredith Kahn, Evryn Kopf, and all of the wonderful librarians at the University of Michigan for your expertise and assistance. Thank you to Vanessa Brouchard and Kay Peterson of the National Museum of American History for your assistance with the Faris and Yamna Naff Collection over the years. Kim Greene and Jeannette Fast Redmond provided much needed editing of the manuscript at different stages throughout the process. Erika Clowes was the best writing coach and motivator that I could ask for. Thank you to Sherri Barnes for indexing and to Steven Baker for copyediting. And, of course, thank you to the fine people at the University of California Press for your stewardship of this project, from fledgling draft manuscript to published book. I especially want to thank Niels Hooper, Naja Pulliam Collins, and Julie Van Pelt.

Completing this book would not have been possible without the love and support of my friends and family. Evelyn Alsultany has been an indefatigable mentor who also became a cherished friend. Your support has meant the world to me. Thank you to Retika Adhikari, Tahereh Aghdasifar, Umayyah Cable, William Calvo-Quirós, Nilo Couret, Kristen Cole, Clare Croft, Anna Fisher, Manan Desai, Jessica Guisti, Jennifer Jones, Nancy Khalil, Aliyah Khan, Heidi Kumao, Scott Larson, Chelsea Lisiecki, Diana Louis, Allan Lumba, Sara McClelland, Victor Mendoza, Yasmin Moll, Jennifer Murray, Diana Ng, Tiffany Ng, Dana Olwan, Cristina Perez, Dahlia Petrus, Ava Purkiss, Deborah Rosenstein, Mejdulene Shomali, Balbir Singh, Antoine Traisnel, and Jessica Walker for the laughs, walks, texts, phone calls, work dates, group chats, meals, memes, and care. I am grateful for my brother, Matt, and my sister, Emily, for your support, kindness, and love. Thanks too for bringing some exceptionally good humans into the family (Erica, Annie, Wendy, Kenyatte, and Barb) and for producing some smaller humans I truly love (Lindsey, Zack, Xavier, and Aaliyah). With words I cannot express, I am infinitely grateful for my father, Ken, who did not live to see the publication of this book but who cheered me on every step of the way. I thank my mother, Connie, who has always been a source of inspiration, love, and kindness. She has never wavered in her faith in me and her support for my work. And finally, all of my love and gratitude to Katie, who has stood by me and cared for the human beyond the scholar for so many years. Thank you for sharing your deep well of compassion with me.

• • •

Parts of the introduction appeared as "Why Arab American History Needs Queer of Color Critique" in the *Journal of American Ethnic History* 37, no. 3 (Spring 2018). Parts of the introduction and chapter 1 appeared as "Narrating Arab American History: The Peddling Thesis" in *Arab Studies Quarterly* 37, no. 1 (Winter 2015), which was reprinted in *Sajjilu Arab American: A Reader in SWANA Studies*, edited by Louise Cainkar, Amira Jarmakani, and Pauline Homsi Vinson (Syracuse, NY: Syracuse University Press, 2022). An early version of chapter 2 appeared as "An Archive of Difference: Syrian Women Peddlers and U.S. Social Welfare, 1880–1935" in *Gender and History* 28, no. 1 (March 2018), which was reprinted in *Arab American Women: Representation and Refusal*, edited by Louise Cainkar, Suad Joseph, and Michael Suleiman (Syracuse, NY: Syracuse University Press, 2021).

Throughout this book, I use the term "Syrian" to refer to Arab people coming from the region of Greater Syria under the Ottoman Empire (or "Ottoman Syria"). Ottoman Syria, also called Bilad al-Sham in Arabic, covered the geographies of present-day Lebanon, Syria, Israel/Occupied Palestine, and parts of Jordan. "Syrian" is also the term these migrants used to refer to themselves during the time period described in this book, in English and later in Arabic. They also referred to themselves as "Arab," primarily in Arabic.

In addition to "Ottoman Syria," I use several additional terms to refer to the region from which these individuals migrated, including the "Middle East" and the "Levant." At times, I also use the "Middle East and North Africa" (or MENA) to refer to a broader geographic region, as well as "Southwest Asia and North Africa" (or SWANA). As a term, SWANA repositions part of this region as being within the Asian continent and reorients it away from the perspective of Europe.

Arabic in the text follows the *International Journal of Middle East Studies'* simplified system for transliteration, with all diacritical marks removed except for the ʿayn and the hamza. Transliterations of names appear with the spellings that those individuals themselves used where applicable. I am indebted to Ryah Aqel, Iman Ali, and Raya Naamneh for their translations of Arabic texts in chapters 2 and 3. I am responsible for any interpretive errors based on these translations.

Introduction

In 1940, a Syrian American medical doctor ran for Oklahoma's seventh district seat in the US House of Representatives. The candidate, Dr. Michael Shadid, had been born in 1882 in Marj'ayoun, a town in the southern part of what is known today as Lebanon. At the time of Shadid's birth, it was part of Ottoman Syria, a large province in southwestern Asia. When Shadid came to the United States in 1898, he worked as a peddler, like many other Syrian migrants at the time. Peddlers traveled either in groups or alone. Some peddlers remained within a city's limits, while others spent days, weeks, or even months traveling the surrounding countryside. Syrian peddlers sold everyday items, such as needles, thread, linens, belts, and soap. They also sold what Americans thought of as exotic commodities, such as silks, perfumes, rugs, and rosaries from the Holy Land.

Years later, after using the money he earned from peddling to attend medical school, Shadid had his own private practice in Elk City, Oklahoma, and was active in local socialist politics.[1] In 1940, for his first of two runs for Congress, he ran as a socialist. The following editorial was published during that campaign in a newspaper based about fifty miles north of where he lived. At that point, Shadid had lived in Oklahoma for almost thirty years, and his medical practice tended the health needs particularly of farmers.

> Down the street he comes, a man apart, knowing no friend; his queer dress, his hooked nose, his broken speech and queer mannerisms set him aside from the rest—the peddler of rugs. On his arm, a gaudy display of rugs and scarfs [*sic*], gleaming like jewels in the sunlight. Sparkling tinsel and glistening silk, yet alas, they bear no blessing of a known manufacturer, a thing made only to sell through the picturing of the faults of others. Bearing a guarantee of a foreigner who you will perhaps never see again. Nor are the political rugs exemplified by the candidacy of Dr. M. Shadid of any better quality. These rugs too glisten in the light of hard times; they are smooth, but what lies under the surface?—Will they, like the peddler's rug, fade, will they become a thing forsaken, dirty, unfit to have around? After the first washing, what will we

> have? . . . No American parentage glorifies this person, and no American philosophy
> blesses his doctrine. We need no off-color Jews as congressmen, nor do we need off-
> color capital-baiting lines of thought in our national make-up.[2]

By using the figure of the peddler as a metaphor for empty campaign promises, this editorial cast Shadid as an untrustworthy and unqualified candidate. The figure of the peddler was an easy image with which to express fears of socialism and the foreign and to discredit Shadid. Many years had passed since the brief period when Shadid worked as a peddler, but linking him to the peddler figure also diminished his career as an accomplished medical doctor. Consider the threat that he posed to the incumbent of five years to warrant this vitriol. Shadid was defeated both times he ran for Congress, but he enjoyed a base of support that earned him the second highest vote count in each election. In fact, in the second election, Shadid was so close behind the winner that he called for an official recount, a request that was denied.[3]

The strategy of highlighting Shadid's foreignness was predicated on a genealogy of Orientalism that cast the Syrian or Arab peddler (and the "Oriental" more broadly) as someone deceptive and manipulative, as someone with no roots in any community and with no loyalty to the United States. The "glistening," "gleaming," and even "gaudy display" of the peddler's rugs and scarves was part of the allure of Syrian and other foreign peddlers; the peddler brought "exotic" items to the doorsteps of working- and middle-class Americans, particularly women.[4] Customers were both excited and repelled by the commodified cultural and racial difference that peddlers sold. Invoking the strong associations of peddling with Ashkenazi Jews, this editorial also embedded Arab difference within anti-Semitism. The editorial called Shadid an "off-color Jew" as a way to differentiate him from Americans, in both racial and ethnoreligious terms; the hooked nose was a common anti-Semitic representation that circulated widely in print depictions of Jews.[5]

The editorial also described the peddler as "queer." Dress and mannerisms (both marked here as "queer") widely index a gendered personhood: our historically and socioculturally specific understandings of femininity, masculinity, and other gendered embodiments. The common usage of the term "queer" at this time was synonymous with "odd." However, by the 1940s, "queer" was also associated more broadly with sexuality—particularly connoting male effeminacy and sexual deviance.[6] The queerness in this editorial was a strangeness that highlighted the Syrian peddler's cultural and racial inferiority to the communities in which he peddled, and the editorial looped that difference back to the flamboyance of the peddler's display. Each of these indices of difference relies on the others for meaning and power. They cannot be disaggregated; they produce one another. Arab peddlers in the United States were rendered knowable to Americans through such discursive practices, which emphasized their cultural and racial deviations from whiteness. But these cultural and racial differences were replete with sexual and gendered embodiments. Arabs were thus sensationalized because of the perception that Arab sexuality and gender was fundamentally different from white American heteropatriarchy, which reinscribed them as racially different.

The experiences of Shadid and the accusations leveled against him are indicative of the complexities of early Arab American racial histories. Shadid was both successful and ostracized. He had access to many opportunities afforded only to white Americans, and he was a naturalized US citizen. Syrians were able to naturalize without legal contest after they successfully litigated their racial position among "free white persons" in 1915.[7] That case, *Dow v. United States*, asserted Syrians' right to naturalize as US citizens, a right based on a "racial prerequisite" of whiteness. In a series of naturalization cases in the early twentieth century, the boundaries of whiteness were policed and expanded to reinforce excluding Asian immigrants from claiming US citizenship.[8] Syrian petitioners experienced different outcomes: some were able to naturalize and others had their petitions contested by the state. Ultimately, Syrians were one of the few groups of non-European petitioners to be granted naturalization rights and to have those rulings upheld in appellate courts.[9] Thus, *Dow* ended the question of whether Syrians were eligible for naturalization and ruled them to be legally white. Due not only to the varying outcomes of the Syrian naturalization cases throughout this period but also to the often contradictory reasoning judges employed to reach those decisions, Syrians have been called "the courts' ultimate poltergeist."[10]

Despite the legal victory in *Dow v. United States*, Syrian Americans' whiteness remained provisional long after 1915.[11] Borrowing Robert Orsi's concept, Sarah Gualtieri suggests that this provisional whiteness is more accurately characterized as a racial "inbetweenness." This inbetweenness is evident in the life of Dr. Shadid and others like him, which shows how Arab Americans could be subject to racialized violence even as they enjoyed a whitened access to wealth and privilege. For instance, for some time, Shadid advocated for a return to his native country because of his experience with racial discrimination. After he was targeted by the Ku Klux Klan in his town in 1927, he wrote to the Syrian American magazine the *Syrian World* to discuss racial discrimination against Syrians and to advocate returning to Syria. Shadid's letter spurred a debate about racism and Syrians' belonging in the United States that continued for several months in the magazine's pages.[12]

Shadid, like many other Arab immigrants of his time, was a racially liminal subject. He experienced legal classification as both nonwhite and white at different moments in his life in the United States, and the records of his life show that he enjoyed some of the material privileges that whiteness afforded while also experiencing racial marginalization. Shadid was married and had biological children, and both statuses (as a married man and a father) were integral to conceptions of idealized US citizenship. Still, his racial liminality called into question his compatibility with white Americanness, regardless of the presumption about any sexual practices based on his marital and parental status, which resembled normative

American heterosexuality. But when Shadid was maligned as a "queer" peddler of rugs, this foregrounded his threatening foreignness through an Orientalist understanding of sexual and gender difference. Syrian racial liminality—and specifically the uncertainty regarding "Arab" and "Syrian" as racial categories in the late-nineteenth- and early-twentieth-century United States—hinged on a complex and fluid entanglement of both Syrian and white American sexual norms.

The main intervention of this book, *Possible Histories*, is to examine both the discursive and material histories of what I call the *queer ecology of the Syrian peddling economy* in order to unravel this entanglement. The queer ecology of peddling is a descriptor that names the peddling economy as broader and more interconnected than has traditionally been defined (as explained below). It is also a conceptual framework, specifically a queer analytic, that allows me to address the sexual, racial, and gendered implications of the Syrian peddling economy in the late nineteenth and early twentieth centuries and in the production of knowledge about the Arab American past. This conceptual framework attends to the contingent and curated nature of historical narratives. It asks, in other words, what was possible in these histories and what has been occluded from them. These are *possible histories* and I use a practice I call *historical-grounded imagining* to explore them. In the pages that follow, I map and analyze the figure of the Syrian migrant peddler and the scrutiny this profession received in order to show how dominant ideas about sexuality are imbricated in Arab American racial histories. As this book shows, the policing of Arab American labor practices—which existed at times in tension and at other times in alignment with white norms of sexuality, gender, and class—produced the figure of the Syrian peddler. This polarizing figure, I argue, was a target of white supremacist heteronormative anxieties. Later, Arab Americans recuperated this figure as a heroic pioneer of early Arab American history, a discursive move that obscures this troubled history and the central role of heteronormativity within it. Historical-grounded imagining is a method for reclaiming and reexamining this queer past.

Peddling was an ecology of laboring practices, interdependence, and intimacies that buoyed the Syrian American migrant community in its earliest years. Contrary to dominant narratives, peddling did not consist only of a traveling salesperson or only of a network of peddlers and those who supplied them with goods. The laboring practices of peddling also included stationary work that many Syrian women undertook, such as operating boardinghouses where peddlers would stay and crafting handmade items for peddlers to sell. In my view, broadening the scope of peddling labor practices is crucial because the true scope reveals the extent to which peddling relied upon Syrian women not only as peddlers but also as those who labored in multiple ways to make peddling a profitable occupation. The array of laboring practices also included those family members, again often women, who stayed home while peddlers left to sell. They took care of children, did other unpaid domestic work, and prepared community meals of celebration when long-distance peddlers returned. A subargument of this book is that peddling was a system of interdependent labor and care that produced new kinship structures and economies, not all of which fit into heterosexual family structures. I also show how peddling enabled forms of intimacy that were specific to peddling (chapter 4). Through my specific theorization of the *intimacies of peddling*, I have developed another major intervention of this book: integrating an analysis of embodiment and erotics into Arab American history. This analysis of embodiment and erotics also provides the basis for considering the possible histories that have been occluded from community historical narratives.

The American[13] and Syrian responses to this queer ecology revolved around racial difference, sexual and gendered propriety, and the ways that peddling work blurred the idealized boundary between public and private life. In turn, both Syrians and white Americans used these assessments of difference and propriety to index the capacity of Arabs to be modern. Were peddlers pioneers who ushered Arab immigrants into a modern, capitalist, and (white) American life, as some Arab American scholars and activists would later have us believe? Or were they anachronistic vernacular capitalists, after Ritu Birla, who threatened the structural position of white Americans?[14] Or were they both? These largely critical discourses have positioned Syrian peddlers as, at worst, lawless creatures who would disregard moral frameworks to make money or, at best, wayward individuals whose actions threatened the reputation of the entire community.

The queer ecology of peddling is an important site for illuminating the relationship between sexuality and race in Arab American history because of the temporary and transitory nature of peddling work and because of its dependence on interactions between Syrian migrants and non-Syrians that took place away from large Syrian communities, where scrutiny regarding social norms was certain. Looking at this early history of Syrian Americans also reveals the deep entrenchment of Orientalist conceptions of Arabs in the American psyche and the extent to which these ideas are tied to sexual normativity. In addition, the sexual dimensions of Arab American racialization in this period are visible not only through Orientalist tropes but also more broadly through discourses of modernity. Amira Jarmakani calls these discourses the "metanarrative of modernity," as they explored "the universalizing, Eurocentric assumptions that are often smuggled into the notion of modernity."[15] In other words, racialization in this context also scrutinized the extent to which Syrians were capable of embodying the characteristics of US citizenship in particular and had the capacity for self-governance in general.

QUEERING ARAB AMERICAN RACIAL HISTORIES

Possible Histories intervenes both thematically and methodologically in the production of Arab American racial histories. Sarah Gualtieri's groundbreaking work has explored how this population was positioned dynamically between the racial categories of white, Black, and Asian during this time.[16] Indeed, when Arabs from Ottoman Syria first came to the United States in the late nineteenth century, they found themselves in a new place in which the racial logics of white supremacy and settler colonialism were among the most central organizing features of society. This book expands this understanding by analyzing how they also brought with them ways of enacting intimacy, desire, and sexuality that frequently did not align with the framework of normalcy outlined by white, middle-class, and Christian American modernity. Although gender and women have increasingly been a focus of scholarship on Arab Americans, sexuality remains not just an underexplored topic but an absent analytic; discussions of gender are limited to cisgender women and often remain embedded within the logic of compulsory heterosexuality.[17]

Possible Histories brings Arab American subjects to queer studies by conceptualizing the ecology of peddling as a queer analytic. The queer ecology of peddling operates along multiple epistemic registers throughout this book. I contend that peddling was an economic network; a transitive sexual, gendered, and racialized system; and a historical reading practice that asks after the uses of historical narrative making. As an economic system, peddling was the transactional exchange of goods for money. It revolved around transitory labor practices that were supported by stationary work, such as operating boardinghouses and making things at home for peddlers to sell. It was also supported by a transnational network of suppliers, and it generated money that supported families separated by transatlantic migration. As I explore in chapters 2 and 3, some Syrians also associated peddling with sex work, and rumors circulated that Syrian women were not offering merely physical goods for sale. Syrians peddled the fantasy of their racial difference in the transactional nature of their work. The encounters between Syrian peddlers and their customers often crossed differences of race and gender. Peddling is fundamentally transactional, as an exchange that depends on and activates sensibilities of trust. American commentators (and some elite Syrians, as chapter 3 demonstrates) frequently questioned the reliability and authenticity not only of goods but also of the peddler. Was this lace actually made in Syria? Did this rosary truly come from Palestine? Did this peddler really lose her husband, leaving her with four children to feed on her own? From these questions of origins, reliability, and truth, we get also the derisive definition of "peddling," meaning to sell goods that are questionable in quality.

Finally, the queer ecology of peddling is also about a transient relationality that opens up analytical registers of the sexual and the erotic. The relations between peddler and customer were often fleeting, and the work of peddling was expected to be temporary. Historical narratives have relied on that time-limited expectation to imbue peddling with more respectable meanings as an occupation. Ironically, this transient relationality also foregrounds Arab migrant erotic embodiment and intimacy in the relations among peddlers on the road, between peddlers and their customers, and among those who tended to the home and community while peddlers were away (discussed in chapter 4).

I conceptualize peddling as a queer analytic to explain its slippery and transient nature. Peddling operates with multiple purposes, being neither strictly a form of labor nor a metaphor. Much like the term "queer" itself, peddling defies singular or stable categorization. As a queer analytic, the queer ecology of peddling offers a lens for mapping and analyzing the complex and transitive nature of peddling work, as well as the shifting, contradictory discourses that interrogate, praise, or deride it. Using peddling in this way allows me to ask, What is unstable, unexpected, or unruly about peddling? What possibilities of encounter and intimacy did peddling open up? This concept is not just specific to Arab American history; it extends beyond the realm of what those outside the field of Arab American studies may view as a parochial ethnic history. For instance, in queer studies, we might ask how particular methods and theories are peddled, how those knowledges are validated, and what other knowledges are occluded in that process.

The queer ecology of peddling effectively opens onto questions of method through its emphasis on the slipperiness of historical narratives and knowledge production. I depend particularly on historical-grounded imagining (which term I use to refer to a body of methodological interventions by queer studies, postcolonial studies, and Black studies scholars) and on a tradition of queer affective method. (I discuss these methods in more detail below.) Peddling also functions as a framework for analyzing the historical narratives placed on peddling and peddlers in order to ask what those narratives have obscured and what power they have accrued. A particular kind of recuperative and respectable history of early Arab Americans has often been peddled in which women appear as the spousal extensions of peddlers, men play the lead roles in the migration story, and Syrian immigrants effectively become white. I am peddling a different history here, leaning on the rubric of possibility, to center sexuality and gender without the assumption or expectation of heteronormativity. The analytic guiding this book—the queer ecology of peddling—uncovers a history of Arab American engagements with and investments in whiteness that are simultaneously engagements with and investments in heteronormative sexual politics. Mobilizing this queer analytic brings Arab American subjects and erotics to queer studies, something that remains at best infrequent at the time of this publication.

Some of the greatest differences between Syrian and American (usually white) ideas of sexuality were most visible in hegemonic American representations of Syrian peddlers. For instance, as late as 1981, Roget's Thesaurus included in its listing for "Arab" the following terms: vagabond, hobo, tramp, vagrant, hawker, huckster, vendor, and peddler.[18] These synonyms form an example of the mark that peddling made on the ontology of Arabness in the United States and the English-speaking world more broadly; but they also associate Arabs with a sexually debased transience synonymous with "hobo" and "tramp."[19] In addition, unlike other immigrant communities in which peddling was a common profession among men, Syrian women peddled in significant numbers. This reality, along with migration itself, began to shift the typical family structures and norms in Syrian diaspora communities. Peddling thus became a site of controversy regarding women's reproductive labor in the family. It also allowed Syrians the possibilities of living differently as they gained physical distance from their diasporic communities. Norms regarding sexuality—particularly sexual activity, sexual relationships, and marriage—became especially fraught in the diaspora as the sustainability of Syrian marriage traditions dwindled. Away from the disciplining mechanisms of Syrian American communities, long-distance peddling in particular opened up possibilities for people to live out and express their desires in different ways.

The racial position of Middle Eastern immigrants and their US-born descendants has been described in different but overlapping conceptual frames, such as "in between" white and nonwhite, "not quite white," "racial hinges" and "racial loopholes," and "white before the law but not on the street."[20] This lack of fixity indicates that race is a fundamentally unsettled concept in relation to Southwest Asian and North African diasporas in the United States. These diasporas include a range of racial experiences; they include those who predominantly experience the privileges of whiteness and those who predominantly experience anti-Blackness. Yet this difficulty of categorization, as well as the unstable nature of race, is an additional reason why the history of Arab Americans is such a rich site for exploring how sexuality (in conjunction with gender, class, and religion) interjects in and modifies that racial vicissitude.

Because this migrant community has navigated white supremacy and Orientalism, we cannot rely on traditional historical methods alone to know things about sexuality in this history. To attempt to do so risks reinscribing the community and its experiences in a heteronormative framework produced through both elite Syrian and hegemonic American ideals. This framework is sedimented by normativity and is therefore perceivable in archival collections. Many collections chronicling Arab American lives have been donated and curated within the context of depicting a certain kind of legible, normative existence—a sameness—that demonstrates their positive contributions in the United States. For Arab Americans, social histories of early Arab America can signify that "we've been here, we've survived, we existed and exist still" in the face of violent rhetoric and criminalization that denies our place in the United States—and, for some, in our ancestral homelands as well. Sometimes these histories can answer the claim that Arabs are essentially different from and incompatible with Americans. To this claim these histories can respond: "We were (we are still) just like you." This dual outcome of representational politics simultaneously affirms and assimilates. Emma Pérez traces this dual tendency as specific to ethnic history writing, in which documenting the existence and contributions of minoritized communities builds armor against institutional oppression. At the same time, the constant comparison of ethnic groups to whiteness prompts Pérez to ask, "Can we salvage history from sameness?"[21] This dilemma arises from a specific problem: projects of historical recovery are embedded and implicated in liberal forms of personhood that rely on a racialized universal of the human.[22]

This sameness hinges on certain normative ways of being that are predicated on class, sexuality, gender, and proximity to whiteness and Christianity. When we look at materials that have been collected in that spirit of positive contribution, we need instead to interrogate and make visible those disciplinary mechanisms of respectability. Yet limiting ourselves to exposing these mechanisms is not enough. *Possible Histories* works in the traditions of scholars of queer history, particularly those who chronicle the lives of queers of color, as well as scholars who think about the records of histories of systemic violence and the lives obscured by such records. In this book I assert that we must imagine possible desires, intimacies, and pleasures that Arab Americans have experienced other than those evidenced by archival records—including those that were not constrained or disciplined by either American white supremacist heteronormativity or Syrian sexual normativity.

In the rare cases when sexuality is a central analytic in relation to Arabs and Arab Americans, it typically appears with a contemporary focus.[23] But this book shows that sexuality has always been a central question framing what happens to Arabs in a US context, even when the terms of sexuality have changed in relation to the human.[24] Arab Americans have been racialized through Orientalist concepts of culture that cast Arabs as the opposite of Americans and American culture.[25] In the contemporary moment, the supposed backwardness of Arab culture is often articulated by narrating the oppression of Arab women, queers, and transgender people, as though this kind of oppression is endemic to Southwest Asia and North Africa and is an exceptional feature of Islam. Viewed through this Orientalist lens, Arab sexuality appears repressed and oppressive. Before the Cold War, however, Americans and Europeans articulated this backwardness differently. Namely, they perceived Arab and Muslim societies as being oppressive to women mainly because of men's licentious behavior.[26] The idea of the harem looms large in representations of women in Arab societies, as an "imaginative space through which to project masculinist and heteronormative fantasies of erotic desire and male power, as organized around male access to and possession of women."[27] The Euro-American fantasy of the Orient as a sexual paradise for white men continues to reverberate, even amid contemporary representations of the Middle East as being sexually repressed and repressive. Today's echoes of earlier representations function as "nostalgic foils for US progress and as imaginative figures through which to grapple with shifting power relations between the United States and the Middle East."[28] This analysis further emphasizes the necessity for everyone to take up questions of sexual normativity in relation to whiteness and white supremacy, because these questions have affected people regardless of their actual desires, behaviors, or identifications.

The history of Syrian American peddling effectively shows how race is imbricated with sexuality, gender, class, religion, and other forms of power and difference. Primarily, the material and discursive history of what peddlers experienced and how they were understood by others reveals the suturing of race to sexuality, gender, and class. *Possible Histories* relies on a range of source materials to explore this central topic, including Syrian American periodicals, mainstream American newspapers, census data, social welfare case studies, literature, and the collections of Arab American families and organizations. In addition, I challenge the historiography of Arabs in the United States, which indicates that the profession of peddling and the figure of the Arab peddler have been recuperated precisely through logics of whiteness, upward class mobility, and heteronormativity.

ARAB MIGRATION AND THE LOGISTICS
OF PEDDLING

Arabs began to migrate voluntarily to the United States in the 1870s.[29] This migration was officially curtailed with the passage of the 1924 National Origins Act, which restricted southern European and eastern European, as well as non-European, immigration by means of a quota system. These limitations stemmed the flow of Arab immigrants through Ellis Island. However, both Louise Cainkar and Sarah Gualtieri have documented numbers of Arab migrants entering the United States from Latin America even after the 1924 limits were imposed.[30] The majority of these Arab migrants came from the Ottoman region of Greater Syria, and they were predominantly Christian (of Maronite, Melkite, and Eastern Orthodox denominations). A small number of Druze, Muslims, and Jews were also among this migrant community. The number of Syrians living in the United States throughout this period is unclear; estimates range from as few as 46,727 (in the 1910 census) to as many as 200,000 (in the estimation of Philip Hitti in his 1924 book, *The Syrians in America*). This uncertainty is partly attributable to the fact that Syrians were initially recorded by immigration officials as coming from "Turkey in Asia" and were counted with all Ottoman subjects. After 1899, Syrian migrants were recorded separately under the label "Syrian," but Syrians were still often misidentified as Turks, Assyrians, Greeks, or Armenians.[31] Interestingly, Syrian migrants began to adopt the use of the term "Syrian" for themselves, in English, once the official US classification changed.[32]

This Syrian movement to and through the United States took place in the context of various types of migration. First, a history of internal migration within the Ottoman Empire predated transatlantic migration.[33] Ottoman subjects, including but not limited to Syrians, migrated for seasonal labor, for upward career moves to urban centers, and as a result of war and conflict. War also contributed to an influx of refugees into Syria from outside the Ottoman Empire; as a result of the Ottoman-Russian Wars of 1853–56 and 1877–78, more than one million Muslims from the Caucasus left the region as refugees. Tens of thousands died during the process of resettlement, and those who survived settled eventually in Bulgaria and Syria.[34] The international Syrian migration that began toward the end of the nineteenth century largely resulted from a changing global economy and its effects on the local silk industry.[35] This migration included significant numbers of Syrians who resettled in and moved through Central and South America, greatly surpassing the number of Syrian migrants in the United States.

From the beginning of Syrian migration to the United States in the late 1870s, pack peddling was a popular form of employment for Syrians. Peddling did not require much capital to begin and was open to anyone, regardless of one's knowledge of the English language. City peddlers might have carts and stay in one place, or they might travel door to door for the day and return home at night. Long-distance peddlers traveled in groups or alone and left for days, weeks, or even months at a time to travel the surrounding countryside or over longer distances. Just as Syrians themselves were found throughout the Americas, the routes of peddlers were likewise not confined to the United States, particularly for those peddling near the more porous US-Canadian border.[36]

Syrian peddlers sold an array of household dry goods and notions (small household items) as well as commodities that they marketed as being from the Middle East. Some of these goods may have been imported, while others were made more locally. The money that peddling brought in ran the gamut: some peddlers struggled and were always poor (or found different work), whereas others made money more easily. For many Syrian migrants, peddling allowed them to amass wealth quickly, which they often sent home to family members in Syria, used to return to Syria to live, or used to purchase land, a house, or a business in the diaspora. For others, peddling was not the lucrative career they had hoped for (or had been told to expect by their compatriots), and they moved on to other pursuits.

Syrians were not the most numerous in the peddling profession. Ashkenazi Jews predominated, especially German Jews, continuing a common profession in the Jewish diaspora. The linkage of European Jews with peddling is also the most recognizable association when it comes to immigrant peddling in US history. Other immigrant groups also peddled. For instance, Bengali Muslims who were rooted in Black and Creole communities of the US South were peddlers during the same time period as Syrians.[37] Syrian peddlers shared similarities with both Ashkenazi Jewish and Bengali Muslim peddlers. Stereotypes of Syrian peddlers often used the same anti-Semitic language that described Ashkenazi ones, most notably that they were greedy and manipulative. Like Bengali Muslim peddlers, Syrians capitalized on the increasing popularity of items from the "Orient" by selling things like lace and silk alongside the household staples buyers would expect. But what differed was the prominence of Syrian women in the peddling population and the ways that Syrian peddlers, regardless of gender, were viewed and discussed in sexualized terms.

Although they were not the only immigrant group to peddle in the United States, Arab migrant peddlers in the United States were unique in several ways. First, Syrian Americans, both individually and as a community, had a "deep and broad" identification with peddling—whether they themselves were peddlers or not.[38] Syrians knew that many of their kin peddled, and they knew that Americans associated them with peddling. Peddling has had a central place in Arab American historical narratives as being the key to the success of Syrian migrants' integration into US society, because it enabled the dispersal of Syrians beyond ethnic enclaves, because it was often an easy way to earn money, and because it allowed for contact between Syrians and other US residents.[39] Second, a significant number of Syrian women peddled, including young girls and women who were single, married, divorced, or widowed. As a result of her extensive research with second-generation Arab Americans, historian Alixa Naff estimated that up to 80 percent of Syrian migrant women peddled at some point in the United States.[40] Syrian peddling was already a form of gendered labor and attracted scrutiny as such; it has been described as an occupation whose effects on family structures produced nontraditional living arrangements between women.[41] Such arrangements of support usually happened when long-distance peddlers, often men, were away from home for long periods of time. Because of women's significant role within the ecology of the peddling economy, including working as peddlers themselves, peddling was thus a contested topic in early Syrian American communities and among American commentators, and it provoked great disagreement about the place of Syrians in the United States and the effects of migration on Syrian communities.

Jacob Rama Berman writes, "The narrative of the Syrian pack-peddler is so central to the way in which the pioneer generation has been historicized that no scholarly account of the years between 1880 and 1924 exists in which the figure does not appear prominently."[42] Indeed, the peddler has appeared so frequently in chronicles of early Arab American life that by the 1980s, some scholars began to note that stories of Arab American peddlers had long suffered from blatant romanticization. Indeed, from folkloric tales to obituaries, Arab American communities recirculated tropes that fit neatly into an American Dream narrative. An immigrant ancestor arrives on US shores with little to his name (the gender here is intentional). A wealthier Syrian compatriot running an import business or a dry goods store supplies him with a pack and goods to sell. He sets off to make his way, quickly earning beyond what he could have imagined, and soon he has enough money to send to his family overseas, perhaps to marry or bring over a wife, and to start his own business. In archives and written histories about Arab American communities, peddling is often imbued with these positive characterizations: how hard peddlers worked, how ingenious they were in finding a way to earn money despite their lack of means, and how much peddling demonstrated their entrepreneurial and capitalist compatibility with American society. Still, as far as many Americans were concerned, peddlers were transients; Americans "looked down on peddling as an activity to be followed by the destitute rather than as a first step in the economic success of an immigrant group."[43] Peddlers were untethered and lacked a known rootedness of place and reputation. As transients, peddlers could be threats to US settler or other colonial structures of heteronormative family, propriety, responsibility, and property ownership. Through the Second World

War, transience and the anxieties transferred onto unattached men were also heavily associated with nonnormative sexuality.[44]

The glorified tales of the peddler pioneer have been tempered by historical research that shows the life of a peddler to have been much more precarious. Many peddlers indeed acquired wealth quickly through this work, but they also experienced hardships from the physical elements, the skepticism of strangers, and the burdens of white supremacy and nativism. Others found no luck in peddling or were too discouraged by its physical demands, and they moved on to other pursuits. Although peddling has had a prominent place in the narration of Arab American life, Syrian workers were actually more numerous in textile mills throughout this migration period, particularly younger and unmarried women and girls in the northeastern United States.[45] Syrians also worked as miners, farmers, bankers, and autoworkers and in many other professions. Despite this statistical evidence, however, the figure of the peddler and the economic network of peddling emerge as central features of the early Arab immigrant success story.

Migration and peddling had tremendous effects on the practice of endogamous marriage in the Syrian community. Those men who migrated on their own in the early years frequently left behind wives and fiancées in Syria. Even if they did not, they may have been promised to someone back home as a future spouse. But migration and peddling work brought possibilities for different kinds of lives than were possible in Syria, particularly where family and intimate relationships were concerned. In the Arab diasporic press, community leaders raised concerns that male peddlers would abandon their familial obligations by breaking engagements, abandoning wives and children, or maintaining multiple families in separate locales.[46] These fears were not paranoid worries; they were founded on reports of such transgressions that made it back to those families who expected migrating men to adhere to typical community practices. Some returning single men were even asked to provide proof that they had not married while in the United States.[47] Naff acknowledged the heterosexual infractions of some male peddlers and reassured her readers that "the majority of single peddlers remained well within cultural bounds." Those who did not, she suggested, succumbed to "nontraditional marital solutions," such as marrying outside the community, taking common-law wives, or engaging in "temporary marriages" with American women.[48]

Although these deviations from heterosexual norms were widely discussed, the prospect of homoerotic or homosexual encounters was unsurprisingly absent from community accounts and scholarship. However, Syrian peddlers were migratory laborers in a time of frequent same-sex encounters among migratory men in the United States and of the public outcry surrounding such encounters. Regardless of whether this prospect was explicit in the minds of Arab Americanist scholars, the expectation that transient peddlers should become settled business owners was particularly related to paradigms of a heteronormative settler economy—a paradigm of US national culture that permeated the Arab immigrant community as it sought to survive in a new home. These connotations arose in the context of the period during which Syrians migrated, and during which public worries about tramps, hobos, and migrant workers mirrored the same concerns about the abandonment of heterosexual marriage and the nuclear family.[49] Some of the anecdotes of cultural misunderstandings that Naff provided were also rife with unease about gendered boundaries and sexual roles. For instance, one of Naff's interlocutors recounted a story of a Muslim peddler who employed an Arab method to implore a local farmer to house him for the night: he kissed the man's beard. In response, the farmer beat the peddler until his peddling partner saw the beating and intervened.[50] The possibility of an accidental and homoerotic act is the silent character in this anecdote and is the reason for the violence wrought upon the peddler. This cultural misunderstanding was, of course, laden with the normative mechanisms of sexuality and gender.

Despite all the anxieties they embodied at the time, peddlers eventually came to represent the compatibility of Syrianness with Americanness. Despite the efforts even of discerning scholars who were critical of such intellectual revisionism, ideologies interweaving class, gender, sexuality, religion, and race have often undergirded the available scholarly narratives in the service of a normative rendering of Arab American subjectivity.

ARAB AMERICANS, QUEER (AMERICANIST) STUDIES, AND HISTORICIST METHODS

Possible Histories is guided by a number of methodological traditions: discursive and material historicist inquiry using traditional historical methods, cultural studies analysis informed particularly by feminist studies and queer of color critique approaches, and historical-grounded imagining, which seeks to destabilize and broaden what we know about the past. These methods allow me to address a wide range of implications from this history and to respond to both the uses and limitations of historical methods for examining race and sexuality in Arab American history. The task of historicizing a minoritized community brings the necessary exclusionary choices of the research process (that is, deciding what is important and what is peripheral) into collision with the wider political lens through which that history will be understood: specifically, the frameworks of power that led to the community's marginalization in the first place. I engage with the published scholarship and archival collection of Arab American historian Alixa Naff among many other sources. Although others have researched and continue to research this history of Arab migrants from the Levant, Naff's legacy—both in constructing a narrative about peddling in this early community and in leaving future generations a wealth of archival materials—is unparalleled. As I depend on her scholarly legacy, I simultaneously contend with the normativizing implications of her curatorial choices, in both the community-based scholarship she produced and the community-based archive she constructed.

Historicist methods can produce a kind of trap in which we rely on only those records that can be corroborated as the ones that produce meaningful knowledge about the past. Because these records are often produced by the state or reflect the unit of the family, they can reinforce the respectability politics of sameness. Alternately, when they are state institutional records, they can reinforce the criminalization or pathologization of a population. Finding untold histories and reclaiming them is thus, in the present, a powerful tool for responding to delegitimizing structures of power: structures that position minoritized communities as being inferior to or outside hegemonic society. While understanding that usefulness, we must also interrogate the sexual, racial, gendered, classed, and religious foundations of sameness upon which that strategy rests.

So much precludes historical certainty regarding basic (yet significant) details of peoples' lives, as well as the contours of many peoples' thoughts, desires, and senses of self. For Arab Americans, the details include names and birthdates. Immigration and census officials have demonstrated great difficulty in understanding Arab names and naming conventions. Historically, Arab immigrants may have used varying transliterated spellings of their name; they may have changed their own name to a more Americanized version; or their name may have been changed upon entry into the United States. The ubiquity of certain Arab names can also make it difficult to distinguish some individuals from one another in the historical record, and birthdates were not always recorded in Ottoman Syria. Immigration, census, and other state records might show approximations that vary across several documents for a single individual. These variations also make it difficult to know whether separate documents refer to the same person or to more than one person.[51]

Historical records often privilege the view of the state, and collected materials have often been individually curated and therefore represent specific viewpoints of what is historically significant and appropriate for inclusion. What, then, would it look like for Arab American history to account for what was possible, rather than only the documented and the conclusive? What is deemed out of reach or irresponsible to imagine when we face a lack of documentation that is considered historically legitimate? This lack is where sexuality can remain elusive as a historicist analytic in communities minoritized by white supremacy and its regimes of sexual normativity. Historical-grounded imagining allows for the complexity and epistemological mess of historical knowledge. It also creates space for the differences in community opinions about various relationships and intimacies, for the wide variation in participants' experiences of those relationships and intimacies, and for the reality of sexual violence and abuse that was also present in these experiences.

Historical-grounded imagining centers on the possible rather than on the conclusive as a way to avoid exclusionary knowledge production about early Arab American communities—knowledge production that often relegates women, gender-nonconforming and nonbinary people, sexual outsiders, and working-class and working-poor people to the margins of history.[52] Both historians and historicist scholars of other disciplines have employed speculation and imagining in thinking about the past. Often these more experimental and polarizing methods are adopted at a time when feminist and queer histories have already been produced in a particular field, often as projects of historical recovery. They build upon, push forward, and sometimes rupture some of those feminist and queer foundations. I am indebted to these scholars, yet I also consider what it means to employ such a method when a project of queer recovery has not first been started.

I use the phrase "historical-grounded imagining" not to stake a claim to a new and distinct methodological practice but to signal my embrace of several methodological approaches working in different historical contexts. Pérez has employed a method she calls the "decolonial imaginary" that she envisions as an interstitial rupturing space, "the alternative to that which is written in history."[53] Pérez's method intervenes specifically in the tendency of ethnic histories to prioritize sameness and similarities with white Americans. Contending with the consequences of what Pérez terms the "history of the same" is urgently needed for Arab Americans, who have unevenly been both beneficiaries and targets of white supremacy. Historical-grounded imagining also builds upon the work of Anjali Arondekar, who urges scholars of sexuality, particularly those working in contexts of colonial domination, to see historical abundance rather than always or only historical lack. Arondekar especially cautions against the recovery model of histories of sexuality and the "privileged lexicon of erasures, silences, and subjects."[54] Historical-grounded imagining foregrounds possibility. Possibility is a rubric of abundance and of endless permutations of historical experience that do not merely fill in the silences but rather give them form, texture, and life beyond scarcity.

I also rely on historiographies of racialized violence (particularly anti-Blackness and anti-Asianness) in this research. This reliance does not presume commensurability between these histories and that of Arabs in the United States but rather incorporates the history of anti-Arab racialization into a larger history of "differentially situated, not equivalent, genealogies of liberalism."[55] In particular, Black studies has produced important critiques of archival methods, as by considering the possibility and consequences of archival research into transatlantic chattel slavery and its afterlife. My use of historical-grounded imagining has also been shaped by Saidiya Hartman's work on the legacies of transatlantic slavery and the Black diaspora. Hartman's work uses "critical fabulation" to consider the lives of those who have been rendered "an asterisk in the grand narrative of history" by anti-Black and misogynist violence. Her method leans on the "capacities of the subjunctive"—doubts, wishes, and possibilities.[56] While Hartman concedes that a historical narrative cannot redress the violence of chattel slavery, she uses the possibilities inherent in critical fabulation to come closer to this redress—an approximation—but also to highlight the impossibility of telling these stories. In *Wayward Lives, Beautiful Experiments* she takes this mode of historicist inquiry further, pressing even more on the generative capacities of imagining by amplifying and expanding on "moments when the vision and dreams of the wayward seemed possible."[57] In this "unthought" history, young Black girls and women "imagined other ways to live and never failed to consider how the world might be otherwise."[58] In *Possible Histories* I lean on these speculative methods to highlight the role of sexuality in the uneven formation of Arab immigrants and Arab Americans as racial subjects, and to produce an imagining of the kinds of desires and intimacies that Arab immigrants and their descendants experienced in the face of white supremacist norms of sexuality.

For decades, scholars of queer sexual cultures have been engaged in questions regarding the necessary methods for historical inquiry into nonnormative sexualities and the utility and power of historical narratives. For US-based scholars, the study of the history of sexuality and queerness was borne of explicitly political projects that sought to recover "histories of lesbian and gay identity formation, community life, and social movement activism" in the midst of the AIDS crisis, ongoing structural heterosexism, and an academy beginning to be shaped by neoliberal multiculturalism.[59] Increasingly, and with the emergence of trans studies, the focus of this scholarship has moved from one of recovering community and individual histories to that of mobilizing "queer" and "trans" as analytical categories that help us understand how sexuality and gender have been contingently shaped—and how these have shaped other categories of difference across time and space.[60] Historians of sexuality and other historicist queer studies scholars have also had to contend with the extent to which "'queer' should remain secured to sexuality as its central object."[61]

This book is situated within these traditions. It concerns the power of historical narratives that implicate sexuality, the question of recovering (albeit with hesitation) queer pasts, the erasure of sexually nonnormative Arab American subjects, and the use of "queer" as a category of analysis. It does so not with the promise of finding queer Arab American subjects that can be recuperated for contemporary purposes, but rather with the knowledge that "queer" itself is both a useful and imperfect category for understanding the imbrications of race with sexuality in this history.

Queer studies scholars have a rich tradition of thinking about what queer methods might be and about the implications of searching for, finding (or not finding), and analyzing nonheteronormativity and queerness. These considerations have been particularly generative with regard to archival formations and approaches to archival methods, ranging from theorizing the quotidian mess of queer lives as an archival practice to the "scavenger methodology" of searching in unexpected places for evidence of queer cultures.[62] I depend especially on these creative and interdisciplinary approaches to method.

At times, a queer method is an accidental one—something unexpected or unintended. Ann Cvetkovich writes that "the accidental encounter is, of course, a form of queer archival method."[63] One such accidental archival encounter—coming across the editorial against Michael Shadid's congressional run—is what prompted my own study of the Arab American peddling economy. The accidental prompts a cascade of questioning and, if one is lucky, a reorienting of foundational assumptions. In this case, the editorial that cast the peddler as a "queer" figure forced me to revisit and revise my understanding of how Syrians were received in the United States and how the peddler functioned in Arab American historical narratives as a response to that reception. Like other queer studies scholars, I embrace the unexpected and the accidental in my work, asking what conditions have produced certain archival appearances. I employ "queer" not as a particular subject that I am looking for but as an analytic for thinking about which practices and encounters may have threatened the racial regimes of heteronormativity at a given moment. As a reading practice, queer functions through hesitation, "through a caution to name or decide in advance what an archive of absences or a rhetorical entanglement will yield up."[64] This queer method is not divorced from the sexual, however; on the contrary, it is open to desire, "always partial, only a potentiality, an opening onto other worlds yet to come."[65] To achieve this sensibility, when I encounter archival materials, I look for things that are "off," for moments of hesitation, for things that appear strange. I look for the possibilities of ambiguity, excess, and multiple interpretations in the ways that Arab Americans have been constituted and have constituted themselves. In other words, I intentionally use my own affective responses to archival materials in the research process.

I draw, too, from the rich body of work known as queer of color critique. Grounded in a genealogy of women of color feminist critique and engaging with queer theory, ethnic studies, and migration studies, this scholarship examines "how intersecting racial, gender, and sexual practices antagonize and/or conspire with the normative investments of nation-states and capital."[66] Queer of color critique is a methodology, a theoretical position, and a political stance.[67] As a body of scholarship, it has focused largely on queer Black, Asian American, Native, and Latinx cultural production, political economies, and movement. The colonial encounters among Europeans, Africans, and indigenous peoples of the Americas form one originary point for the material and discursive violence that marked some as normative and others as deviant, animalistic, and other—primarily through racial, gendered, and sexual logics.[68] Queer of color critique scholars have articulated how nonconforming and nonnormative sexualities and genders have been racialized through this historical process and how this gendered and sexual racialization has contributed to the reproduction of social science, policy, and the state's regulation of its inhabitants. Nayan Shah names this historical phenomenon queer of color "estrangement."[69] Scholars who engage in queer of color critique have also intervened in the racial dimensions of queer theory and the normative formations of queerness, noting that queer theory has tended to presume whiteness in queer subjects and that its authors' whiteness has shaped the theory they have produced.

This presumption has meant not only that queers of color have been over-looked but also that how queerness itself has been theorized has been defined by whiteness and white supremacy without tacit acknowledgment. This epistemo-logical perspective presumes a severing of sexuality from race and other forms of difference, a severing that is not possible. *Possible Histories* proceeds from the assumption that different regimes of sexual normativity exist globally and that those regimes collide and contend with one another through forms of racialized imperial and colonial dominance. I focus on that collision and trace how norma-tive and nonnormative forms of Syrian sexuality became nonnormative in the US context. In this light, queerness, as a conceptual frame, potentially implicates a range of desires and practices that affect all racially minoritized subjects under white supremacy, not just those who appear to be "gay," "lesbian," or "queer."[70] In addition, the Eurocentric origins of the heterosexual-homosexual binary and what we have come to understand as "queer" can obscure the multiplicity of normativ-izing sexual structures.[71]

Possible Histories continues in the generative tradition of queer of color cri-tique by intervening in conversations about the appropriate, expected, or norma-tive subjects of queer theory. The Middle East and North Africa and its diasporas are belated geopolitical arenas for queer studies, as described by Keguro Macha-ria. Scholarship that only recently has paired Arab (or Arab American) studies with queer theory marks a delayed or undeveloped arrival in "queer modernity."[72] Studying queerness and Arab subjects at this moment confronts one with the feel-ing of catching up with the rest of queer theory. It also means that, because the field has already done so much theorizing of the category "queer" and of sexual non-normativity, the sites of this research may feel "uninteresting to mainstream queer studies."[73] These impressions of belatedness also speak to the Orientalism within queer studies, which perceives queer Middle Eastern and North African lives as developmentally in the past. Middle Eastern and North African queers (and our attendant political concerns) are thus positioned as needing to "catch up" with the modern, Eurocentric queer subject. Indeed, like much of the Global South and its subjects, Arabs are expected at best to provide examples of queer theory concepts but not to generate more theory or to challenge the models that the field has constructed. Arabs provide "the exemplars, but rarely the epistemologies."[74] Yet, as Kadji Amin tells us, it is precisely because the queer in Arab and Arab dia-sporic sites functions differently than canonical queer theory that scholarship on the Global South and its subjects has been marginalized in queer studies.[75]

I am cognizant of the fact that a project which centers Arab diasporic sub-jects residing in the United States still risks a recentering of the Global North as the site(s) of theory production, the sites that "matter" to queer studies. My own position as an Arab American and as a tenure-track faculty member in the US academy reinforces that tendency. Still, these subjects and many of the sources they left behind were transnational ones in affiliation, in affect, and in physical circulation. They were and remain deeply rooted in the Levant itself, as well as in other parts of the Syrian diaspora, such as the Caribbean and Latin America. The Middle East itself is a "historically, politically, and economically deeply transnational region."[76] Arab American studies, too, is fundamentally a transnational intellectual and political project. This stems from the transnational affinities of Arab Americans themselves, as well as the intellectual necessity of drawing on Arab and Middle East studies scholarship in conceptualizing Arabness and Arab communities in diaspora. This intellectual necessity loops back to those transnational affiliations and also stems from a lack of engagement with and legibility of Arab Americans from within US ethnic studies. This relationship between Arab and Arab American studies, however, is not one of neat, reciprocal exchange and power. While Arab American studies must depend on Middle East area studies to a certain extent for its legibility as a field, Middle East studies has not historically been concerned with its diasporas and their intellectual, cultural, political, and economic trajectories. Arab American studies also risks recentering diasporic Arab American concerns and positionalities and situating them as equivalent to those in the Middle East and North Africa itself.

The region of the Levant from which these migrants came, as well as the framing of the regional, also serves as a queer site in this project. Although some scholars have imposed a Lebanese national frame on this history, given that the majority came from an area that became part of the nation-state of Lebanon, this imposition erases other, minor subjects of this migration. In addition, at the time of their departure, these emigrants had affinities and networks that traversed the region of Ottoman Syria and beyond, to other parts of the Ottoman Empire and still other Syrian diasporas in the world.[77] This population also held a range of political perspectives that included loyalty to or acceptance of the Ottoman sultan, anticolonial sectarian nationalisms, and anticolonial pan-Arab nationalism.[78] Much of the scholarship that documents these views examines the perspectives of elite and literate men. We do not have an accounting of the possibilities of nonnational and nonimperial perspectives on home, belonging, affiliation, and governing among these migrants.

As a formation outside a nation, the regional itself stands in as a queer model in contrast to the modernity of the nation-state and national consciousness.[79] A queer conceptualization of extra- and supranational spaces, like diaspora and region, allows for a decentering of national affiliation and nationalism.[80] Gayatri Gopinath posits that the regional is "a spatial category [that] simultaneously animates notions of linear temporality and modernity, where the region is often figured as premodern and atavistic in relation to the modern nation."[81] Despite the ideological claim to nationhood espoused in Arab nationalism, the category of Arab is multiple and contested, one that contains hierarchy and difference. Rather than allowing for a latent or presumed nationalism of "Arab" or "Lebanese" to reassert itself in this analysis, I press on other forms of affinity and use the term "Syrian" as a nonnationalist, diasporic identity. This usage does not discount the presence of nationalisms among Syrians but rather provides space for nonnationalist affiliations as well. Using this nonnationalist framing also moves the conversation about diasporic communities beyond a dichotomy of authentic versus assimilated, wherein notions of retention or loss of culture map neatly onto a distinction between Arabness and Americanness. Disrupting such notions of authenticity also "troubles the Orientalist representation of an explicitly homophobic 'traditional' or authentic [Arab] culture."[82]

As with the conceptualization of region itself, Eurocentric discourses of modernity have positioned Syrians, as well as other Middle Easterners and North Africans, as if they are located in another time.[83] If Middle Easterners and North Africans are out of (modern) time, then their diasporas are out of time and place. We can then understand that queer (Americanist) studies' continued indifference to queer Arab American scholarly and political projects is, in and of itself, an endeavor of queer modernity. Reconceptualizing Arab American histories and cultural production as part of queer critique fundamentally alters the terms of time, space, and entry into a queer modernity upon which queer studies is built.

The Syrian migrants this book focuses on may be mundane or even undesirable subjects of queer theory. They may not resemble what we typically understand to be queer. They may have been complicit with white supremacy in their efforts to survive in the United States. If they were alive today, some would assert that they were heterosexual. Some may be reluctant, recalcitrant, or unheroic subjects.[84] They are not idealized or necessarily subversive.[85] Their positioning as being potentially undesirable is the result of racial and geopolitical normativities that have developed within queer theory. To address this problematic result, Amin proposes that we allow "queer" to "come not only to *mean* but also to *feel* differently than it does now."[86] This project *feels for* queer in eclectic ways, working against paradigms that posit the impossibility of queer Arab histories.

OUTLINE OF THE BOOK

Possible Histories argues for the centrality of sexuality to understanding early Arab American racialization through four chapters. Chapter 1 outlines how the figure of the male Syrian peddler must be understood as a queer figure of Arab American and American history, by tracing the slippages and dissonances between Syrian peddlers' popular representations and their own accounts of peddling experiences. In literature, popular music, and news media, Syrian peddlers—particularly men—have been depicted as the bearers of exotic excitement, a source of seductive danger, and the manufacturers of deceit. The encounter between a swarthy Syrian man and a naive white woman at her doorstep has played out repeatedly in these representations. The threat of this racial and sexual encounter was ever present. The use of Orientalism in defining the sexual difference of peddlers reveals the anxieties that Syrian peddlers evoked about white racial purity, masculinity, and sexual normalcy. The experiences of peddlers bore out these anxieties, as can be seen through an examination of archival legacies of long-distance peddlers. These sources also demand that we reckon with the opportunities peddling opened for a variety of sexual experiences outside heterosexual monogamous marriage. I use the occasion of tracking down one of my own peddler ancestors and considering his possible deviations from heterosexual monogamy to demonstrate a queer affective method. Chapter 1 focuses on one representation of Syrian peddlers, which continues to reverberate decades after its debut and holds a significant place in the cultural imaginary of the United States: the musical *Oklahoma!* and its peddler character, Ali Hakim. I explore three iterations of this cultural work: the 1931 antecedent to the musical, *Green Grow the Lilacs*, written by the queer Cherokee playwright R. Lynn Riggs; the 1943 stage musical *Oklahoma!* by Richard Rodgers and Oscar Hammerstein II; and the eponymous 1955 film version of *Oklahoma!* Mirroring the trajectory of many Syrian Americans over time, the iterations of these cultural works demonstrate how peddlers were encouraged to assimilate by ceasing their movement and marrying white settlers. However, based on the representations of peddlers in news media and from their own recounting, they remained threatening as racial and sexual outsiders.

Whereas chapter 1 focuses on the effects that popular culture representations of Syrian peddlers have had on actual Syrians, chapter 2 shows how the economy of Syrian peddling was scrutinized through women's participation in it. Syrian women contributed to the sustainability of peddling as a profession by making things at home for peddlers to sell, by operating boardinghouses where peddlers could stay, by caring for children and family elders while peddlers were away, and by working as peddlers themselves. To investigate women's participation in the peddling economy, this chapter relies primarily on social welfare records in which Syrians were both aid recipients and social reformers themselves. This analysis shows how Syrian women's peddling practices were at odds with norms of white, middle-class femininity and threatened some Syrians' claims of whiteness, thus revealing the contours of a sexual economy of the Syrian migrant family. By this, I mean that the measures taken to discourage women from participating in the peddling economy emphasized that women's labor in the Syrian immigrant family should be essentially reproductive. At critical moments, I use the practice of historical-grounded imagining to counter the omissions and characterizations of official records. Chapter 2 also illuminates internal Syrian dynamics of class and its intersections with sexuality and gender by examining Syrian women both as clients of social welfare and as social reformers themselves.

Chapter 3 continues the thread of Syrians' internal debate about peddling and traces it through the pages of the Syrian American press. Whereas the first two chapters illuminate marginalizing discourses about Syrian peddlers and begin to shed light on responses internal to the Syrian community, the third chapter shows how Syrians produced self-normativizing discourses about women, marriage, and sexuality in Syrian migrant communities to make sense of and resist how they were perceived in the United States. Over a period of roughly thirty years, the Syrian press focused on Syrian women peddlers, always imagined as unsupervised and unaccompanied by men in public spaces and as thus threatening the idealized Syrian American identity that these elite Syrian migrants (the editors and readers of the Syrian American press) were crafting. By reiterating several arguments about the dangers that peddling posed to women, to the Syrian community, and to the community's reputation, writers claimed a link between peddling and an aberrant female sexuality. These debates index an elite migrant community's concerns about the parameters of normative Syrian sexuality as refracted through white and middle-class American ideals.

Finally, chapter 4 examines Arab American sexuality, gender, and race—not from the perspective of threat, violence, and policing but rather from the perspective of pleasure, particularly those homosocial and homoerotic pleasures enabled by the very work of peddling. This chapter asks, How can we account for these pleasures historically, when little evidence of Arab American homosexuality exists in our historical records? Using photographic materials from the Faris and Yamna Naff Arab American Collection, I ask what historical traces remain of sexual non-normativity in Syrian peddler communities, given that most collected materials have been assembled to present a "respectable" image of Arab immigrants. In response, I conceptualize homosocial and homoerotic pleasure within the realm of what was possible—a more expansive view of pleasure than searching for an Arab American homosexual subject. I examine a series of gender-segregated photographs of peddlers from the 1920s that foreground multiple connections of pleasure between men or between women in Syrian American communities. I imagine the pleasurable possibilities of Arab American history that peddling enabled and consider the ways that some Syrians may have resisted the self-normalization of their elite counterparts in the press.

1

Traveler, Peddler, Stranger, Syrian

Queer Provocations and Sexual Threats

The wild plum-blossoms fluttered in the lane,
*   Like fairy lace hung out to dry,*
After the playful coming of the rain
*   From a clear sky.*

The Syrian peddler shook the clinging drops
*   Of water from his heavy pack,*
With laughter that the farmer at his crops
*   Must bend his back.*

The men were plowing in a black-loamed field,
*   And they were far enough away*
To leave the house safe for a wife to yield
*   To his display.*

A bashful farmgirl met him at the door—
*   Her mother looked up in surprise.*
Quickly he spread his wares upon the floor,
*   Peddler-wise.*

Bright-colored silks and laces billowed out
*   In airy grace from skillful hands. . . .*
The girl had in her eyes the weary doubt
*   Of lonely lands.*

The woman's eyes were brighter—having seen,
*   She sighed, "Put back the pretty stuff—*
My daughter's only twelve, she'll be sixteen
*   Soon enough!"*

—GLENN WARD DRESBACH, "*THE SYRIAN PEDDLER*"

As Syrian peddlers traveled through rural spaces of the United States and interacted with people outside their own immigrant communities, curiosity and anxiety grew about their presence. Such feelings were often expressed in popular portrayals of the Syrian peddler, particularly Syrian men. Peddlers appeared in poetry, short stories, novels, and children's books, as well as in the news media. Regardless of the format, all of these genres put Syrian difference on display for the American public in two distinct ways. First, Syrian peddlers brought what was understood as exotic difference to the doorsteps of aspiring-middle-class Americans via the goods that peddlers offered for sale as well as their own racialized bodies. While household staples such as sewing materials, soap, and linens were essential in a peddler's pack, so were items like Jerusalem holy water, rosaries, lace, and silk that elicited fantasies of far-off places. Second, male Syrian peddlers supposedly posed a sexual threat to the women who purchased their goods. The manufacturers of this threat imagined white women and their daughters, the epicenter of the domestic middle-class idyll, being home alone and defenseless against the seductions of the peddler and his wares. Recurring through these themes of difference was the idea that manipulation and seduction—qualities particular to the Oriental character—were central to the peddler's economic success.

Glenn Ward Dresbach's 1924 poem "The Syrian Peddler" demonstrates such an imagined scenario. The peddler, who has escaped the toil of working the land, laughs that the farmer "must bend his back." (The irony here is that that peddlers' packs were often quite heavy and carrying them around was physically taxing.) While the (men) farmers are occupied, the peddler can take advantage of the women of the home. The scene that Dresbach describes between the peddler, a mother, and her daughter is one of seduction. The language of "yielding" signals that the peddler's sales display is a temptation for both the mother and the daughter. The mother's caution that the young daughter will "be sixteen / Soon enough!" points to the daughter's impending sexual maturity. Is the daughter imagined to be ready to yield to the peddler's goods or to the peddler himself—or both?

The curiosity and anxiety about Syrian peddlers thus also contained underlying desire for this racially and sexually different figure. The Syrian peddler was at once alluring and deviant. This positioning, along with the numerous possibilities for different sexual intimacies enabled by long-distance peddling, makes the Syrian peddler a queer figure—one of sexual excess, one threatening to white settler heteronormativity.

This chapter traces the lineage of the Syrian peddler as a queer figure through the archival legacies of long-distance peddlers and the representations of Syrian peddlers in popular culture. In short stories, poems, plays, and other literary works, Syrian peddlers, particularly men, are depicted as the bearers of exotic excitement, sources of seductive danger, and manufacturers of deceit. The encounter between a Syrian man and a naive white woman at her doorstep plays out repeatedly in these representations. The threat of this racial and sexual encounter is ever present. The use of Orientalism and questions of modernity in defining the sexual and gender difference of Syrians reveals the anxieties that peddlers evoked about white racial purity, masculinity, and sexual normalcy. The experiences of peddlers themselves also bear out these anxieties, albeit in different ways. They also demand that we reckon with the opportunities that peddling opened for a variety of sexual experiences outside heterosexual monogamous marriage.

Syrian peddlers were facilitators of settler colonialism: they made the stealing of Native lands in the American West and Midwest more feasible for white settlers by providing the convenience of access to goods that rural areas often lacked in comparison with cities. But at the same time that Syrian peddlers played a crucial role in this process, their perceived racial and sexual difference threatened the white-held power in the communities that they helped to shape. The peddlers were queer figures in a landscape struggling to normalize itself according to a middle-class, white American ideal. Remembering these figures and understanding the labor, desire, and anxiety associated with them interrupt the racialized nostalgia of US settler colonial history, as well as the narrations of early Arab American history that ignore sexuality as a formative rubric.

This chapter examines representations of male Syrian peddlers in popular media and shows how these depictions betray racial and sexual anxieties about the presence of Syrian immigrants within US society. The Syrian peddler became a vessel for white American concerns about the economic position of white business owners, the purity and virtue of white women, and the overall demographic changes in the American citizenry. The figure of the peddler proved highly flexible for these purposes. The anxieties surrounding peddlers hinged specifically on the notion of a racialized sexual difference inherent in Syrian and other Southwest Asian men. At the same time, desire surfaced along with these anxieties, stemming from the fabricated exoticism of the so-called Oriental. I focus on a very specific iteration of these instances of representation—the musical *Oklahoma!* and the original play that preceded it—because they allow a comparison of the portrayal of the Syrian peddler in the same story across different temporalities of Arab American history. Through these artistic works, the figure of the Syrian peddler has surreptitiously reverberated in US popular culture for decades.

Taken alongside these representations, the social history of Syrian peddlers both allows an analysis of these representations' effects and forces us to grapple with questions of what we can know, how we can know it, and how we might strain beyond those limitations with regard to peddler sexuality. Moving between the material and the discursive here, as well as between social history and the literary and representational, also connects and blurs the fictive and the real.

I thus stitch a thread in this chapter between discursivity and embodiment. That is, the knowledge produced through textuality is related to the material experiences of Syrian peddlers through the desires involved in spectatorship (of the plays and musical discussed herein), readership (of local papers that sensationalized

Syrian peddling life), and research (my own). For example, we can imagine that the readers of local papers who learned about the arrival of Syrians and their strange customs were both titillated and repelled. Audiences of *Oklahoma!* delighted at the sinewy and seductive trickster nature of the peddler character. And I, the researcher, navigate my own desire to locate, name, and substantiate sexual excess in my own family history—and in the historical records of other Syrians—through historical-grounded imagining. These queer desires of spectators, of readers, and of the researcher (myself) motivate the engagement with embodiment. Desire is a way to approximate embodiment, preventing an intellectualization of discourse; and these multiple queer desires are where those threads of discursivity and embodiment loop together.[1] "Queer" here may look and feel differently than what we are used to. Following Kadji Amin, I use queer as a method that is, at its core, multiply affective and multiply historicist.[2]

A MOVING TARGET: VIOLENCE ON THE ROAD

Syrian peddlers experienced both physical and discursive violence in their lives in the United States. In the news clippings I examine below, I detail an aversion to (and sensationalizing of) peddlers. That averse outlook ranged from suspicion to mistrust to outright fear—and, in some instances, to unacknowledged desire and fantasy. At the core was an anxiety about the strangeness of Syrians and the rootlessness of their transient labor. Dierdre Moloney notes that the anxieties provoked by immigrant peddlers, including Syrians, stemmed from their economic position and its perceived consequences: "As economic middlemen, [peddlers] traveled extensively across borders rather than being rooted deeply in one community. As such, they could not be easily contained or monitored, and posed a metaphorical threat to U.S. citizens."[3]

These anxieties had emotional, social, and physical repercussions for Syrians. But Arab American historiography (and the archives from which it draws) does not often dwell on this unease and uncertainty in its telling of peddling experiences. The preeminent social historian of early Arab America, Alixa Naff, doggedly asked after experiences of discrimination and othering when she interviewed first- and second-generation Syrian Americans in the 1960s. Even so, an overwhelming number of her participants denied that they experienced discrimination. Despite the prevalence of such narratives—indeed, such fiction—every so often an interview is clearly shot through with longing and pain, in which the violence of separation from the land of one's birth and of the encounter with white supremacy refuses to remain submerged. Elias Lebos provided one such interview.

Born in the village of Rachaya, Elias Lebos first came to the United States in 1896 at the age of twenty-nine. After arriving in New York, Lebos went directly to Fort Wayne, Indiana. Fort Wayne was a known supplier hub for Syrian peddlers, where newcomers could be trained to take up the work quickly and be equipped with goods to sell and routes to travel. Whenever Lebos and a group of other Syrian men left from Fort Wayne, they walked about sixty-five miles over the course of the week. They slept in farmhouses during the week and in boardinghouses in a town over the weekend. Every Saturday, they wrote to their supplier with a list of goods they needed and where they would be the following Saturday to receive those goods. Lebos peddled like this for approximately two and a half years, sending a hundred dollars a month back home to his family, until he returned to Rachaya.

He came to the United States again in the early 1900s and spent considerable time peddling in Minnesota. Remarking on this second peddling stint, he exclaimed in an interview: "No terrible experience passed me by. Sometimes a town would be too difficult for us or sometimes difficulties would be too much or we would be kicked away by customers or get so tired we couldn't walk any more or there'd be mud and puddles and rain—and suffering—Leave it to God how we suffered."[4] Lebos thus listed various ways the vague "difficulties" posed an impediment to this way of making a living. What made a town "too difficult," and what made those difficulties "too much"? In reading that they would be "kicked away by customers," one can begin to envision the social and physical ostracization that Lebos and his kin confronted. Lebos's recollection blended into the realities of working and traveling continuously outdoors: mud, puddles, rain, and suffering. Lebos then elaborated that the kind of physical difficulties he encountered while peddling were also social and racist in nature: "In Minnesota, the Bohemians, Swedes, and Norwegians would chase me to kill me." At the time, Lebos was traveling with four other men, who, like him, had come from Rachaya to the United States. Lebos managed to hide from the men who were chasing them. Once they were gone, he hid his suitcases, climbed a tree, and strapped himself to it with rope so that he would not fall if he fell asleep. He stayed there through the night and realized that he was completely alone only the next morning. About his companions, Lebos remarked: "We don't know if they were killed but no one ever heard from them again. They vanished." Once he was on his own, he got sick: "I don't know what my sickness was—fatigue, depression, neglecting [my] health. Who knows. Many of us experienced illness and depression."[5] Such a firsthand account of racist violence and of the profound effect it had on Syrian immigrant health is quite rare in the archives. More often than not, Syrian immigrants and their US-born children either minimized racist othering or characterized their experiences as being devoid of racism altogether.[6]

For other peddlers, the ostracism they encountered came at night, when they looked for shelter. Essa Malooley, who also came from Rachaya, recounted difficulties he had in finding a place to sleep on his peddling trips: "We slept at farmers' houses. Yes, many times I was turned away because maybe they were afraid of peddlers or something. No, they didn't turn me away because I was an Arab. They never asked me what I was. Peddlers looked poor."[7] Malooley remained certain that he was not turned away because he was Arab; it was because he was a peddler. But poverty and class are also racialized; and an accent, a darker skin tone, and a markedly non-European phenotype would have signaled foreignness. Malooley, then, was turned away because of multiple forms of assumed or actual difference between himself and his potential customers.

In another example, the brother of Alice Abraham left from Cedar Rapids, Iowa, to try his hand at peddling. She recounted in an interview that he almost froze one night because "no one would give him a place to sleep." Finally, he asked a farmer to let him sleep in his barn, but the man made him come inside instead, where he could be more easily surveilled. While sleeping indoors might seem more ideal than spending the night in a barn, the farmer proceeded to walk around with a gun in his hand the whole night. Alice's brother was not able to sleep that night and was determined never to peddle again after that trip.[8]

Others recounted similar experiences, including a Druze Syrian man whose life story was published almost a decade after his peddling days. Ed Aryain (born Mohammed Aryain) remembered that although he encountered many hospitable homes during his peddling trips, there were "many times which were far worse," including being "turned down at dozens of houses," doors being slammed in his face, an angry man telling him to go away because "his kind" was not wanted. Years later, Aryain still remembered how much these incidents hurt; they continued to haunt him.[9]

The physical violence that Syrian peddlers feared was not merely hypothetical. Beginning in the late 1880s, news articles described violence against peddlers occurring in rural areas. In one example, a Syrian peddler went missing in 1891 in Pennsylvania. The peddler's son found his father's peddling pack abandoned on the Susquehanna River bank. Spots of blood were nearby. The son suspected that the father had been murdered for the money he carried on him from selling his goods.[10] In another example, a married couple peddled together in West Virginia. After they took separate routes, the husband disappeared. The wife believed he had been murdered for his money and goods.[11] Other peddlers were beaten or murdered and then robbed: "Two bullet holes in the [peddler's] body told the tale of [his] ending" in Tennessee.[12] In West Virginia, two men were convicted of killing a Syrian peddler; one was given the death penalty (a sentence that a new trial later changed to a life sentence). Papers reported that the man had said "the damn peddlers ought all be killed."[13]

In this last instance, the two perpetrators of violence were white men. In every other instance, however, if the assailants were identified at all, they were invariably Black, Native, or Syrian. An 1893 news report from Mason County, Washington, told of a Syrian peddler killed by a stray bullet, but some believed he was murdered. He and another Syrian had just left the Skokomish Indian reservation in the area, where they had sold jewelry. The report proclaimed that the "cheap, trashy jewelry carried by the peddlers is just the thing to please the Indian fancy and that robbery might have been the incentive."[14] In Meridian, Mississippi, another Syrian peddler was brutally murdered and robbed. The news article reported the gory details in this way: a group of white men found the peddler's body and then traced the blood back to a house where four Black men were found dividing the peddler's money. The Black men—the presumed assailants—then "disappeared, and it is stated that they were put to death."[15] On their face, these articles collectively show that all sorts of people—not just white Americans—could harbor animus for Syrian peddlers and act upon it. But the paucity of named white assailants is suspicious, all the more so given the swift "justice" that followed in the many cases in which assailants were nonwhite.

How does this violence matter for thinking about Syrian peddlers and sexuality? The threat that Syrian difference posed to Americans was always predicated on a sexual difference—that is, Syrian peddlers' ability to persuade and entice, via the goods they sold, was closely linked to the idea that they could persuade sexually as well. In the post–Civil War era, when anxiety over miscegenation was reaching its apex, racist violence was inextricably linked to sexual and gendered panics.

PEDDLERS AS PESTS: RACIAL CAPITALISM, WHITE GENDERED FEAR, AND DISCURSIVE VIOLENCE

White Americans' fear of Syrians also contributed to discursive violence against them in the press, often manifesting as alarm about Syrians' arrival and their work as peddlers. One category of early articles, from the 1880s and 1890s, includes sensationalized reports of groups of Syrians arriving or being detained at US ports of entry. Headlines like "Masters of Mendicants" and "'Sanctified' Arab Tramps" contributed to a discourse that said all Syrians were beggars and shiftless transients.[16] One 1885 article described Syrians as "the class of Arab tramps that periodically come over to the United States and make a begging tour through the country. When they see a policeman, they pull out a bundle of beads and pretend to be selling."[17] Another article reported on a camp of Syrians who stopped in Louisville, Kentucky, on their way to California. Remarking on their strange customs and having interviewed local residents about them, the reporter commented, "They are queer and the children run from them." Local residents feared that the Syrians would kill them in their sleep.[18]

As Syrian populations increased in the early twentieth century, local papers sometimes described peddlers as a type of nuisance to white residents and white businesses. For instance, one newspaper printed its own definition of a peddler: "He invades peoples' homes and persuades them to buy what they do not want."[19] In Guthrie, Oklahoma, retailers attempted to raise license fees to drive peddlers from town.[20] Indeed, Syrians were frequently mentioned in the press when they were arrested and fined for peddling without a license. The imposition of licensing was one way that small towns attempted to prevent peddlers from competing with local brick-and-mortar businesses.[21] In El Paso, Texas, the local paper aggressively characterized the rise of Syrian business ventures ("Syrians Grabbing the Business of El Paso").[22] In the Oklahoma Panhandle, newspaper editors plainly told residents not to buy from Syrian peddlers. After speaking with two Syrian peddlers who told them that business had not been good of late, the editors asserted that "our people" had merchants who already served the community well. "Stick to your town and her business people," they proclaimed; "they are the fellows who stick to you. The others 'stick it' to you."[23]

These warnings and mischaracterizations of peddlers enacted a kind of "white sovereign entrepreneurial terror" in which, following Kyla Wazana Tompkins, capital and whiteness as property are sutured, "making entrepreneurialism and whiteness coeval terms predicated upon a biopolitical logic that metes out death and propertylessness, hunger and debility as natural outcomes for those against whom whiteness is wielded."[24] These reactions to Syrian peddlers can also be understood through the distinguishing framework of "legitimate" versus vernacular capitalists. Rather than circulating capital "for the benefit of the public," the peddling ecology relied on kinship networks for labor and recirculated capital largely within those same family structures.[25]

These discursive characterizations echo in the recuperative measures taken by early Arab American scholarly and community activist texts. Many of these works noted that peddling was a temporary profession that suited Syrians' intentions of returning home after earning money rather than remaining in the United States.[26] Narrative maneuvering, however, could transform this fact of convenience into evidence of Syrians' propensity for and commitment to capitalism. A 1985 edited volume published by the Arab Anti-Discrimination Committee took issue with the "persistent notion" that Arabs immigrated to be peddlers and that they were "predisposed toward entrepreneurial activity."[27] Emphasizing Syrians' entrepreneurial nature and clever adaptability in peddling work became a strategy for responding to these historical discourses that maligned Syrian peddlers. Naff commented on this same tendency: "In Arab American folklore, stories about immigrant entrepreneurs are second in popularity only to stories about immigrant peddlers. We have liked to think of our forefathers as independent businessmen who disdained to work for others and had the courage, against all odds, to strike out on their own."[28]

Peddling was consequently viewed as the starting point in a trajectory that ended in "success and middle-class status."[29] Regarding some peddlers' transition to opening brick-and-mortar businesses with the capital they made in peddling, Naff called these shifts "evolutionary stages" in peddling: "They were no longer the humble pack peddler. They saw themselves and acted as 'classier salesmen dealing with classier people.'"[30] In a settled business and personal life, one would own a physical storefront, cease the frequent travel that peddling entailed, and engage in marriage and reproduction—all things that were part and parcel of assimilating into white, middle-class Americanness.

These narratives attempted to reposition the peddler as a capitalist at heart: not a threat but rather someone compatible with white American capitalism. "Syrian immigration and rapid modernization were fortuitously compatible," Naff argued, and the Syrian peddling sector "revitalized . . . an anachronistic enterprise and made it function successfully within a technologically oriented economy."[31] Naff situated Syrian peddlers as having filled a niche opened by the rapid industrialization of the late nineteenth century—specifically, the gap created by the isolation of rural communities from goods and services as urban populations swelled. In linking peddling with capitalism and entrepreneurship, these narratives revised the labor of peddling, and the economy that supported it, to be normative in the US context.

Other scholars have noted that Syrian peddling was merely a product of the opportunities available to them, in particular the possibilities created by a racially segregated economy. In places like Mississippi and Alabama, Syrians peddled to the Black communities that white American entrepreneurs ignored. This strategy also forced Syrians to acknowledge and navigate the crosshairs of racist, nationalist, and in some cases anti-Catholic prejudice. Joseph Schechla noted that although Syrians in Mississippi interacted with Black Mississippians through peddling, they did not identify with them, contributing instead to maintaining the color line.[32] For Maronites in Alabama, this system brought both dangers and benefits: "Certainly they, especially the darker-skinned Lebanese, experienced painful moments: every time they used public facilities they faced possible challenges to their race; similarly, each farmhouse that a peddler approached required the reestablishment of racial identity and the possibility of anti-foreign and anti-Catholic prejudice. At the same time, the Lebanese benefited from segregation: racial bifurcation promoted their economic ascendance."[33] In El Paso, Texas, and surrounding areas, Syrians peddled to working-class Mexican Americans to such an extent that the Spanish term *árabe* became synonymous with merchant.[34] Some Syrians on both sides of the US-Mexico border crossed it to peddle to their customers.

The press's discursive violence that positioned Syrian peddlers as threatening to white capital also relied on stoking white gendered fears of Syrian sexuality. A lengthy article published in 1898 examined the influx of "undesirable" immigrants coming through Ellis Island. Focusing on Syrians in particular, the author described Syrian peddlers as pests throughout the South and West who were able to skirt immigration laws by "complying with the letter of the law" through their marriage claims. Upon arrival at Ellis Island, the author claimed, each Syrian would find an "immigration husband" or "immigration wife"—that is, another Syrian who would pose as a spouse for legal entry requirements: "A Syrian woman with a child is considered specially valuable as a peddler in the streets of towns. The husband who meets her is not likely to know how old his wife is, when or where she was born, or even her name. . . . But he never fails in demonstrations of family love. He is most passionate in outward devotion to his immigration wife." An illustration of a tarboush-wearing man embracing a woman who holds a baby accompanied this section of the article, with the reiterating caption "He never fails in demonstrations." Immigration officials whom the report quoted were convinced that a single Syrian man would pose as a husband for up to five or six women, who were then by law allowed to enter the country.[35] This article implied not only that such Syrians were skirting immigration laws but that Syrian men used this trick also to engage in sexual relations with multiple women simultaneously.

Although fictional representations of such fears focused on the potential seduction of white women by peddlers—as, for example, in the poem that opens this chapter—news reports focused on the fear that Syrian peddlers would sexually assault white women customers. Several articles specifically highlighted fraught interactions between Syrian peddlers and white women, amplifying white fears of racialized sexual violence. A 1918 article told of a Syrian peddler "prophet" in Washington, DC, who also offered healing services in the form of charms and amulets. Though sensational to a white American clientele, amulets were commonly used by Arab women.[36] Two days before the article's publication, Waharaud Barakat had come to the home of Estrella Keyes to sell laces and embroidery. After Barakat "hinted at occult powers," according to the article, Keyes asked him to come back later and then notified the police. Once he returned, the two discussed Keyes's inability to have children. Barakat then gave her a collection of charms with instructions for their use and promised that they would help her become pregnant. The article called this interaction between Barakat and Keyes a "séance" and reported that he attempted to embrace her after she paid him five dollars for the service. The woman then cried out, and the police, who were hiding in an adjacent room, arrested him. He was charged with "telling fortunes without a license" and with assault.[37] Another article, from 1910, accused a Syrian peddler of setting fire to a woman's home in Lehi, Utah. The unnamed peddler had previously visited the woman to sell his goods. She accused him of "attacking and assaulting" her. He was arrested and convicted and spent two months in jail. The paper reported that, while incarcerated, he vowed to have his revenge upon his release.[38]

Another report, from New York in 1905, told of the attempted lynching of a Syrian peddler after he was found alone in his tenement room with two young girls. An Irish mother went looking for her eleven-year-old daughter one day when she had not come home after school. After asking others in the neighborhood, she was directed to the room of an older Syrian man. Inside, she found her daughter and another girl, aged nine, alone with the man. Police apprehended him, but the girl's father attempted to lynch him in the street. As the father tried to rally the crowd of onlookers to assist him, he yelled, "Are ye men or Syrians?" The father's hypothetical question sutured normative binary gender to sexuality by juxtaposing manhood against the depraved and violent sexuality of Syrians that this story implied.

Instead of assisting in the lynching, the mother and other onlookers prevented the father from inflicting any more violence on the Syrian man. This shocking report—reprinted across the country, including in Oklahoma and Arkansas—featured a drawing depicting the lynching scene.[39] Collectively, these reports centered on the fears of white consumers and produced for readers a "pleasurable fiction of threat at any moment, facilitating the performance of a grotesque and melodramatic victimhood."[40]

One article depicting the racialized and sexualized fear of peddlers perhaps best embodies the racial contradictions Syrians experienced in the United States. In August 1903 nineteen-year-old Rasheed Saliney, a jewelry peddler, was being held in the Greer County jail in Oklahoma for the "attempted assault" of one of his customers: a white woman named Effie Witt.[41] According to census records, Saliney had arrived from Syria only the year prior. Although the alleged assault had taken place in nearby Roger Mills County, Saliney was taken to Greer County because police feared that he would be lynched if he remained where the alleged assault took place. The encounter between Saliney, a Syrian man, and Witt, a white American woman, was a racialized, gendered, and sexualized encounter. The accusation of assault (assumed to be sexual) and the fear of a lynching point to the historical structures that positioned men of color, particularly Black men, as sexually predatory toward white women. Yet the fact that police moved Saliney to another county complicates a simplistic narrative of the Arab immigrant at odds with white American power. This move was a protective measure; in some sense, the local police were aligned with (or at least sympathetic to) Saliney. That he was moved to a county where other Syrians, including relatives, lived meant that he would have recourse to support there, rather than remaining in a place where he may have known no one and had fewer possible allies.

The unreliability of these sensationalized accounts, along with the difficulty that Americans had with Arabic names, makes verifying these events and their aftermath a process of repeating dead ends. Regardless of the accounts' veracity, however, each of these press appearances of Syrians highlights the anxieties white settlers had about Syrians' sexual excess, apparent lack of desire to become US citizens, and transience. In many cases, but not exclusively, these accounts demonstrate the vulnerability of Syrian men as peddlers, in contrast to the threats they were assumed to pose to white women. By reiterating Syrian men's removal from Syrian wives through migration and peddling, this discourse was one of "deviant heterosexuality."[42] However, peddling in the diaspora did open new possibilities for living out one's sexuality differently, such as by delaying or refusing marriage, taking on multiple wives in different locations, or experiencing sexual intimacies not sanctioned by heterosexual marriage. While inflammatory, these media narratives also highlight the ways Syrian men could become untethered from community sexual norms on their peddling routes.

TRACKING DOWN PEDDLER SEXUALITY:
FAMILY FICTIONS

These media representations show how sexuality was on the minds of Americans as they confronted the difference of Arabs in their midst. There is a blurriness here between representation and the materiality of historical experience. Because these media stories are sensational, fantastical, violent, and titillating, it would be easy to cast all of these representations as based purely in Orientalism and white supremacy and to carve out an oppositional understanding of Syrian migrant sexuality— perhaps one that fit better with white, middle-class sensibilities of the time. But to do so would ignore the material realities of peddling and the opportunities it created for exploring new sexual encounters and erotic lives.

If these articles represent a set of complex realities about Syrians, migration, and peddling, then, as historical artifacts, they indicate that migration and long-distance peddling did enable some Syrian men to break the sexual expectations set for them. Indeed, historical evidence corroborates this indication with regard to migration. For instance, Sultana Alkazin came to Philadelphia from Beirut around 1901. She arrived with her three children after her husband—who had emigrated sometime before—sent for them. To her surprise, however, she found that her husband was now with another woman, with whom he had fathered children. Her husband hoped that they would all live together, but for Sultana, this was not acceptable. So she took her children and moved to Atlantic City, New Jersey, which had an established Syrian peddling community.[43] Religious leaders were similarly concerned about the opportunities for different sexual intimacies that transatlantic distance enabled. They witnessed some men abandoning wives or engaging in "extraofficial polygamy" in the Americas. When men returned to Syria to marry, some leaders required "letters of certification" indicating that they had not already taken wives abroad.[44] How the absence of a wife was certified, and by whom, is unclear.

My great-great-grandfather may have been one such man. George Karem—son of Karem, who was son of Michael—was born in Hamat, in the northern part of present-day Lebanon. The names of the women from whom George Karem descended have been omitted from the family tree and from oral retellings of the family's history, reinforced by patriarchal naming practices. In the late nineteenth century, George and one of his sons came to the United States, staying first in Louisville, Kentucky, where he had relatives. From there, he peddled throughout the South. All of his children had also been born in Hamat, and they and their mother, Mary, came one by one to the United States. Mary and her youngest son, Nick, were the last to arrive. But by the time they arrived in Louisville to join George, he was nowhere to be found.

The first time I asked a family member what happened to George Karem, I was told that he had died in Vicksburg, Mississippi, which had an established but small Syrian community. I made a notation next to his name on the family tree: "died in Vicksburg, Mississippi." My mother remembered that her father (Philip, a grandson of George) told her this, but no one can confirm when or how George died. Several years later I asked again about George. My great-uncle, another of George's grandsons, said that after establishing himself with steady work in the United States, George was supposed to send for his wife and children—but he never did. All his family knew was that he was "gone." A cousin who attended a medical convention in Alabama about thirty years ago added fuel to the rumor when he returned and told the family that several people had either mistaken him for another Lebanese American man who was local or asked him whether he was related to a local Lebanese American family.[45]

Attempts to trace this history or corroborate any of these possibilities lead in circles. This section narrates my circuitous attempts to verify what happened to George Karem and the role that the ecology of peddling played in his disappearance. Using my own family history allows me to foreground the affective nature of historical-grounded imagining—the queer method I use—in examining the ecology of peddling. By explicitly tracing my own route through the archival research process regarding my ancestor, I make visible my own desire and analytical decisions and reiterate the suturing of discursive and embodied histories to one another.

One possibility is that, by 1900, George was living in Louisville, having arrived in the United States two years earlier. The 1900 census lists a George Karem as a notions peddler (that is, a seller of small, household items) who lived at the home of his cousins, Salaam and Karem Shaheen, with cousin Karem's wife and children and another cousin, who appears on the census as Narzna). All of the adult males in the household worked as notions peddlers. The census also indicates that George had been married for five years by this time and that he was born in 1873. The document makes no mention of the son who had supposedly immigrated with him. However, if this is the correct George Karem, this listing opens additional and unexpected questions. The life of George's wife, Mary, and their children are traceable and verifiable. They first appear in the 1920 census, though they had all immigrated by 1907, according to the youngest son's naturalization papers. Mary was born in 1854, according to her death certificate. If we take this George Karem to be the correct one, this birthdate put Mary at more than twenty years her husband's senior. And the birth years of George and Mary's known children make this arrangement more interesting—or make this George Karem unlikely to be the correct one. George and Mary Karem had five children: Karem George (born 1882), Isaac (born 1884), Foshmiah (also known as Fannie, born 1885), Jameelah (born 1890), and Nicholas (the aforementioned Nick, born 1895). Given the dates of the children's births in relation to their parents, however, either the first four children were from a previous relationship, or George and Mary had them out of wedlock. The former is more likely, as George would have been only nine years old when the first child was born. So we can conclude that this is the wrong George Karem.

Another possibility in the census records is a George Karem who appears on the 1910 census as living in Louisville. This George was also a peddler, was born in 1869, and had been married for fifteen years. He was a boarder at the home of another Syrian family. If this second prospect is the correct George Karem, he would have been slightly older than the George in the 1900 census—but he would still have been significantly younger than his wife, and there are the same issues with the timing of children's births.

Or could we consider the George Karam who was born in 1863 and died in 1910 in Bangor, Maine?[46] His gravesite has a tombstone, but no other evidence of his life seems to be traceable through traditional archival methods. At the turn of the century, a few hundred Syrians were living in Maine, and the largest group lived in Bangor.[47] If this third prospect is the correct George, then it seems more plausible that all of George and Mary's five children were his biological offspring. His death in 1910 would also track with his family's arrival in the early twentieth century without having further contact with him. But Bangor is a long way from Vicksburg.

One of several other possibilities was Karem George Karem, sometimes written as Karem George, who was born in Hamat and lived part of his life in Vicksburg. He married Azizie Mfarge in Vicksburg in 1911 and became a naturalized citizen in 1920. The two later moved to Santa Monica, California, and had five children together. California may have been far enough from Kentucky for George to live a new life with his new family. But the excitement of finding this potential match (given the name, birth location, and residence in Vicksburg) had clouded my judgment. I had overlooked this George's birthdate and eventually realized that this was the oldest son of the correct George Karem. Of course, then, one simple but unsatisfying possibility is that George Karem left no historical trace in either US government or Arab American community records.

Given the ubiquity of the names George and Karem, and the common inversion of them due to the difference in Syrian and American naming practices, my repeated attempts to track historical evidence of George Karem's life in the United States have over and over again given me hope that he can be found—and over and over again proved fruitless. My desire to find George Karem in the archives is so strong that every instance of revising or proofreading this chapter has resulted in another round of archival searching and verification. But this process has also opened questions of how possible it might have been for an immigrant to change his identity, forge a new life, and leave an old one behind, all in a strange land not of his kin. Left with this information, we are given options of disavowal and of probability. What was more probable, and on what do we base this assessment?

As I began my foray into census and immigration documents, I acknowledged my desire to find the archival proof of his familial abandonment. I suspect that George Karem was a bigamist; I want to know this and substantiate it. I am reminded of Saidiya Hartman's words that "the loss of stories sharpens the hunger for them."[48] Yet, even as my own scholarly inquest turned toward his life, what surfaced was perhaps an equally, if not more, riveting question regarding the life of George's wife, Mary. Given the possibility of a sharp age difference between Mary and George, several questions surfaced. Could Mary have had a husband before George? Or a lover out of wedlock? Could any of her children have been the product of sexual violence? Would any of those possibilities have diminished her chances of securing a future through marriage? Few people in my family seem to remember or recount a significant age difference between George and Mary—an age difference that is culturally and historically constructed. Perhaps George's disappearance facilitated the forgetting of this important detail. Perhaps along with it, the details of Mary's life before her marriage to George succumbed to forgetting as well. Perhaps there was no age difference at all, or perhaps it was not seen as socially significant at the time.

Once I began to ask about Mary, rather than George, I learned another piece of family scandal. Apparently, Mary had an affair with the husband of Fannie, her eldest daughter, who was recorded as living with her in the 1930 census. After this affair, Fannie's husband fled to South America. The listing of Fannie as widowed on the census can be traced to her husband's flight. The normalization of George and Mary's union and George's "death" may have occluded intergenerational knowledge about the realities of the village economy in Syria, including negotiations about marriage, family relationships, and sex that fell outside what was deemed traditional. Most certainly, those who knew the origins of Mary and George's relationship crossed the Atlantic as well, but the articulation of this knowledge may not have. In this sense, a focus on Syrian men and sexuality does not necessarily mean that Syrian women are absent; rather it means that we must look for them (and their sexuality) in different places and by different means.

While many details of my ancestors' lives can be verified through census records, city directories, and other vital documents, the aspects of their lives that point to sexual nonnormativity are harder to pin down through traditional historical methods. These details linger in incomplete and sometimes intentionally obscured family histories and in speculation passed down through the generations. Perhaps George Karem had betrayed his duties as a husband and a father. Maybe Mary Karem was sexual in ways that exceeded the bounds of community expectations. We can say with greater certainty that with sex and relationships came control, obligation, and discipline. These truths also point to the labor of peddling as a crucial factor in this sexual excess. Because peddling facilitated the physical distance between him and his diasporic kin, this profession enabled and masked George Karem's (potential and actual) deviations from heteronormative community obligations.

Despite the small size of the Syrian community, male Syrian peddlers appeared frequently in US popular culture. The majority of these appearances reiterate the same set of ideas about Syrian peddlers that the press echoed, including the excitement engendered by the goods they offered, their propensity to manipulate their customers, and the seductiveness and unreliability of their Oriental sensibilities. In the second half of this chapter, I turn to the literary iterations of the Syrian peddler in the play *Green Grow the Lilacs* and the derivative musical and film productions of *Oklahoma!* in order to delve into the meaning produced by fictional representations of Syrian peddlers and to consider how these representations shaped the possibilities that Syrians saw for themselves in the United States. Both *Green Grow the Lilacs* and *Oklahoma!* showcase the same sexual and racial anxieties about peddlers that we find demonstrated in press coverage and personal accounts of Syrian peddlers. The different role and resolution of the peddler's story lines in these texts, however, further highlight the liminality and malleability of Middle Eastern racial positioning and the central role of sexuality in it.

A PEDDLER ICON: ALI HAKIM

Few would recognize the best-known representation of a Syrian peddler on stage and screen, even though it continues to circulate as part of US popular culture today. Rodgers and Hammerstein's 1943 musical *Oklahoma!* exemplifies the portrayal of the peddler as an exotic and manipulative threat. It also—at its inception—cemented the image of the Syrian peddler in the public imagination for years to come. Set in what was called Indian Territory in the early 1900s, shortly before the state of Oklahoma was admitted to the United States, the plot revolves around settler matchmaking, feuds between cowboys and farmers, and glorified narratives of US democracy and the western frontier.[49] *Oklahoma!* was revolutionary for the American genre of musicals, as it was the first to fully integrate musical numbers into the plot. It was also the longest-running show of its time. With its first production in 1943, *Oklahoma!* became an instant success; it ran for five years on Broadway, for three years in London's West End, and then for another ten years in the United States with a second company.[50] *Oklahoma!* continues to be performed today in amateur as well as professional productions. In 2007, the 1955 film version of *Oklahoma!* was added to the National Film Registry, which catalogs films of cultural, artistic, or historic importance to the nation.

Amid an almost entirely Euro-American cast, *Oklahoma!* features a lone non-European figure: the Persian peddler, Ali Hakim. While this Southwest Asian migrant figure's presence could be viewed as an anomaly in the midst of American homesteading life, he was anything but. Indeed, immigrant peddlers were a common feature of rural life from the latter part of the nineteenth century into the early twentieth century. Despite his character's description as Persian, Ali Hakim is commonly perceived to be an Ashkenazi Jewish character because of the stereotypes he embodies and because of the association between peddling and Ashkenazi Jews. However, *Oklahoma!* was based on a play written more than a decade earlier by queer Cherokee playwright Lynn Riggs: *Green Grow the Lilacs*. In Riggs's play, the peddler character was Syrian and was modeled on an actual Syrian peddler from Riggs's childhood in the Cherokee Nation. Despite the character's Syrian origins, however, the Arabness of the peddler has not been critically analyzed.

The character's journey from "Syrian" to "Persian" in the development of *Oklahoma!* is somewhat of a mystery. The character started as a Syrian peddler with no name in Riggs's play; but in the first two drafts of the musical, the peddler became an Armenian by the name of Kalenderian Kalazian.[51] How and why Rodgers and Hammerstein departed from "Syrian" and arrived at "Armenian" is unclear, but soon enough "Armenian" also disappeared and the peddler became Ali Hakim, the Persian. Tim Carter, who has extensively chronicled the life of *Oklahoma!* speculates that the Armenian background was dropped because the first director of the show, Rouben Mamoulian, was himself actually Armenian.[52] The shift away from an Armenian character here was an acknowledgment of the caricature of the peddler. In addition to these nationality labels, the peddler character was also referred to as "Turkish" in correspondence regarding casting.[53] None of these sources acknowledge the Syrian peddler from Riggs's original play.

Although the rationale for each change in the national origin of the peddler is unknown, the coherence among the changes is clear. Rodgers and Hammerstein made decisions that enabled the peddler to retain his Middle Eastern origins (as written by Riggs) and simultaneously imbued him with what they understood as (Ashkenazi) Jewish stereotypes. The positioning and analysis of Ali Hakim as a Jewish character who is also assumed to be of European origin has proceeded through three routes. First, the character of Hakim has been described as a white ethnic whose storyline is a lesson in assimilation for American Jews. Second, some of the most prominent actors to portray the peddler character (including its earlier version in Riggs's play) have been Ashkenazi Jews, including Joseph Buloff, Lee Strasberg, and Bruce Adler, all of whom had ties to Yiddish theater traditions. Finally, Ali Hakim has been understood as an authorial figure representing his Jewish creators, Rodgers and Hammerstein.[54] Susan Kollin notes that the "often overlooked history of struggle" of Arabs and Iranians in the United States "has been frequently set aside in scholarly readings that position the figure of the peddler as a stand-in for other marginalized groups in America."[55] What, then, does it mean that a Middle Eastern character was a permissible and effective vehicle to convey Jewish stereotypes? And what is the significance of rendering the Syrian origin of Riggs's character negligible? Rather than taking the Middle Eastern trait of the peddler as a metaphor, I account for both the Arab origins of the peddler and the Ashkenazi Jewish influence on the creation of Ali Hakim, revealing the interdependence of early Arab (and more broadly Southwest Asian and North African, or SWANA) and Ashkenazi Jewish racializations in the United States, as well as the sexualized dimensions of Arab racialization.[56]

Although the character of Ali Hakim in *Oklahoma!* has been linked to stereotypical representations of Jews and was recognizable to American audiences because of the prominence of Jews in peddling professions throughout the nineteenth century and into the twentieth, I analyze the Arabness of the peddler to reveal two interventions.[57] First, the interdependence of Jewish and Arab racializations surfaces and necessarily levels a blow to the ontological dichotomy between Arab and Jew. This dichotomy originates in Zionist rhetoric; its maintenance upholds the displacement of Palestinians and the denial of Palestinian sovereignty, as well as the narrative that Arab (and other Middle Eastern and North African) Jews can only find belonging in Israel.[58] Second, taking seriously the peddler character's Arabness highlights the figure's queerness, sexual anxieties, and these anxieties' centrality to Southwest Asian racialization. My analysis shows that the jokes relating to Ali Hakim's effeminacy and sexuality in *Oklahoma!* cannot be separated from the character's racialization as Arab and Southwest Asian. These jokes function to render the peddler queer, both by questioning the normativity of his sexuality and gender and by setting him apart from the settler community. In addition to relating to the peddler's ethnic background, this queerness stemmed from the anxieties about transient labor and homeless men that grew in the first half of the twentieth century.[59]

In the two decades before the state of Oklahoma was established, the white settlers who came to Indian Territory were emboldened by the doctrine of manifest destiny. They saw themselves as would-be yeomen, entitled to produce a life from the land and to own the land that they worked.[60] Their whiteness was the key to this entitlement. But when many of these poor white settlers became tenant farmers, rather than landowners, this sense of entitlement fueled both the white radicalism of labor struggles and the rise of the Ku Klux Klan in the early decades of twentieth century.[61] The concept of settlement encompassed not only staying put but also private property ownership, business practices tied to that property (e.g., farming or running a store), and, significantly, heterosexual marriage and reproduction. Syrian peddlers were economically useful in this setting by providing goods to white settlers in spaces where goods were not easily accessible. In this context, Syrian peddlers, as racially ambiguous members of the Oklahoma and Indian Territory landscapes, were not especially urgent sites for white nationalist investment. Their economic usefulness outweighed the threat they posed to white supremacy.

Despite this mixture of usefulness and racial insignificance, however, the transient practices of peddling and the sexual implications of that transience were unsettling. This is an example of peddlers' liminal racial position. Their small numbers, in addition to the uncertainty regarding their race, shielded them from a certain amount of white supremacist targeting. But they were not clearly white enough to exempt them completely from racialized violence. The anxieties about Syrian male peddlers point to their transgression of each of these elements.

While *Green Grow the Lilacs* gives little attention to the Syrian peddler character's story, *Oklahoma!* resolves the anxieties surrounding Syrian peddlers through their inclusion in the community: an inclusion via forced sexual, gender, and economic assimilation. This resolution is an example of how a specific hetero-normative economy was essential to the settler colonial project.[62] Examining the social history of peddlers in Oklahoma and other rural spaces adds context for understanding how these fictional representations accrued meaning.

MINOR ENCOUNTERS: LYNN RIGGS'S *GREEN GROW THE LILACS* (1931) AND *KNIVES FROM SYRIA* (1925)

Riggs's plays are filled with the characters of his childhood in the displaced Chero-kee Nation. Riggs was born in 1899 near Claremore, in what would later become Oklahoma, to a Cherokee mother and a white father who was a naturalized Chero-kee citizen. Riggs's mother died in his childhood, and his father remarried another Cherokee woman, who raised him.[63] He had a difficult relationship with his father. Riggs spent most of his life living between Santa Fe and New York City, but the life of his imagination remained with his childhood home.

When asked about the characters of his youth, Riggs wrote:

> It so happens that I knew mostly the dark ones, the unprivileged ones, the ones with the most desolate fields, the most dismal skies. And so it isn't surprising that my plays concern themselves with poor farmers, forlorn wives, tortured youth, plow hands, peddlers, criminals, slaveys—with all the range of folk victimized by brutality, igno-rance, superstition, and dread. And will it sound like an affectation (it most surely is not) if I say that I wanted to give voice and a dignified existence to people who found themselves, most pitiably, without a voice, when there was so much to be cried out against?[64]

Riggs was a queer, mixed-heritage Cherokee playwright who wrote in the first half of the twentieth century. It is not a stretch, then, to propose that his childhood was one in which he felt outcast, and thus it is not surprising that he wrote about others who were outcast as well. Kirby Brown describes Riggs's oeuvre as "one Cherokee's attempt to contend with the chaotic aftermath of allotment and statehood during the early decades of the twentieth century."[65]

Riggs wrote *Green Grow the Lilacs* in 1929; it was first produced on Broadway in 1931. It ran for sixty-four performances (approximately two months), toured throughout the Midwest, and was later nominated for a Pulitzer Prize.[66] The play tells of the courtship between Laurey Williams, an orphaned landowner who lives with her widowed Aunt Eller, and Curly McLain, a local cowboy. The central obstacle to their love is Jeeter, a farmhand living and working on Laurey's property. Riggs's play included a number of folk songs, which were later replaced in *Okla-homa!* by Rodgers and Hammerstein's musical score.

The unnamed peddler appears in only two scenes: first when he comes with Ado Annie to visit Aunt Eller and Laurey, and then in the following scene, when he sells Jeeter a knife. The character of the peddler is unnamed in the script and described as "Syrian." He first enters the play as he is traveling his peddling route accompanied by Ado Annie. His character is constituted immediately as dishonest, manipulative, and seductive. Aunt Eller is furious with him for having sold her, during his previous visit, an eggbeater that was promised to do much more than beat eggs. In response, the peddler mocks her fury by offering her another one. Laurey is concerned about Ado Annie's naivete and reminds her that peddlers are not to be trusted with matters of the heart. Laurey cautions Ado Annie against a relationship with the peddler: "You don't want to git to like a peddler man *too* good, Ado Annie. You hear me? They got wives in ever' state in the union."[67] Signaling that the sexual danger of peddlers was common knowledge, this statement mirrors many people's anxieties about the purported detachment of peddlers and other migratory men from their home communities and normative family structures. As the peddler greets Laurey, he excitedly remarks how much she has grown up and kisses her along her hand and arm. Laurey rebuffs his flirtatiousness, but Riggs's stage directions indicate that she is "a little pleased, in spite of herself."[68] Laurey has a back-and-forth with Ado Annie, again marking the peddler as a primarily sexual being. Laurey asks Annie, "Is that the way he talks to you?" When Annie replies, "Aw, he don't talk to me," Laurey exclaims, "Mercy, whut does he *do* to you!"[69] Significantly, this scene takes place in Laurey's bedroom, where they have gathered to look at the peddler's goods for sale. The peddler may have a scheme to be alone in the room with the young women, as the script has him suggest to Aunt Eller that he has merchandise for her outside with his horse. Aunt Eller exclaims, "Not gonna leave you and two girls in no bedroom, all by yerselves."[70]

The seduction surrounding the peddler is equally about his merchandise and his uncommon origins. Laurey works herself into an "abstracted ecstasy" when dreaming aloud of the things she'd like to have. Laurey's monologue delves into the close associations among middle-class white femininity, desire, consumption, and fantasy: "Want things I cain't tell you about. Cain't see 'em clear. Things nobody ever heared of. . . . Not only things to look at and hold in yer hands. Things to happen to you! Things so nice if they ever did happen yer heart ud quit beatin', you'd fall down dead. They ain't no end to the things I want. Everything you got wouldn't be a starter fer me, Mister Peddler Man!"[71] Laurey's desires are simultaneously material, bodily, and spiritual, alluding to the exotic ("things nobody ever heared of"), the experiential ("things to happen to you"), and the insatiable ("they ain't no end to the things I want") as essential components of the existential questions of Laurey's life. The language of her monologue mirrors the rising importance of commercial consumption and its constructed connection to emotional fulfillment in the cultivation of a white, middle-class femininity.[72] Although Laurey is not presented as middle-class, she has inherited land from her parents and exhibits an aspiration to upward mobility through the items and life she desires. The acquisition of exotic items was a way for the working classes to demonstrate their middle-class ambitions. Each of these desires could also be sexual. Merchandise from the so-called Orient, particularly items associated with the Ottoman Empire, invoked the sexualized space of the harem.[73]

The labor of the Syrian peddler, then, helped constitute his buyers as white, middle-class (or middle-class-aspiring) American women. Both the body of the peddler—in its racialized and sexualized form of difference symbolizing "the East"—and the goods the peddler provided contributed to this labor. Cosmopolitanism, or the display of knowledge of the world beyond one's local confines, was essential to this consumption, and a racial and imperial hierarchy was part of that cosmopolitanism.[74] Syrian peddlers and the cultures they represented (for consumption) could be desired, but they still had to be reviled; the desire created by the nexus of US empire, Orientalism, and capitalism did not allow an equilibrium of power. Vivek Bald's scholarship on Bengali Muslim peddlers working in the United States during the same time as Syrian peddlers shows a similar process of desire and revulsion. Bald describes the peddlers as operating "on a thin edge between Indophilia and xenophobia."[75]

The racialization of the peddler in Riggs's play is typical of other popular portrayals of Syrian peddlers. The peddler is described in the stage directions as "a little wiry, swarthy Syrian . . . very acquisitive, very cunning . . . his beady little eyes sparkling professionally."[76] In production photographs from the Theatre Guild's 1931 staging of *Green Grow the Lilacs* (see figure 1), Lee Strasberg, the actor playing the peddler, appears to be wearing dark eyeliner, facial hair, and makeup to darken his skin. The eyeliner accentuates his "beady little eyes," and the styling of the facial hair invokes racist representations of East Asian men. Here, the peddler is an Orientalist representation of Southwest Asian immigrants. Although the peddler was played by a well-known Ashkenazi Jewish actor in this production, the stage makeup turned the Ashkenazi into the Syrian.

Green Grow the Lilacs was not Riggs's first portrayal of a Syrian. Described as "a comic melodrama of Oklahoma country life," his one-act play *Knives from Syria* (1925) also has a peddler character. It too takes place near Claremore, but about twenty years after the setting of *Green Grow the Lilacs*. Given that it is a one-act play, its characters and plot are not greatly elaborated, but the central theme of unattached women in Oklahoma is the same. A woman and her daughter live alone and survive with the help of a farmhand. The daughter is betrothed to the farmhand but becomes interested in a Syrian peddler (again, unnamed) who visits them frequently. The peddler has written to the daughter and expressed his interest in her; the mother is disgusted by the prospect, but the daughter's desire for the peddler (and the life associated with his transient work) grows. While the daughter is excited by the travel that marriage to a peddler would offer her, the mother warns her that a Syrian peddler would beat her and that they would not have a place to live.[77] The climax of the story occurs when the peddler returns to town and shows the mother and daughter a collection of Syrian knives, among other merchandise. When they see the knives, both mother and daughter fear that the

FIGURE 1. "Laurey's Bedroom Scene. L to R: June Walker (Laurey), Ruth Chorpenning (Ado Annie), Lee Strasberg (Peddler) and Helen Westley as Aunt Eller Murphy." Theatre Guild production of *Green Grow the Lilacs*, 1931. Photo by Vandamm Studio©, Billy Rose Theatre Division, The New York Public Library for the Performing Arts.

peddler was the perpetrator of a recent attack against their farmhand. In an absurd twist, the threatened mother relents and allows the daughter to marry the peddler. When the mother learns that the farmhand was attacked by someone else, she regrets her decision, as she has lost her daughter to a man she abhors. However, her daughter is eager to leave behind what she feels is a boring life and vows never to return. The play thus revolves around the daughter's fascination with and desire for the peddler and around the mother's paranoia about the danger he poses; these foci underscore Riggs's familiarity with Syrian peddlers and the ways their potential customers received them. In one sense, his plays are well versed in the Orientalism of settler culture and its intertwining of desire with violence.[78]

Syrians had a documented presence in what later became the state of Oklahoma as early as 1874, though they did not appear on census records until 1900.[79] Because the earliest documentation described the birth of a child to Syrian parents, Syrians were likely in the region even before this date. The Riggs family themselves, including Lynn and his mother, knew Syrian peddlers.[80] The specificity of the Syrian peddler was important to Riggs's creative remembering of Indian Territory and Oklahoma, but that specificity was lost on audiences and reviewers.

Reviews of the original run on Broadway in 1931 and the tour in 1932 show that *Green Grow the Lilacs* was generally well received. Strasberg, who played the peddler in the original cast with the Theatre Guild of New York, was rarely mentioned. Many reviews did not even mention the peddler role, and those that did simply referred to the character as "a peddler," without ethnic description. This corresponds to the way the peddler is listed in the cast of characters (as "A Peddler"), though the dialogue refers to him as Syrian. Some reviews either changed or erroneously described the peddler's background. A review of the Baltimore production with the original cast described the setting as one in which "the difficult business of subduing the Indians and the soil had been completed by the pioneers' children" and says that "the Jewish peddler who appears in this play was bringing the first frills of a civilization which lay just over the horizon for the prairie folk."[81] In this case, the knowledge that Strasberg was a Polish-born Jew, and that peddling was associated in particular with Jewish immigrants, may have overridden the plot's own indications that the peddler was Syrian. In another instance, a review of the production in Pasadena, California, mentioned the "Hungarian peddler," who was played by a different actor altogether.[82]

Only a single review mentioned the peddler's Syrianness, and obliquely at that. One *New York Times* article charted a genealogy of Riggs's playwriting and his arrival with a hit in *Green Grow the Lilacs*. The piece mentioned *Knives from Syria* and stated that the essence of each of his subsequent six plays can be found in this "experimental one-acter": "For here is the peddler, a brother to the one in 'Green Grow the Lilacs,' who with his samples of an outside world's adornment stirs romantic longings in an Oklahoma farm girl."[83]

The sparse attention that these reviews give the peddler accords with the character's relatively small role in the play. One could say that this disappearance in the press mirrors the Syrian peddler's disappearance from the actual plot of *Green Grow the Lilacs*. Although Rodgers and Hammerstein's musical adaptation, *Oklahoma!*, depicts a fairly homogeneous, white settler community, the actual demographics of Indian Territory at this time were drastically different. David Chang's research on nation, race, and landownership centers on Oklahoma in the nineteenth and early twentieth centuries precisely because of its racial diversity. The story of Oklahoma is the story of a "violent transformation" of Native, Black, and white settler relationships to the land, as all three groups had significant presences in both Oklahoma Territory and Indian Territory from the mid-nineteenth century through the 1920s.[84]

The dispossession of Native land is central to Chang's account. The indigenous nations that had lived in the area when Europeans first arrived were displaced after the Indian Removal Act of 1830, as the US government forced tribes in the southeastern United States to relocate to this ever-diminishing area of land designated "Indian Territory." The Choctaws, Chickasaws, Creeks, Cherokees, and Seminoles were forcibly moved along what is commonly known as the Trail of Tears and resettled in the area that would become Oklahoma. Black Americans also came to this area, in multiple ways. Some escaped slavery in the South and found homes with Native tribes; others were enslaved by Native nations who sided with the Confederacy; and still others came here upon their emancipation, with hopes of owning land and starting new lives. White settlers called "boomers" began coming to this area illegally to take land after the Civil War, when those nations that sided with the Confederacy were forced to cede land to the US government.[85] Boomers attempted to steal, lease, or otherwise occupy indigenous lands in this region. In 1890 the US government named these lands Oklahoma Territory, which was on the western border of Indian Territory, and opened it for homesteading by settlers.

The story of *Oklahoma!* erases not only this landscape and its history but also the likelihood that Riggs's characters were themselves meant to be Native.[86] In contrast to the demographic reality of Indian Territory at the turn of the century, Rodgers and Hammerstein emptied the geography of *Oklahoma!* to make it "the vacant landscape of the myths of dominance."[87] Chang suggests that white settlers in Oklahoma were more concerned with Native and Black claims on the land than with a small immigrant population and questions about its whiteness.[88] This insignificance is mirrored in Riggs's play, in which the Syrian peddler is irrelevant after two scenes. Like peddling itself, the Syrian facilitates something else—in this case, the story of a community in which he is an outsider. Syrian peddlers were significant enough for Riggs to include them in two works, but they were not the focus of his creative vision.

ADAPTING THE "LAND OF DOMINANCE":
OKLAHOMA! (1943)

Rodgers and Hammerstein's *Oklahoma!* is commonly understood to be a musical about American unity and the doctrine of manifest destiny, created to provide uplifting and reassuring entertainment during World War II.[89] The musical adaptation kept close to the original plot of *Green Grow the Lilacs* and preserved much of Riggs's text in its script. The names of the major characters remained the same throughout the play and the musical, with two exceptions: Jeeter Fry in *Green Grow the Lilacs* became Jud Fry in *Oklahoma!* and the nameless peddler in the former became Ali Hakim in the latter. Three principal characters were also added to the musical: Will Parker is Ado Annie Carnes's suitor, who competes with Ali Hakim; Andrew Carnes is Ado Annie's father; and Gertie Cummings is Ali Hakim's eventual wife. The storyline involving these characters is essential to the expanded role of the peddler in the musical adaptation.

Although the majority of the characters in the story are portrayed as fully accepted members of the community, two are clearly cast as outsiders. The first is Jud, portrayed as a violent man and a potential sexual predator. Although Jud's racial origins are not made explicit in the musical, scholars have variously interpreted his character as symbolizing "bad" Jewishness or Blackness.[90] The second outsider, the peddler, is the antidote to the violence of Jud's storyline. Rodgers and Hammerstein greatly expanded the role of the Syrian peddler—now the Persian named Ali Hakim—for the musical. Ali Hakim's role is that of the jester, providing comic relief for the audience while simultaneously embodying the anxieties about peddlers and Southwest Asians that persevered through the early twentieth century. His storyline is secondary, as it chronicles his flirtation with Ado Annie and her involvement with Will.

Ali enters the story in the same fashion as the peddler does in *Green Grow the Lilacs*: traveling with Ado Annie and stopping at the home of Aunt Eller and Laurey. Instead of taking place inside Laurey's bedroom, the scene occurs outside, in front of the house. As with Riggs's Syrian peddler, Ali's seductiveness is situated between revulsion and excitement. Aunt Eller and Laurey are skeptical and are repulsed by him—but when he shows them what he has for sale, their abhorrence melts away. Once Ali tells Aunt Eller about the lingerie from Paris he can sell her, she stops berating him and instead invites him inside the home for a meal. The peddler's seduction thus extends to his wares; even those who are suspicious of the quality of his merchandise and the integrity of his sales pitch, like Aunt Eller, are eventually seduced into buying something.

Ali's associations with manipulation, comedy, seduction, and fantasy are solidified throughout the first act of *Oklahoma!* But the seductiveness of the peddler himself, and particularly his masculinity, is undercut in this version by several elements. First, Ali's love interest, Ado Annie, is portrayed as a clueless flirt who would leave Ali behind if only she knew better. In *Green Grow the Lilacs*, Ado Annie is not supposed to be an attractive woman; the stage notes describe her as "an unattractive, stupid-looking farm girl."[91] Yet in *Oklahoma!* she is as attractive as the lead, Laurey. She still retains the cluelessness of Riggs's character, but the musical's emphasis is more on her sexual proclivities. She is portrayed as sexually open, dim-witted, and morally naive. In both versions of the character, Ado Annie is not a respectable woman: she is hypersexual, and her sexuality is not aimed toward reproduction. Thus, one can infer that she is with Ali Hakim because, as her solo musical number suggests, she "cain't say no," rather than because of his appeal as a mate. In addition, when Ali greets Laurey and kisses up and down her arm, the Laurey in *Oklahoma!* is affronted. She exhibits none of this flirtation's "secret pleasure" that we find in Riggs's stage notes. In the move from 1931 to 1943, the Syrian/Persian peddler has lost some of his desirability.

Ali's seductiveness is tempered by a second factor: his role as the musical's comedian. An earlier version of the musical included certain comedic lines that connected gender to Ali's racial difference from the white settlers. In the earlier version, Ali opens the song "It's a Scandal! It's a Outrage!" with the spoken lines: "Friends, / Out in the east, / Out in the east, / A woman's a slave. / She is bought, / Rented or leased. / Then she's taught / How to behave!"[92] In effect, these lyrics set

Ali apart from the other men of Claremore by invoking his imagined relationship to hyperpatriarchal norms of the Islamic East. These lyrics' specific references to enslaving, purchasing, and teaching women "how to behave" invite images of the harem, well known to American audiences by the 1940s. This song is the only one that Ali performs, and it creates a momentary intercultural patriarchal identification between Ali and the male settlers. After Ali has ended up engaged to Ado Annie despite his desire to be single, the men lament together the growing independence of women and the diminishing freedom of men. Ali's difference from white Americans is thereby established through various maneuvers that signal his gender, sexuality, and culture as being distinct and deviant from those of the United States. These lines were cut from the final stage version of the song, but a similar jab at Middle Eastern patriarchy ensues when Ali jokes about the number of wives Persian men have, calling his brother who has only one wife a "bachelor."[93]

In addition to playing the jester, Ali practices a seduction that offers hints of sexual nonnormativity as well. In one scene, he gives Ado Annie a "Persian goodbye" in front of Will, her white settler fiancé. The joke is that the "Persian goodbye" is a long, passionate kiss. At this point in the story, Ali has been trying to convince Ado Annie that Will is the right husband for her, trying to avoid marrying her himself. As he sings Will's praises, she asks him, "Do you love Will too?" And after Ali gives Ado Annie his "Persian goodbye," he jokes that Will could be the next to receive one. The suggestion of queerness in this joke, by highlighting Ali's failure with women, undermines any possible normative masculinity of the peddler.

In *Oklahoma!* Ali's fate is continually at the mercy of the women he seduces—or, more accurately, at the mercy of their fathers. Ado Annie is convinced that because Ali wants to find "paradise" with her upstairs at the Claremore hotel, he must want to marry her.[94] In keeping with her character's cluelessness, Ado Annie gladly tells her father the details of their courtship. She says that Ali calls her his "Persian kitten" because they have "soft round tails."[95] As a result, Annie's father points his shotgun at Ali to force him to agree to marry her. Ali escapes by maneuvering Ado Annie and Will together instead, but later he ends up tricking himself into marriage with another woman, Gertie Cummings. Gertie is distinguished by her piercing, nervous laughter and is clearly portrayed as not the most sought-after woman in the community, which in turn reflects negatively on the peddler's desirability. In an echo of Ali's earlier misfortune with Ado Annie, the union with Gertie is arranged at gunpoint by Gertie's father. Earlier drafts of *Oklahoma!* also introduced another character (cut from the final version) to play opposite Ali: a Mexican woman named Lotta Gonzales, who is described as "sexually active."[96] While racialized differently than Ado Annie, Lotta Gonzales is also hypersexual and nonreproductive, thus underscoring Ali's deviance in relation to the women in his life. In those drafts, Ali's relationship with Lotta is solidified by the end of the play, a plot move that would have also reinscribed Ali's brownness and blocked his assimilation into the white settler community. Both story lines (the initial draft

FIGURE 2. "Joseph Buloff (Ali Hakim), Celeste Holm (Ado Annie Carnes) and Ralph Riggs (Andrew Carnes) in *Oklahoma!*" St. James Theater, 1943. Photo by Vandamm Studio©, Billy Rose Theatre Division, The New York Public Library for the Performing Arts, 1943.

involving Lotta, and the final version with Gertie) involve taming women's sexuality through marriage and, more broadly, disciplining desire—making desire, and especially women's sexual and relationship choices, a major concern of the plot. Both story lines also position the peddler's love interests as less desirable than the female lead, Laurey.

The costuming and body language choices for Ali Hakim also signal his deviation from normative masculinity, as evidenced in the production photographs of the original Broadway cast. In figure 2, Ali's sexual and gender differences are best seen in contrast with Ado Annie's virulent father, Andrew Carnes, and in contrast with Ado Annie as well. The picture depicts the scene in which, after he finds out about Ali's intentions with Ado Annie, Andrew tries to force Ali to marry her at gunpoint. Andrew's monochromatic dark suit jacket, pants, and boots denote an unambiguous masculinity, compared with Ado Annie's light-hued dress and tiers of ruffled fabric. Ali also wears a suit, but his looks unlikely to ever get dirty. His clothing is fancy, in the style of a dandy: entirely patterned in plaid edged with dark piping. The characters' body language mimics this contrast. Andrew's stance is wide-legged, and he points a shotgun in Ali's face. Ali's body is languid, approaching the shape of the letter *S*. Rather than holding a gun or another weapon, Ali holds a walking stick, which droops toward the ground. He is not bracing for a fight but rather pointing, or perhaps wagging, his finger in Andrew's direction. Phallic gestures of varying states abound in both men's postures.

In his gendered visual and bodily presentation, Ali Hakim is thus situated between Ado Annie and Andrew Carnes. Not a woman but not fully a man either, in appearance he is more associated with a dandy than with a farmer or a cowboy. This indeterminate positioning echoes the 1920s' discourses about the sheikh character and the fears of increasing effeminacy.[97] It also builds upon earlier histories in which Arabness and Middle Easternness were discursive vessels through which to express anxieties and fears about other marginalized populations. The figure of the "street Arab" is a prime example. Beginning in mid-nineteenth-century Britain and later in that century in the United States, poor boys who were in public view without parental care, who were either working or just existing on the streets, were characterized as "Arabs" because of their wildness, their lack of supervision, and their apparent lack of rules governing their lives. The starkest example was the use of "Arab" to characterize other nonwhite racialized groups who were similarly deemed "lawless" and "ungoverned."[98] Films like *The Sheik*, released in 1921, used Arab characters (who were coded either racially or culturally as Arab) as a way to express anxieties about the place of Italian immigrants and their offspring in American society.[99] In this latter example, as well as in Rodgers and Hammerstein's Ali Hakim, the Arab or Middle Eastern figure was also a sexualized one, and that sexuality depended on the gendered ambiguity of Middle Eastern masculinity.

Ali's queer masculinity is thus inseparable from his placement in the community as an Oriental foreigner. Despite Rodgers and Hammerstein's intention to create a thinly veiled Ashkenazi Jewish character, the queerness of this figure—his seductiveness, simultaneous effeminacy, and failures with women—underscores the character's Southwest Asian origin and the Orientalism of his creators. The threat of Ali Hakim as both a sexual predator and an effeminate deviant, all embodied in the same individual, is enabled through Orientalist genealogies of cultural difference.[100]

Just one year after the end of the US tour, following eleven years of performances since the debut of *Oklahoma!* on Broadway, the film version was made. The movie's script and musical numbers stuck closely to Rodgers and Hammerstein's stage version. While the first two stage iterations of the peddler were played by notable Jewish actors (Lee Strasberg and Joseph Buloff, respectively), the 1955 film features a well-known non-Jewish actor, Eddie Albert. Albert, a character actor who played a range of leading and supporting roles, was not associated with Jewishness or indeed with any particular ethnic characters. Scholars who have examined the transition from musical play to film assert that by the time the film was produced, the character was so well established that the producers found it no longer necessary to make him overtly Jewish.[101] The film's Ali is also no longer effeminate like the one in 1943. Nor is his appearance altered to make him look Middle Eastern, as in the 1931 staging.

Beyond his Persian designation, the only thing that differentiates Albert's Ali from the rest of the Claremore community in the movie is his profession as a peddler and his foreign accent (which is not consistent through the film). Ali's ethnicity in the film functions as an accessory; for all intents and purposes, he is (or has become) white. Also, the peddler's one musical number, "It's a Scandal! It's a Outrage!," was cut from the film. Although the queerness of Ali Hakim was mitigated in the film version by eliminating his effeminacy, the jokes about the "Persian goodbye" and his love for Will remain. He is also still portrayed as a sexual predator. In the beginning, rather than meeting Laurey either inside or outside her home, Ali encounters her swimming in the nearby lake. Laurey scrambles to cover herself with a towel as Ali approaches and begins to remark upon how grown-up she is. As he kisses up her hand and arm, Laurey is visibly affronted, rebuffing Ali's advances in a show of feminine propriety. This difference from both Riggs's play and the stage version of the musical marks Ali Hakim as a clear womanizer. However, his sexuality is no longer intertwined with his supposed non-European origin. As his race is whitened, his sexuality is also whitened, or normalized.

Both the authorship of *Oklahoma!* and the time when it was written illuminate the reasons for the differences between the musical and Riggs's play where the peddler is concerned. Whereas Riggs wrote during the Great Depression, was influenced by his indigeneity, and sought to tell stories of the people he knew in childhood, Rodgers and Hammerstein wrote during World War II and were influenced by their own immigrant and Jewish heritages. In 1943 the United States was at war. American unity, the persecution of Jews under Nazism, and the potential expansion of US empire were all important ideas in popular culture. Rodgers and Hammerstein were two of a number of Jewish artists who helmed American musical theater in the 1930s, 1940s, and 1950s. Andrea Most argues that theater during this time was the primary venue through which Jews could articulate their vision of America and carefully insert themselves "as accepted members of the white American community."[102] Most notes that the settling-down of Ali Hakim in the film version of *Oklahoma!* may also have had to do with the impact of Zionism on Rodgers and Hammerstein. Zionism offered the promise of a utopic Jewish state, which was presented as a place where Jews could "return to the soil, become farmers, and claim the land as their own."[103]

In addition, at the time *Oklahoma!* was created, the United States had not yet recovered from the roving army of men looking for work during and after the Depression and their association with perversion. If anything, the Depression-era anxieties surrounding hobos and tramps grew into a full-fledged panic about homosexuality during World War II, as the number of veterans in transient populations grew. Officials feared that these numbers would skyrocket after the war, allowing for increased roaming of the unattached and their abandoning of familial responsibilities.[104] The GI bill was created for this purpose, for "settling men down after wartime." In this legislation, the first prohibitions against homosexuality also appeared, as the "vague opposition between mobility and settlement [was] hardening in a clear line between homosexuality and heterosexuality."[105] The musical's uneasy humor about the peddler's potential for queerness, as well as his unrestrained flirtatiousness with women, fit into this rubric of national panic. *Oklahoma!* both spoke to this anxiety in American audiences and appeased them by heterosexualizing and domesticating all elements of sexual deviance in the story, all the while reaffirming American superiority. Later revivals of *Oklahoma!* went on to revise its racist, anti-indigenous, and heteronormative plot, including a 2018 version that changed the characters' genders and sexual orientations. That particular revival recast Ali as bisexual.[106] Susan Kollin notes that many of these attempts at recuperation have come at the expense of the still-Orientalist peddler character.[107]

In Indian Territory and the early days of Oklahoma statehood, Syrian peddlers inhabited contradictory positions. Their economic services were useful, but their racial and cultural difference, seen as a kind of queerness, was threatening to normative American national identity. If the queerness of the peddler was a barrier to the early Syrian immigrant's integration into white settler societies, forcing the peddler to assimilate through his sexual and economic practices would ostensibly allow him this access. Rodgers and Hammerstein's *Oklahoma!* illustrates this resolution with the peddler, in what is perhaps its most significant deviation from Riggs's *Green Grow the Lilacs*. Specifically, while the peddler does not appear in Riggs's play after the first two scenes, in *Oklahoma!* Ali Hakim's flirtation with settler women continues. Ali evades marriage to Ado Annie only to find himself trapped in a commitment to Gertie Cummings by the end of the show. Once she announces her marriage to him, Gertie explains: "Ali ain't goin' to travel around the country no more. I decided he orta settle down in Bushyhead and run Papa's store."[108] The settling here is literal, meaning that Ali must stay put, now living and working in the local community rather than coming and going as he pleases. Reflecting the sexual anxieties about transient male laborers during this period, the settling indicated here also concerns Ali's life as a bachelor and womanizer. Margot Canaday notes that, in the context of the national panic regarding migratory populations after the Great Depression, "the literal cessation of movement was only a precondition for settling down, which implied not only steady employment and property ownership, but marriage and reproduction as well."[109] Finally, the settling also points to the transition from Indian Territory to the state of Oklahoma, wherein the peddler is ushered into a different role in the settler colonial project.

We can see the centrality of heteronormativity to the white supremacist, settler colonial project in this process of settling. The narrative strategies of early Arab American scholars and community activists are indicative of the sexual politics of settling as well. These narratives posited peddling as a temporary endeavor that quickly enabled transient Syrian pioneers to become permanent settlers who operated businesses, married and had children, and contributed to the communities in which they lived. This trajectory thus operated within a binary of transient versus settled. For this binary to function, peddling had to be a temporary endeavor, a profession performed out of necessity and ingenuity. This trajectory might appear in the formulation of going from "Peddlers to Store Owners" or "Peddlers to Professionals," or perhaps as a settling-down like "Peddlers Find a Home."[110] As peddling routes produced many small Syrian communities across the midwestern and southern United States, Alixa Naff argues, theirs was a process of "piecemeal transition of transients into citizens." The presumed subject of these narratives, however, was a Syrian man, and he was expected to conform to a particular sexual framework. The transient (peddler) was unattached and thus able to live out sexual relationships in a number of ways, while the citizen (business owner) was married (or looking for a wife) and ready to reproduce his sexual, settler citizenship. In these ways, the overarching binary regarding transience and settlement operated through several other overlapping binaries, each masking these sexual imperatives: ethnic enclave versus dispersed settlements, Syrian nationalist versus American citizen, working class versus middle class, transient versus settled, and migrant versus citizen. All of these binary articulations contributed to an implicit spectrum from Arab or nonwhite to white, and from transient to settler. The route from one to the other was also a sexual one.

The narrative resolution of *Oklahoma!* is a process of assimilation, whitening, and settling for the male Southwest Asian peddler: through his profession and business practices, his mobility and residence, and his sexuality. The musical's resolution offers a striking contrast to the experiences of violence that Syrian peddlers articulated, and it offers a glimpse of how the possible route toward whiteness for Syrian immigrants was anchored in disciplining sexual norms and in taking on a new role within US settler colonialism. For Syrian women, as the following chapter shows, the responses to their roles in the ecology of peddling were mired in both Syrian and white American essentialist ideologies of womanhood that necessitated women's sexual role within the Syrian immigrant family.

2

"A Woman without Limits"

Syrian Women in the Peddling Economy

'Abd al-Masih Haddad's 1921 short story, "Timthal al-Huriyya" (Statue of Liberty) is a tongue-in-cheek cautionary tale for the Arab immigrant man.[1] The story's protagonist, Nakhla al-Masoub, brings his young wife, Edma, with him to the United States, where he hopes to enrich their lives economically. Yet, despite being a self-described "lord of the house," Nakhla strikes out financially time and time again and ends up deep in debt. One day, his brother-in-law suggests that if Nakhla were to send his wife out to work as a peddler, his debts would quickly diminish. The brother-in-law convinces Nakhla of this proposal by noting that "in America, women succeeded in work and they even surpassed men." Indeed, Nakhla's wife becomes such a successful peddler that she becomes their primary source of income, and Nakhla eventually becomes the caregiver of their three children. This labor arrangement dramatically challenges Nakhla's masculinity and his sense of self: "His wife continued to be the breadwinner while he raised the children in their mother's absence. He left work, his entire life and his family's life now rested on the shoulders of his wife. . . . After this, Nakhla was no longer a prince in his house, but became a slave to his wife and his children. She became the head of the family and a woman without limits."[2] This transformation and the tensions it introduced feature in an exchange between Nakhla and his wife:

> Nakhla continued to swallow his worries until he couldn't handle them anymore. That same night, the lady Edma returned home from work to look for Nakhla and found the children crying and sniffling. Once she had tended to them, she went looking for her husband, shaking as if her heart was on fire. There, she saw him sitting on a bench in Liberty Park. He was lost in thought, thinking about how he was once a prince in his own land and now a slave in the diaspora. Edma began to humiliate him and lead him to the house, telling him that if he did this again that she would kick him out of the house and would pay someone to take care of her children in her absence.[3]

Such is Nakhla's emasculation: no longer a "prince" of his home and nation, he is chastised by his peddler-breadwinner wife for not taking care of the children. His descent as "a slave in the diaspora" is simultaneously economic, gendered, and sexual. The anxieties Haddad alludes to aligned with discourses about modernity and changing gender norms, discourses in which men feared emasculation by the "new," modern woman.

Haddad's depiction of gendered oppression was not unique for his time. Elizabeth Saylor notes that several Arab migrant writers regularly commented on the situation of women under patriarchal structures. These critiques were, however, somewhat undermined by their overwhelming focus on men's perspectives—as is the case with "Timthal al-Huriyya."[4] Haddad's story hits at the heteropatriarchal structure of the Syrian family and at the disruption and transformation wrought by migration and living in diaspora. To gain insight into Edma's perspective, we must look and imagine elsewhere.

Syrian women were the nexus of the queer ecology of peddling. Their participation in the peddling economy was central to this sexual, gender, and family transformation because their labor had sexual and gendered implications for how they were discursively and materially constituted in diaspora. First, Syrian women peddlers trespassed gendered boundaries of space and labor when they worked outside their homes and traversed public space in the course of their work. Second, all Syrian women who participated in the peddling economy—whether as peddlers, boardinghouse operators, or makers—brought the gendered and classed norms of Syrian motherhood into stark relief. Working outside the home or turning the home into a site of nonreproductive labor called into question a Syrian woman's maternal fitness, in both Syrian and American contexts. Third, the archival legacies of the peddling economy highlight the sexual economy of the Syrian immigrant family. The measures taken to discourage women from participating in the peddling economy emphasized the ideal of women's labor in the Syrian immigrant family as, essentially, sexually reproductive. The fact that, in some instances, Syrian women and girl peddlers were more successful than their male counterparts only deepened this tension.

Syrians also debated internally about the consequences and propriety of women working as peddlers. One consequence of this debate came in the form of frequent gossip about women's and girls' behavior, as well as the threat of gossip ("what will the people say"?).[5] (I examine these internal debates as a form of Syrian community self-policing more fully in chapter 3.) While the concerns about peddling Syrian men were overtly sexual, concerns about Syrian women in the peddling economy were often expressed through the identification and violation of gender norms. It would be a mistake, however, to understand these expressions of gender anxiety as divorced from the sexual. I examine gender alongside sexuality as an analytical tool. This approach does not presume an equivalence or necessary link between sexuality and gender, but rather recognizes that gender remains a "crucial modifier of sexuality."[6] Indeed, the social welfare concerns regarding gendered morality, as explored in this chapter, were always simultaneously concerns about the sexual.

Shifts in the economic and family life of Syrian Christian peasants, who formed the majority of these migrants, actually began before migration.[7] For example, farmers in Mount Lebanon participated heavily in the silk industry, raising silkworms to feed on their mulberry trees. The opening of the Suez Canal in 1869 boosted this sector even more over the following few decades until increased competition from Chinese silk dampened Mount Lebanon's industry. In this context, some women and girls began to work in silk factories, while men continued to work the land. This arrangement has been called a sacrifice of women's honor, offered so that men could retain their own honor, as well as their social status, both of which were based in the land.[8] It may be more accurate, however, to call attention to this process as imbuing the concept of "women's honor" with a kind of flexibility to adapt to these economic changes while still allowing for patriarchal control.

In diaspora, Syrians were presented with relatively fewer options for having a sense of self and doing land-based forms of work, particularly when many of them intended to return to the Levant after making some money. If we accept the premise that some Syrian men's sense of honor (i.e., their sense of heteropatriarchal-based identity) had already weathered some blows in the decades just prior to migration, the lack of land-based but short-term economic opportunity in diaspora exacerbated these issues in Syrian masculinity. Certainly, such a generalization was not absolute. Some Syrians were open to permanent or long-term relocation (and thus a wider variety of work), and others were more adaptable and receptive to these changes in gendered labor than others. In addition, this dynamic may have been particular to those migrants from Mount Lebanon, whereas those from cities like Damascus may not have felt these gendered changes in exactly the same way.[9] But in other cases, such as that of Haddad's characters Nakhla and Edma, women's successes as peddlers were a reminder of these cultural changes and of Syrian men's diminished opportunities to sustain an economically based sense of masculinity within the diaspora. Such differing experiences of these massive gendered and cultural shifts paved the way for women's and girls' behaviors to become the basis for ethnic and nationalist identity in diaspora.[10]

Early Arab American studies scholarship bears out these transformations wrought by migration and peddling. In one of the earliest publications on Arabs in diaspora, published in 1943, Lebanese sociologist Afif Tannous studied emigrants and their descendants from his home region who had relocated to Vicksburg, Mississippi, some fifty years earlier. Comparing the norms of the diasporic community with those of their ancestors and contemporaries in Mount Lebanon, Tannous traced acculturation through family structure, economic culture, social integration, and citizenship and nationalism. He argued that peddling suited Syrians' temporary intentions in the United States because "it did not tie them down to the place permanently" and it allowed for "quick and lucrative results."[11]

Tannous understood the changes in gender norms and marriage customs to be key factors in this process of acculturation. He was particularly interested in fertility rates, the advent of divorce, and the "breakdown of the family unit" from an extended kin household to a two-generation household consisting of a married couple and their children. Peddling, and women's participation in it, was a sharp departure from the "original culture," as were changes in the family living structure: "Complete departure from the original culture has occurred with respect to the subordinate role of the bride in particular and of woman in general. Instead of going to live with her husband's people, the bride now starts her home independently with her husband. She takes full charge of the home. She has also achieved occupational equality. With this goes full economic equality, to the extent of joint ownership of property and business in many cases."[12]

Tannous included an excerpt from one of his interviews with a seventy-year-old woman to illustrate these changes. The woman's husband had come to the United States alone at first, refusing to let his wife accompany him, "saying that it would be a shame on him to let his wife travel to the end of the world in order to earn a living."[13] But when the husband had difficulty with the climate and became sick, the woman left their children with their grandmother and joined him in the United States: "I tried peddling, as soon as I arrived, and succeeded very well at it, making much money. *Then I sent my husband back home* and continued my successful peddling."[14] In the absence of further information about this particular arrangement, we can only imagine the perspective of Tannous's interviewee; perhaps, like Edma in Haddad's fiction, "she became the head of the family and a woman without limits."[15]

Early Arab American scholar Philip Hitti advanced an argument about women's economic utility in his 1924 book, *The Syrians in America*. As soon as Syrians realized "the economic value of the woman," Hitti observed, women began to migrate in larger numbers. In particular, the work of peddling "lent itself more easily to women workers who had freer access to homes."[16] As discussed in chapter 1, that differential access was based on the perceived *sexual* threat of Syrian men and the lack thereof in Syrian women and children. Later studies corroborated this link between migration, women's labor (and peddling in particular), and changes in family life. Two early studies in the 1969 edited volume *The Arab Americans* showed the significance of women in the Syrian peddling economy. In her chapter on Arab Americans in Boston, Elaine Hagopian noted that "some of the best and most successful" peddlers were women, some of whom took up peddling as their husbands moved on to open their own businesses.[17] Safia Haddad argued that the shifts in women's economic position resulting from migration challenged the patriarchal status of men. Haddad detailed the changes in women's "spatial world" (that is, into the public sphere) because of peddling and women's adaptation to commerce inside the home (by making things for other peddlers to sell). These characteristics of Syrian women's labor shifted the traditional structure of gender and the family, but Haddad contended that both men and women knew it was economically useful.[18] No matter what Syrians thought of them, these changes were substantial and the woman peddler became a symbol of them.

To investigate women's participation in the peddling economy, this chapter relies primarily on social welfare records in which Syrians were both aid recipients and social reformers themselves. In their archival legacy, as well as their power to shape public discourse regarding poverty, gender, and citizenship, social welfare agencies reveal a dynamic and inconsistent understanding of Syrian immigrants. Social welfare records reflect the changing and often contradictory opinions held regarding (and to a certain extent, within) the Syrian community and reveal the mechanisms through which Syrians were discursively disciplined into (or expelled from) the US national body. Once Syrians began to appear in US social welfare records starting in the late 1880s, their living conditions, family structures, cultural markers of difference and similarity, and laboring practices became sites of scrutiny. Of course, this development fit with larger discourses questioning the place and assimilability of immigrants from southern and eastern Europe and from across the Asian continent. Although naturalization rights were based on a claim to whiteness, uncertainty persisted regarding Syrians' racial qualifications for citizenship even after the courts settled this question in Syrians' favor in 1915. Thus, in social work records, we can see how Syrians' "degrees of undeserving or deserving" the privileges of Americanness remained in flux.[19]

Moreover, Syrian women in particular populate the pages of social welfare records, for a variety of reasons. First, many of these agencies were, as a rule, primarily concerned with women and children and thus sought contact with women and children from various communities. In some cases, social workers would not aid a particular family without first seeing the woman of the household.[20] Indeed, women and children in general appear more frequently in social work collections than men—whether as social workers themselves, who were overwhelmingly middle-class women, or those whom social workers sought to help. Second, Syrian men who peddled would have been away from home for longer periods of time, and thus women were more likely the ones seeking aid for their families. Women peddlers usually stayed closer to home.[21] Finally, some Syrian men may have felt too vulnerable (and potentially emasculated in that vulnerability) to seek aid from what was usually a female social worker.[22] Children also appear abundantly in social welfare commentary. Their appearance was always an indictment of their parents, and specifically their mothers. Thus, the social welfare commentary surrounding Syrian communities and peddling produced damaging discourses about Syrian women and their families.

The sources used in this chapter include proceedings and reports from charity organizations, articles from periodicals on social work and philanthropy, news media, census data, case files from the International Institutes of Boston and

Minnesota, and the papers of the Syrian Ladies Aid Society of Boston. Agencies of social welfare were a venue through which Syrians sought assistance with employment, health and medicine, money, and in some cases issues more centrally related to immigrant needs, such as English-language classes, naturalization, and family reunification. At such places as the International Institute of Boston, case files show hundreds of Syrians came to the agency's offices for aid or received visits from social workers regarding abandonment or neglect by a husband, physical and sexual abuse, the need for child care, or financial assistance.[23] Other Syrian immigrants attended language and "Americanization" classes or sought help in bringing other family members to the United States. The collections of social work organizations and periodicals are but one set of sources where records on working-poor and working-class Syrian immigrants can be located. The content of such archives often contrasts starkly with community and family-based Arab American collections, whose curation might well have been shaped by donors' desire to preserve a narrative of respectability (as discussed in chapter 4).

Although some outside the Syrian community saw virtues in the Syrian peddler, few social workers seemed to do so, particularly when women peddled. Many in the various fields of social welfare derided peddling as a dishonest and lazy form of work, painting Syrian men as manipulative, Syrian women as pitiful and unruly, and Syrian children as endangered and dangerous. In some rarer circumstances, social workers saw women peddlers as exercising new opportunities for independence and prosperity. Peddling was not something that could be done in isolation. At the very least, it required a supplier of the items for sale. More often than not, peddling was an enterprise that also needed support from other peddlers to ensure safety on the road and to avoid competitive quarrels, as well as support from family members who took care of children and the elderly at home. Moreover, nonpeddling women often made lace or other items for peddlers to sell, or they operated boardinghouses where peddlers would lodge on their long-distance routes. So, although peddling required a degree of disconnect from the community, it is better understood as a highly interdependent system of work. And precisely because this system blurred the classed and Eurocentric boundaries of public and private gendered and sexual labor, it attracted the gaze of the state. The public-private boundary hinged on prescribed gendered and sexual roles and was central to Eurocentric conceptions of modernity. To social welfare workers, the peddling economy became a symbol of Syrians' violation of this boundary and, by extension, called into question their capacity to be properly modern. Peddling was embedded in a web of social welfare scrutiny of Syrians' homes, boardinghouses, parenting practices, intimate relationships, and larger support networks that sustained peddling as a profession.

There are gradations of participation and scrutiny to attend to here. Some peddlers, including women, were praised for their hard work and initiative in finding a way to survive in a strange land. In addition, it is difficult to even make distinctions between "positive" and "negative" representations of Syrian women in the peddling economy, as such characterizations relied on a normative system of evaluation that scripted women's work into binary categories of modern versus traditional and American versus Syrian. Women's labor in the peddling economy was controversial, but it was not universally maligned. Still, social welfare reformers saw peddling as an inherent threat to the family—one that allowed men to abandon their familial duties, women to neglect their children, and children to be exposed to the moral and physical dangers of the streets. Charity and social workers' scrutiny of peddling among Syrians—and particularly among Syrian women—was at once a concern about female gender and sexual normalcy, about the racial classifications of Southwest Asian immigrants and their assimilability, about the policing of public space, and about poor and working-class immigrants who lacked (or seemed to lack) the aspiration to a middle-class, sedentary professional life. Syrian women's adaptability to the norms that social workers articulated for them correlated directly with their perceived fitness for US citizenship, a privileged category predicated on standards of white, middle-class heteronormativity. When social workers pathologized Syrian women for their parenting, homes, and laboring practices, they created an opportunity for others to interrogate Syrian racial, sexual, and gender normativity.

WOMEN PEDDLERS AND RACIAL PRESCRIPTIONS OF GENDER

Syrian women took to peddling in great numbers and, in doing so, challenged both Syrian and white American gendered prescriptions for women and girls. The ramifications of this challenge varied. In some cases, peddling women were a curiosity; in others, they were cause for great alarm.

One 1888 news article implied far-reaching consequences of Syrian women's peddling. A Syrian nun living in Brooklyn was peddling beads door to door to raise money for an orphanage in Syria. She was accompanied by a young boy who served as her interpreter. An onlooker reported her to the police because "her strong masculine features and her big feet led him to believe she was a man." Police detained the nun and the boy until their story could be verified. While police could not confirm the nun's womanhood directly (a fellow religious sister vouched for her), the police were satisfied that her statement as to her intention was truthful and released them both. Still, the news reporter felt certain that the sister was no sister at all—neither a nun nor a woman—and he set out to determine this by interrogating others and tracking his suspect back to her residence. From here, the reporter built a sensational, quasi-anthropological account of his foray into Brooklyn's Syrian neighborhood. His investigation took him from shopkeepers to churches to saloons, and eventually to "batter[ing] at every door he came across" at 57 Washington Street, a boardinghouse where many Syrians lived.

Finally, he encountered "a person who was dressed like one of Barnum's Arabs." Careful to refrain from using any gendered pronouns, the reporter noted the appearance and contents of the room while describing the impossibility of communication:

> Besides the Syrian and the reporter there was in the room an old bedstead, upon which the Syrian sat, and a couple of old chairs, upon neither of which the reporter sat. The floor was bare. There were some pieces of leather straps and a piece of old rope near the window. Some old clothes hung by a hook from the wall. The reporter could not make the Syrian understand that he was looking for the Sister who was said to be living in the house, and started out to look for an interpreter. The Syrian closed the door and locked it.[24]

The reporter discovered later that this person was indeed the sister he had been seeking. Other Syrians continued to vouch for her, but the Catholic church from which the sister was said to have a letter was vehement that they would "not give a letter to anyone let alone these Syrians." The reporter continued his account by reflecting on the mendacity of Syrian peddlers, their propensity to drink "big schooners of beer," and their cheapness. In one store that the Syrian sister was said to have frequented, the shopkeepers said that sometimes other sisters would encounter her there. In those instances, she would "hasten away," causing the shopkeepers to reflect that it was "queer the way she acted." Moreover, when they tried to question her boy interpreter, the two would leave.

How might we think about this historical artifact of a person's life, in this case, the Syrian peddler? Maybe this was indeed a cross-dressing Syrian peddler living in late-nineteenth-century New York City. This could have been a man dressed as a nun, with a story about raising money for an orphanage so that his peddling efforts would be more profitable. After all, Syrian men were perceived to be sexual threats to their (presumed) white women customers, as demonstrated in chapter 1. Women peddlers were received with more sympathy and thus were more likely to make a sale. In some cases, children peddled with fathers to mitigate their perceived threat.[25] We certainly cannot conclude that fabrications of narrative were never used to persuade customers.

But can we also imagine a different reality than that suggested by the reporter? In the absence of archival information about the peddler themselves, we can draw on what we do know about the time and the context to imagine an alternate scenario:

> *Mariam would rise early in the morning, just as the first birds began to chirp. This was her indication that others would rise soon, and her time would no longer be her own. Careful not to make too much noise, she washed her face and pulled on the long robe and habit that was typical for her order. She checked her reflection once and brushed a wisp of hair under her habit. While others tended to think her odd-looking for a woman, she was quite satisfied with the rough quality of her features and her towering*

size. Better to be feared than to be dominated, she thought. Better to be unlikely than common.

She double-checked that her kasha, *her peddling box, was stocked and opened the door. Elias was seated in the hallway, waiting to begin their route. She often wondered if it would have been more prudent to leave him at the orphanage, but he seemed to grow from their adventure. Plus, he hadn't lost his manners or his kindness. She reassured herself.*

Their first stop was the holy store on Barclay Street. They came here on the first Wednesday of every month. Sometimes as they left, they were able to catch customers, drawn by the prospect of blessed rosaries from Jerusalem. The boy called to an older woman who was descending the front stoop, but she hurried away from them as they approached. The two entered the store and saw that a group of Syrian ladies, the Khoury sisters, were gathered near the purchase counter. Upon seeing Sister Mariam and Elias, the sisters whispered in hushed tones and averted their gazes. Mariam felt her cheeks hot as the shopkeeper's curiosity bubbled over. He said something to Elias in English, and Elias's tug at her sleeve indicated it was time to leave. In moments like these, any attempt to satiate inquiring tongues only led to more questions and more suspicion. She didn't want to put Elias in the position of having to defend her, and she wanted to keep her own anger manageable. They left without a word. They proceeded to their next stop, as if nothing had happened.

We can wonder: was her jaw too square, her gait too lumbering? Did she not smile enough? Was she simply taller than the women the reporter was accustomed to? Perhaps she was neither a masculine woman nor a cross-dressing man but a gender transgressor of another sort. We cannot know how this particular historical figure thought of themselves; that barrier to our knowledge is a frustration, but it also holds endless possibilities. The questions about this particular figure—and others—are important, as is the attempt at a response. Regardless of what we might imagine, the answers remain open-ended. We can, however, glean from this remarkable story that Syrian women's peddling constituted a serious transgression of gender for some.

Another instance of reporting on Syrian life, published decades later, hints at some of these implications of gender transgression in women's peddling. In 1911, the *Detroit Free Press* published a piece on the ubiquity of Syrians working as peddlers and of women, in particular, among their ranks. "Kindly-disposed people are distressed at the burdens these women carry," the brief article noted, but, it reassured readers, "eastern women are trained from infancy to carry" such loads.[26] The article continued: "The water jar, which such a woman carries home on her head thrice a day from the fountain, perhaps a hundred feet deep in a valley below her village, is far heavier than her suitcase of embroideries and kimonos. . . . Whatever the disadvantages of peddling, the weight of the pack is not one of them."[27]

This article was excerpted from a series of essays published throughout the summer of 1911 in the social welfare periodical *The Survey*. Written by missionary and editor Louise Seymour Houghton and funded by a grant from the Carnegie

Foundation, this four-part series chronicled the history and life of Syrians in the United States.[28] The standing of Syrian women figured prominently in Houghton's reporting. The excerpt printed in the *Detroit Free Press* spoke directly to perplexed Americans (presumably white and middle-class) who wondered at Syrian women undertaking such physically demanding work. This particular excerpt from Houghton's series—which the newspaper titled "Syrian Peddlers: Eastern Women Trained from Childhood to Carry Heavy Weights"—trafficked in a form of essentialism that was simultaneously gendered and racial. That is, although the proper American woman might be too fragile to undertake such work, the Syrian woman was perfectly capable of undertaking such loads.

If we think about the *Detroit Free Press* excerpt and the investigation of the peddling nun as indicative of the racially gendered unease that Syrian women peddlers provoked, we might even ask if Syrian women peddlers were indeed considered women at all by others. In the eyes of those who believed that proper women limited their labor to unpaid domestic work in their own homes, Syrian women peddlers may have been unruly subjects for categorization.

These violations of gendered behavior were not the only aspect of women's peddling work that threatened Syrians' ability to fit either within Eurocentric visions of gender difference or within Syrian heteropatriarchal family structures in diaspora. The economic independence that women could gain from peddling fueled anxieties about the changing nature of Syrian communities under migration. One second-generation Syrian American told of a woman from Zahle who gained such independence. She came to the United States, and after receiving goods from a supplier, she started peddling. She eventually earned enough money to return home, where she "saw herself as better than her husband and built herself a beautiful home."[29]

Indeed, many women found a particular opportunity in peddling that they may not have found in other work. Historian Alixa Naff's research concluded that "a surprising number [of women] continued [peddling] well into the thirties and forties, long after most men had turned to other pursuits. . . . Some who gave it up returned to it intermittently in times of economic crises, between pregnancies and even after the childbearing age."[30] While Syrian men began increasingly to take on nonmobile jobs after 1910, some Syrian women continued to find economic opportunity and flexibility in peddling. One woman, ʿAqlah Brice Al Shidyaq, immigrated to the United States by herself in 1894, leaving her husband and children behind in Mount Lebanon. After arriving in West Virginia, she changed her name to Mary and began peddling. Despite being illiterate, she learned rudimentary English, Italian, Polish, and Hungarian and built a base of loyal customers.[31] She continued to peddle into her sixties, at which point her sons persuaded her to stop. But as the Great Depression began, she took up the profession once more to aid her family and peddled until she was almost seventy years old.[32]

Some women were eager to leave peddling for the more respectable vocation of marriage and childrearing—and, indeed, there were community and external pressures to do just that. Based on her oral history interviews, Naff claimed that "most gladly gave up peddling to marry and raise a family." She lamented that "no one will ever know how many girls who peddled yearned for some man, any man, to free them from the drudgery."[33] Even so, for other women, the true drudgery may have been a middle-class marriage itself, devoid of their own endeavors outside the home. These women gained pleasure, independence, and self-worth from their peddling work.

Houghton focused overwhelmingly on Syrian women in the remainder of her series in *The Survey*, often describing the merits of women's participation in the paid labor force. In an unexpected passage, Houghton described the economic autonomy made possible by Syrian women's peddling:

> The peddler is a free man—more often a free woman. Why should she give up the open air, the broad sky, the song of birds, and the smell of flowers, the right to work or to rest at her own pleasure, to immure herself within four noisy walls and be subject to the strict regime of the clock? Why should she who has been a whole person, and her own person, become a mere "hand" and that the hand of another? . . . When the woman yields and abandons peddling for less congenial (and usually less profitable) work, she yields not to argument, but to a subtle and keen consciousness that her social standing among these incomprehensible Americans will somehow be thereby improved.[34]

It is possible that Syrian racialization somewhat enabled Houghton's openness here. For instance, the idea that Arabs were exceptionally brutal toward women may have influenced Houghton to view Syrian women's economic independence even more favorably than such independence among other immigrant women. Still, while many frowned on Syrian women peddlers, Houghton saw the numerous benefits that peddling could bring. She critiqued as meritless the social pressures incumbent upon Syrian women to labor differently. Her mention of women peddlers who gave up peddling for other forms of work came from learning about actual campaigns to convince Syrian women to do so. One such campaign was waged in Boston.

SPATIAL BOUNDARIES: GENDER AND SEX IN PUBLIC SPACE

The Syrian community in Boston was much smaller than its New York counterpart but still sizable enough to attract the attention of social workers. Its women peddlers were of particular interest to the Associated Charities of Boston, which in 1899 urged Syrian women to quit their peddling work "for some more self-respecting occupation" (though what other profession would have been acceptable is unclear). Boston social workers railed against what they too saw as peddling's uncomfortable proximity to begging, arguing that peddling simply enabled Syrians to avoid work and relied on their innate proclivity for deceit: "These persons are said to have very little idea of truth, to consider lying a legitimate method of doing business."[35] The campaign went so far as to assert that buying from peddlers "encourages begging, lying, idleness, neglect, exposure, and a further increase of Syrians to 'sweep up money from our streets.'"[36] Despite the Boston charities' best efforts, a follow-up report from six years later suggested, the situation had, if anything, worsened, as Syrians continued to migrate to the United States and take up peddling. The authors of the original campaign had allowed that Syrians could "eventually become useful citizens." But after the men showed their unwillingness to take up factory work en masse, and the women had stubbornly refused to work only within their homes, the second report now described Syrians as "undesirable immigrants."[37] Such was the unpredictable position of Syrians at the margins of whiteness: there were possibilities for incorporation, but there were also dangers that would lead to exclusion. Women's work as peddlers threatened this already unstable positioning.

Houghton referenced the Boston campaign explicitly in her series. She opened the second installment in her reporting by acknowledging that many people associated Syrians with begging and saw peddling as a mere cover for that practice. She refuted this association, citing no evidence for the claim in her research. While conceding that begging may have been common thirty years earlier, she argued that, if so, there was good reason: "For countless generations begging has been in Syria a privileged, if not an honored, calling." Still, Houghton claimed that the "American spirit" turned Syrians away from begging and toward peddling, which she maintained were distinct activities. Closely related to the claim that Syrian peddlers were beggars was the accusation that the Syrian woman peddler was merely the "drudge of an idle husband who lives upon her hard earnings."[38] Houghton cited some examples of women peddlers being "drummers" for their husbands, but how she came to these conclusions is unclear. Nonetheless, social welfare records likewise often reveal this frequent assumption that Syrian women peddled at the behest of their husbands.

The link between peddling and begging predated the arrival of Syrians in the United States. Mid-nineteenth-century ordinances known as "ugly laws" sought to restrict from public view the display of physically disabled and poor people.[39] A typical ugly law prohibited those deemed "diseased, maimed, mutilated, or in any way deformed" from being "in or on the streets, highways, thoroughfares or public places."[40] But gender and sexuality were deeply embedded within understandings of "ugly." For example, such laws often prohibited cross-dressing, distribution of "lewd" material, and any woman acting "lewdly" or in "bold display of herself" as well.[41] In the case of male beggars, the ugly laws concerned the disabled or injured body; but for women, the laws also focused on appearance and "lack of attraction and beauty."[42] Proper femininity was not compatible with public display, so these ordinances explicitly policed how a woman displayed femininity. The category of "unsightliness" used in these ordinances also included anyone nonwhite, disabled or not.[43] A woman's whiteness (or lack thereof) was undeniably linked to her degree of femininity and vice versa; thus these ordinances set white female standards of beauty in stark relief. For Syrian women, simply moving through public space implicated them in this "ugly" history.

Although many in the Syrian community tried to distinguish peddling from begging, the long-held associations between the two activities were difficult to disentangle. The Syrian intelligentsia who did not shun peddling attempted discursively to distance the profession from begging, by emphasizing that peddling was an adaptable and clever form of entrepreneurship. Yet peddling was a transient form of labor (associated with sexual nonnormativity). It confused the supposedly neat Eurocentric boundaries between public and private, and it required performative strategies to make a sale. So, as much as these explanations sought to distinguish between the two, begging and peddling remained linked in the public mind.

Take, for example, the following descriptions of women beggars and Syrian women peddlers, respectively. The first, from 1898, noted how women beggars were typified by their appearance: "Lowest are the door-to-door beggars, 'drifters' or 'floaters,' with the 'blackhoods,' the women who beg on the side streets and in front of the churches and are hard to dispose of."[44] The second description comes from a 1962 interview with a Syrian man who peddled: "Women would wear the black scarves on their heads. Up to 15 of us would leave together daily. You'd see them at the street car stop. A saloon owner used to make fun of them. All packed and dressed funny and going out like gypsies."[45] The black hoods or scarves served to mark women peddlers and beggars visually as the same. The Syrian peddler's own description of the women "going out like gypsies" links peddling to begging through stereotypes of the Romani people. Public concerns about immigrant beggars in particular "played out in contestation over immigrant peddlers," demonstrating the "perpetually thin and wavering" line between peddling and begging.[46] Some leaders from peddling communities even wanted to ban peddling because they felt it reflected badly on the whole community.[47]

Houghton remarked that Syrians "put a hedge around the women, and guard their virtue in the extra-perilous business of peddling. The sense that the eyes of the colony are upon them is a potent influence against bad conduct in man or woman."[48] The only two reader letters in response to Houghton's series reflect this preoccupation with women's reputations and peddling. The first was from a reader who wished to clarify some distinctions between Syrians and Armenians: specifically, that Armenian women were not peddlers. The reader claimed that Syrian women peddlers were posing as Armenians and faking stories of "sorrow and suffering in the recent massacres" to play on the American public's sympathies for the Armenian people. The reader was possibly referring to the 1909 Adana massacres committed by the Young Turks, a precursor to the Armenian genocide during World War I. "There are practically no Armenian women in America who peddle," the reader wrote, "for the Armenian man, no matter how poor he may be, is almost always too proud *to permit his wife or sister* to run about the streets begging or peddling."[49] A woman's labor, the reader emphasized, was the purview of her husband, brother, or father alone.

The idea that it was Syrian men who decided whether Syrian women could peddle reflected poorly on Syrian men, since so many women did peddle. Syrians were constantly negotiating this fine line between women's economic value and women's improper independence. Syrian women who worked in the peddling economy were not properly dependent on their husbands for economic survival. Dependency was stigmatized for single women (as they were thought to be or expected to become public charges), but a certain kind of dependency was desirable for married women.[50] Syrian women peddlers, in particular, were the "bad" kind of dependent, cast in particularly immoral terms. Some of them relied on public assistance to get by; they placed their children in the care of family members or, worse, in the care of the state in order to peddle; and many refused the "help" of social reformers who sought to return the women to their homes.[51] When social work texts discussed Syrian men, the dependency discourse echoed contemporaneous racist ways of characterizing Black men as "unable to dominate" Black women.[52] Syrian men were seen as idle and lazy, in stark contrast to their stubborn wives, who refused to assume white, bourgeois domestic roles. The Associated Charities of Boston's incisive condemnation of Syrian peddling reflects the violation of this hierarchy: "It is not the custom in this country to let the women work and have the men remain idle at home. It is not natural for mothers to leave their children during the day to be looked after by men. When girls and young men go out on the streets to peddle, they fall into bad company; and, as one who understands his people well says, 'they often end by going to houses of ill-repute.'"[53]

The second reader letter responding to Houghton's series came from a social worker in Boston who defended the campaign against Syrian women peddlers by remarking that any negative characterizations of the community were rooted in experience: "When we first dealt with [Syrians] they were treated by every charitable society exactly as other people, but we found them extremely untrustworthy and unreliable. Few employers in Boston have found them satisfactory and they have taken great pains to cheat the charitable societies, which accounts for the feeling existing here."[54] Comparing the streets and homes in the Syrian quarter with those of other nationalities' communities, the reader found the former "the dirtiest that are in my district." But the crux of the letter refuted Houghton's claim that Syrian women who worked outside the home were unmarried (and thus were not neglecting maternal and marital duties). The reader retorted, "We have here many married women who peddle. Some of them have left their husbands in Syria, and some of them, in the testimony of their own educated countrymen, are of immoral character."[55] The implication here was that Syrian women peddlers were physically estranged from their husbands through their own actions and that they had children at home or in Syria who were being neglected in their absence; their "immoral character" pertained to their sexual virtue.

Peddling required navigating public spaces, such as public squares and train stations—sometimes without the company of a male relative. Such activities were viewed as trespassing gendered boundaries and were widely linked to the anxieties surrounding unwed mothers and sexual promiscuity.[56] These spatial anxieties affected the reputation of women peddlers, in part because being in public space without a male relative linked women to sex work. Social welfare records also hint at associations between female mobility and sex work.[57]

Within the Syrian community, rumors of such associations abounded for women who peddled far from home (even though long-distance women peddlers usually traveled with a male relative). Syrian community collections reflect these associations between female peddlers and sex work—but perhaps not for the reasons the social workers imagined. Multiple accounts state that women peddling in Fort Wayne, Indiana, and in Billings, Montana, peddled to sex workers at brothels because the sex workers were kind and purchased finer items from them.[58] On the other hand, within the Syrian community, rumors also circulated that certain women peddled more than just dry goods and would do "humiliating things" to make a sale.[59] Houghton claimed, however, that "the chastity of the Syrian woman, by universal testimony, is beyond question." She continued, "'A Syrian prostitute was never known,' is the testimony of city missionaries, charity organization officials, city magistrates, above all of policemen."[60] Despite these confident assertions, gossip about Syrian women's reputations was ubiquitous, making it difficult to discern when Syrian women actually engaged in sex work and when their laboring practices simply crossed prescribed boundaries for women's sexuality.

As many women of color feminist scholars have documented, the criteria for womanhood and femininity are explicitly linked to sexuality and race. Black feminist scholars in particular have shown that "woman" has historically been "an exclusive, policed, and specifically European gender formation."[61] While the first half of the twentieth century saw a growing concern with male same-sex sexuality among white men in the United States, the parallel concerns of "perversion" and "deviance" for white women centered on abnormal heterosexuality—particularly for women engaged in sex work.[62] These intersectional precedents created a treacherous landscape for all Syrian women who claimed sexual normalcy and whiteness, but particularly for those who peddled.

PEDDLING LABOR AND MOTHERHOOD

The labor that women provided in the peddling economy also provoked anxieties regarding Syrian motherhood. Syrian women peddlers who were also mothers were assessed and judged based on their ability to care for their children while working. If a peddler was married and her husband did not have work, she could leave her children in her husband's care. One second-generation Syrian American

Muslim noted that many women peddled while their husbands stayed at home with the children.[63] At times, another family member or an older child might assume childcare responsibilities. Syrian women could also seek assistance from child welfare organizations that provided day care and long-term care for children. Since normative femininity also depended on particular ideals of motherhood (in both Syrian and American contexts), the scrutiny of Syrian mothers also risked affecting their racial positioning in the United States. Several newspaper clippings from the late nineteenth and early twentieth centuries offer insight into the ways that peddling mothers could encounter pity, derision, and judgment—sometimes all at once—in their work.

A Syrian woman was arrested in Atlanta in 1910 for peddling without a license. License-related penalties were a frequent nuisance for Syrian peddlers, particularly when they moved through different locales and were unaware of local ordinances that governed peddling. Mandating license fees was a common way to discourage peddling.[64] In the courtroom, the judge took pity on this Syrian peddler when he saw "four children hanging to her skirts and a little babe in her arms" and heard that her husband had recently died.[65] But before the judge could release her without a fine, which she stated she could not pay, the arresting police officer told him that a local Syrian man sent women out to peddle and instructed them to give pitiful stories of hardship if they were caught without a peddling license. Upon hearing this, the judge revoked his sympathy and levied a fine on the woman. An onlooker in the courtroom promptly paid it for her, but the news article did not identify the good Samaritan. Of course, we cannot determine the woman's true circumstances based on this news story alone. But we might be reasonably confident that she was aware of how her *performance* of motherhood and poverty might affect how the state dealt with her in this instance.

Another story prompts us to imagine the difficulties a Syrian woman could encounter on her own in diaspora. At the beginning of the twentieth century in Pennsylvania, a newborn child was found stowed in a cesspool, having nearly suffocated. Although the *Scranton (Pennsylvania) Tribune*'s initial coverage of the story reported that the mother had not been found (and no father was mentioned), it remarked that "an Arabian woman gave birth to a child recently, and afterwards disappeared."[66] That woman was Mary Tamar. In subsequent coverage, the paper noted that Tamar was a peddler and, upon hearing that the child had been found, she "took her wares and left her home."[67] Her husband was living in Jerusalem while she was in the United States, and she initially denied that the child was hers. Eventually, she was found, arrested, and reunited with the baby. At that point, she admitted to having birthed her. Shortly after this, the child died.

Through the circumstances of transliterated and altered Arabic names, as well as the transient nature of peddling work, Tamar eludes the probing confirmation of historical inquiry. Given that just three clippings examine this specific nexus of gender, labor, race, motherhood, and child welfare, the many silences in this news coverage beckon us to ask after the possible experiences of Tamar and her child. Namely, how did she become pregnant? What consequences did she fear from becoming a single mother to a child, presumably conceived out of wedlock? Caring for a newborn and peddling were already incompatible activities; but overlaid with the threats of violence, poverty, or social ostracism, as one might imagine for Tamar, they would have been untenable.

What other options did a peddling mother have? The Syrian Women's Union of New York saw many Syrian women struggling and opened a nursery for Syrian babies in 1899.[68] Observing that women were taking very young children with them while peddling—"carrying a child on one arm and a basket on the other"—some wealthier Syrian women in New York raised funds to open the nursery, enrolling twenty children under the age of three in its first year.[69] Women who peddled over longer distances than day peddlers did might well have gone months at a time without seeing their children. Litia Namoura's mother was a peddler in New England who placed her children in boarding schools while she was away. Namoura and her brother were placed separately, and her mother visited them twice a year.[70] Although these options were available, some Syrian families made use only of American charity organizations to shield themselves from Syrian community gossip. In 1921, members of Boston's Syrian Ladies Aid Society were visited by an American charity worker who ran a nursery. She said that they had many Syrian members who left their children in this nursery's care rather than seek aid from Syrian sources.

Syrian mothers who peddled and placed their children in others' care were especially singled out for criticism. A 1901 government report on immigrant communities was incisive when assessing Syrian immigrant parenting practices. The report claimed that Syrians' experience with American missionaries exposed their "intrinsically servile character . . . , [their] ingratitude and mendacity, [their] prostitution of all ideals to the huckster level. No sooner are they landed than they seek the commitment to institutions of such of their children as have not attained working age."[71] Although such a generalization is clearly hyperbolic, some Syrians did make use of child welfare services, particularly when their work did not permit them to look after their children.

The outcome of placing a child in this kind of care, however, varied widely. One particularly haunting story illustrates the risk that came with using such services. In 1884, Dibi Musa left her son and husband behind in Al Munsif and traveled to New Orleans. She was pregnant when she left and gave birth to her baby after arriving. Being without family and needing to work, she left her newborn in the care of Catholic nuns "on the promise that they would care for her while Dibi peddled in the countryside."[72] When she returned from her trip, the nuns told her that her baby had died. Because she never saw a grave, she remained unconvinced of the nuns' story and "lived with the anguish of not knowing the true fate of her only daughter."[73]

Like the other archival traces presented here, this story opens up many questions. On the surface, one might read it as reinforcing the opinion expressed in the aforementioned 1901 government report. Syrians come, they place their children in institutions, they go off and peddle, and disastrous consequences ensue. Certainly, if this woman was knowingly pregnant when she traveled to the United States on her own, one might indeed question her fitness as a mother. But she was unlikely to have undertaken such a hardship intentionally. Indeed, if she had been visibly pregnant, she would likely have been turned away upon her arrival in the United States, on the grounds that she was liable to become a public charge.[74] We must also consider that she might only have learned of her pregnancy after leaving home or only upon arriving in the United States. What choices for survival would she have had then?

Ideas about proper motherhood were of central importance to social workers, who regularly visited homes to assess living conditions and the health of children. Feminist scholarship has shown how social welfare from the late nineteenth century into the twentieth century functioned overwhelmingly as an area of a gender-based politics for middle-class women reformers.[75] As immigration swelled in the second half of the nineteenth century, US nativism responded to changing demographics by developing a "social geology of citizenship based on race."[76] "Maternal practice" and reproduction were the focus of anxieties regarding the production and maintenance of the right kind of Americans. These concerns stemmed from the assumption that character came explicitly from lineage. For many reformers, motherhood was deeply rooted in concepts of assimilation and vice versa; accordingly, reformers prioritized immigrants' assimilation over exclusion.[77] When social reformers entered Syrian homes, every detail could be scrutinized, recorded in case notes, and shared with other social welfare organizations.

At the 1916 National Conference of Social Work, a self-proclaimed "child saver" gave a soliloquy about unsafe home conditions for children: "You know all too well the homes, the over-crowding, the late hours, the tea and coffee drinking, the peddling, the home industries, the home where both the parents go out to work or the mother to play bridge, the lack of proper discipline."[78] The speaker made no explicit mention of immigrant or working-class homes because no mention was needed; the evocation of crowded living quarters, "tea and coffee drinking," and other vivid details called on attendees' shared understanding. Similarly, a social worker giving a presentation on medical casework at the same conference expressed many of the same concerns while discussing a twelve-year-old Syrian boy with a heart condition. The boy's home life was considered at odds with his rehabilitative needs: "A poor home in an overcrowded foreign neighborhood, a large family of children, the father dead, and the mother with little intelligence and no control over her family." The boy was placed in a boarding home for children; but soon after, "the mother demands the return of the boy to the unhealthy, overcrowded, Syrian quarter, where he can again run wild on the streets."[79]

BOARDINGHOUSES AND NONREPRODUCTIVE
LABOR INSIDE THE HOME

Boardinghouses starkly demonstrated the blurred boundary between public and private in Syrian homes. Some Syrian families took in boarders for additional income, yet doing so invited the critical gaze of not only social reformers but also peers in the Syrian community. Boardinghouses were essential in the peddling economy because they supported long-distance peddlers and offered some mothers a means of financial gain while they stayed home with children. The presence of additional people in the home, however, risked tarnishing any image of domestic normativity according to both American and Syrian ideals. Syrian communities had a word in Arabic, *fadiha*, meaning a "scandal with sexual overtones," that referred specifically to having boarders in the space of the family home. Boardinghouses were also often designated as houses of ill repute or "ill fame" in social welfare records.[80] For women who ran boardinghouses, which often housed peddlers and other transients, having strangers in their homes invited gossip and risked a visit from a concerned social worker. Women and girls were at the center of boardinghouse controversies, as their reputations were always at stake. Young girls' sexuality was at risk with nonrelative men in the house, and mothers were at fault for having strangers in their homes. Unmarried women, as well as women who were physically separated from their husbands due to migration, were particularly vulnerable to gossip.

The discursive anxiety surrounding boardinghouses can be seen in the case of the Said family, whose lengthy case file with the International Institute of Boston chronicles its contact with the social welfare organization from 1925 to 1935. The Saids and other Syrians' primary point of contact with the organization was Victoria Karam, a Syrian American and social worker.[81] Wedad Said, a Protestant, and Salem Said, a Druze, had both been married previously, and each had children from those marriages.[82] Before their marriage to each other, boardinghouses provided a critical subsistence for Wedad. After the death of her first husband, she and her two sons lived with her sister, who ran a boardinghouse. Karam noted that this particular boardinghouse was known to be "somewhat immoral," but her case notes did not include any details. During that time, Wedad's sons were taken away from her. Karam's notes surmise that the other social worker involved in removing Wedad's sons "got to know about [the sons] through his aunt." This detail implied that the woman running the boardinghouse—Wedad's sister—had already attracted the attention of social workers. After her sons were taken, Wedad bought a house, which she used to run a boardinghouse herself.[83] There Wedad met Salem while he was staying at her house as a boarder. Once they married, he convinced her to sell the boardinghouse and put the money toward their family.

Years later, when Salem alternately could not find work or refused to look for work, the Saids took out a loan to purchase a new boardinghouse with a basement in which they could live. Living with them at this time were Salem's four daughters from his previous marriage, one of Wedad's sons from her first marriage, and their two daughters together, both under the age of one. In December 1926, the youngest baby died of pneumonia, and Karam's notes imply that the death resulted from neglect. In previous visits, Karam had noted that the two youngest children seemed "too pale" and that they were not able to go outside enough because Wedad was busy running the boardinghouse.

Wedad apparently grew frustrated with her husband's lack of employment in contrast to her own full load of work. As Karam put it, Wedad "has to take care of the whole boarding house and the washing and besides care for his daughters and their meals and at the end all her work is not appreciated and she does not have a cent in her pocket while he loafs around and does not make any effort to work."[84] Although the boardinghouse revenue enabled the family to get by, Karam tried to convince Wedad to stop working and devote all her energies to her children and her home. But Wedad refused, because her husband was not bringing in any income. That their home was the generator of their revenue was of great concern to Karam and the other social workers in her network, despite the fact that the boardinghouse (and alternately Wedad's sporadic work outside the home) provided the only income supporting the family.

For another family, the boardinghouse was a central feature of tragic events. Due to poverty and a tumultuous marriage, Mary and Najeeb George came in contact with the International Institute of Boston in 1925. Najeeb was disabled from a work-related accident and was diagnosed with a psychological condition. Mary was living separately with their children but returned to her husband when she was granted legal guardianship over him. Karam's notes reveal that Mary had relationships with other men, who at times also housed her and supported her financially. Karam also noted that several of Mary's children were born out of wedlock.[85] Eventually, Mary and Najeeb divorced, and Mary left with their youngest two children. She opened a boardinghouse and had a third child; she did not remarry. This case file ends after one of Mary's children was beaten by a boarder and died from the injuries. Here, the boardinghouse served as the catalyst for Mary's failed motherhood: the death of a child due to violence from a stranger in the home.

Boardinghouses were thus reliable sources of income but also potential sites of violence. One case illustrates both the violence that a boardinghouse could bring and the community policing of women's sexuality. Ramza Hamaty, a forty-year-old Syrian woman who had a husband and son in Syria, ran a boardinghouse in Boston. In 1926 one of her boarders, a Syrian man, raped her and she became pregnant. When she went to the hospital just before giving birth, Karam, the Syrian social worker, was called to interpret for her. Hamaty "was almost crazy at seeing a Syrian," fearing that knowledge about her situation would spread. She wanted to place her baby for adoption, but she initially refused to talk to Karam, "saying she is lost now that a Syrian knows about her." Based on Karam's notes, Hamaty had an intractable fear of Syrian knowledge of (and gossip about) the violence done against her and her unplanned pregnancy. Karam wrote, "Then there was the question of the baby, which is as black as coal and very ugly, thus there would be no hopes of adoption according to Mrs. Hooker [another social worker]."[86] In addition to capturing the violence done to Hamaty in the course of her boardinghouse work, Karam's notes reveal one way that anti-Blackness within US society, and both colorism and anti-Blackness in the Syrian community, operated at this historical moment. Without giving further details, Karam noted that the baby was adopted and that the woman continued to live in fear that her community would find out.

Another Syrian woman's boardinghouse was the site of gossip among social workers and presumably her community as well. Having separated from an abusive husband, Noura Jibrail struggled to support her two children while operating a boardinghouse. She rented out the first floor and all but two rooms on the second floor; she and her children lived in the two rooms. The chain of communication between Boston social workers led to a visit from Karam. Karam had been told by a Denison House social worker that Jibrail was "rather friendly" with a young male boarder she saw in the home. The social worker thought that she should "be careful about her reputation." When Karam visited to see for herself, she too was suspicious of this boarder and encouraged Jibrail to ask him to leave. Jibrail was ill at the time but was still working to run the house and take care of her children. Karam even spoke with Jibrail's husband about her situation. He wanted Karam to help her "live in a house by herself and thus save herself the gossip and the work as she was in weak physical condition."[87]

Gossip and rumors are fuel for the imagination. The most compelling aspects of such communication, for the purposes of historical knowledge production, do not revolve around the veracity of the gossip (as my many thwarted attempts at historical verification perhaps signal). Rather, a more fruitful inquiry delves into their function as a vehicle for transmitting cultural information about sexuality. Gayatri Spivak calls rumor a "subaltern means of communication" for which no origin can be traced. The claims within the rumor are irrelevant. Rumor is not error; it is errant. It signals transgression and relays information that is "always assumed to be pre-existent."[88] Similarly, Clare Potter writes that rumors and gossip, particularly concerning sexuality, can be characterized as "truths that are not factual."[89] The anxieties, gossip, and in some cases sheer alarm surrounding peddling mothers and women who operated boardinghouses indicate that Syrian women's labor in the peddling economy blurred the idealized separation of public and private space, according to both Syrian and white American norms.

Similar gendered and sexual dynamics occurred in South Asian migrant communities in the Pacific Northwest during the same time period. While South Asian women were present in these communities in far fewer numbers compared to their Syrian counterparts, Nayan Shah writes, "the rumors of unmarried women living among men fostered an image of sexual immorality and a wholesale absence of respectable domestic culture, making it impossible to distinguish between the bunkhouse and the brothel."[90] Indeed, some women running boardinghouses were accused of really running brothels. One boardinghouse in Fort Wayne, Indiana, was remembered colloquially by a fellow Syrian as "Mary Malooley's house of prostitution."[91]

When Syrian women put their children in someone else's care in order to peddle, they were accused of neglect. When they allowed strangers (often other peddlers) to board inside their homes, their own living spaces and parenting practices were scrutinized. Working outside the home prevented women from receiving aid, but aid alone was not enough to support a family when they did stay in the home. Leaving children unattended in order to work was grounds for child removal. Sending older children out to work so that a woman could stay home to take care of the rest of the family was neglect. Taking in boarders was considered highly immoral, and receiving any kind of help from a nonrelative male was assumed to be linked with sex work.

Of all the choices that women considered to support their families, few stoked the flames of Syrian community self-policing more than operating a boardinghouse. This self-policing, maintained through gossip, reinforced ideals of Syrian respectability. At the same time, Syrian respectability intersected with and was refracted by the pressures to conform to white American sexual and gendered norms. A thread of presumed heterosexuality may be implicit in this collection of stories of Syrian mothers, but this thread points not just to the idea of failed motherhood but also to the possibility of failed heterosexuality, including both errant heterosexuality (i.e., sexual encounters outside marriage bonds) and sexual bonds among women. In the early years of the twentieth century, increasing attention was paid to the category of so-called normal sexuality and its opposite, "deviance"; for women, this trend meant increased attention to so-called deviant heterosexuality.[92]

CLASS AND SYRIAN MOTHERHOOD

The case of the Said family, whose boardinghouse came under scrutiny as discussed earlier, also reveals some stark differences in class, motherhood, and labor in the Syrian American community. When the social worker Karam visited the Said family in May 1925, she had been told by another agency's social worker that Wedad and Salem Said were having difficulties with their eldest son, George, and needed an interpreter in order to place him in a juvenile institution. Upon visiting, Karam learned that Salem Said did not get along well with George, who was actually one of Wedad's sons from her previous marriage. What began as an issue of father-stepson strife, continued into many other difficulties as the case file narrative unfurled. As the family's life came under the gaze of the social welfare agency, the parents' marriage and parenting styles, their work habits, the children's behavior, and their overall home life all became areas requiring regulation and discipline.

The twenty-nine typewritten pages of case notes plus the correspondence among social work agencies also show how the Said family's interactions with the International Institute were embedded in a larger context of accessing social welfare services and networking among social workers in the Boston area. On the back of the intake form appears a list of dates and names of other agencies accessed: "6-10-25 SSE, 5/24-21 State Temporary Aid . . . 2/11/22 S.P.C.C. . . . 2/25/26 Children's Aid Ass'n., 12/2/19 Industrial Aid Society."[93] These notations were made not merely for the record; they provided information on how much or little the family used social welfare services and also enabled social workers to share information about particular families across agencies. In this instance—in which the adults in the family did not speak English and the International Institute social worker spoke both English and Arabic—Karam also provided a good deal of information to other social welfare parties, which were unable to gain the same level of access to the Said family's lives. Within the ten years during which the Said family was in contact with the International Institute of Boston, members of the family experienced unemployment, physical and sexual abuse, the births of two children, the deaths of two children, illness, changes in residence, and the death of Salem, the father and husband.

Ostensibly, the relationship between this agency and the Said family began because they were experiencing troubles with George, Wedad's eldest son from her first marriage. But the case notes do not make clear whether the Saids wanted help from a social welfare agency. The notes simply indicate that the interest of a social work student brought the family to the attention of the International Institute. Indeed, the relationship between the father and the stepson had so deteriorated that the son had been found delinquent, and Salem was so troubled that he "had no mind for work." But once the situation piqued the interest of the Syrian social worker, the son's behavior became just one of many family issues perceived to need reform. As the son was scrutinized, so were the parents. Karam wrote that Salem, the father, had "led a low and immoral life" as a gambler and womanizer before his current marriage to Wedad. Her notes frequently describe chastising him for a lack of ambition and for his failure to bring in money for the family.[94] In interpreting these notes, we must balance the social worker's classed perspective with Salem's unknown perspective. But his lack of work, for whatever reason, required Wedad to keep the family afloat. As a result, Karam was particularly concerned with Wedad's mothering, her relationship with her children, and her management of the house. Her marital troubles also made frequent appearance in Karam's notes, including Wedad's desire to leave her family and Karam's counsel against this action.

Contact between the International Institute of Boston and the Said family diminished significantly when Karam herself got married, had a baby, and went on maternity leave. The agency's other social workers remarked in the case notes,

"Since we lost our Syrian worker in April 1929, we have had but slight contact with the family."[95] Even after Karam returned to the organization, now named Victoria Abboud, contact was not nearly as sustained as it had been previously for five years, and it was often made now by the other (non-Arab) workers. At the 1930 Family Welfare Society conference, representatives from a group of agencies convened to discuss the Said family's case. The representative of the Society for the Prevention of Cruelty to Children (SPCC) felt that it had "never got at the bottom of the difficulties in the Said family" and questioned the veracity of information procured from the family members themselves. Victoria Abboud continued to appeal to Syrian community members and organizations for aid on the family's behalf, but to no avail because "they felt that Mr. Said was lazy and using money he received foolishly and that he should provide for his children." By this time, the oldest daughter was again in foster care, and workers reported that "she hardly ever comes to see her family." Salem Said died in 1933. After a short session in a juvenile girl's facility, the next eldest daughter followed the oldest daughter into a foster home; notes report that she "does not want to go home; Mrs. Said does not want her there, so she is placed in a [foster] home."[96] Despite a sustained and detailed engagement with the Said family over a ten-year period, no more news of the family followed this development.

We have no comparable record of Victoria Abboud's own home life and parenting choices. During the course of her work with the Said family, as noted, she also became a mother, and the contrast between the two mothers' experiences reveals the classed gulf that existed in Syrian migrant communities. Abboud, born Karam, was twenty-one years old when she came to the United States from Beirut in 1922. She was single, appeared to be traveling alone, was college educated, and could speak Arabic, English, French, and Turkish—all of which signal that her background was one of relative wealth and status. In Beirut, Karam had worked with an orphanage, and her trip to the United States was initially for the purpose of fundraising for those children. She began working with the International Institute of Boston in 1924, which led her to also work with the South End Denison House in 1925.[97] There, she and Amelia Earhart worked with the Syrian community, with Earhart teaching English and Karam translating into and from Arabic. Karam attended Simmons College in Boston, where she received a certificate in social work. In 1928, as mentioned earlier, she married Alfred Abboud, and the couple went on to have two children.

Abboud's total career in social work spanned five decades, including supervising social workers for the Federal Emergency Relief Administration, which was formed during the Great Depression. Her 2001 obituary (she died at the age of ninety-eight) described her as "a social worker who dedicated much of her life to helping impoverished children, battered women, and immigrant families."[98] While Abboud took leave of her social work responsibilities to devote full-time attention to her newborn son in 1929, Wedad Said never had a moment's rest from the urgent need to bring in income for her family. Even after giving birth to her fourth child in 1916, Wedad was immediately concerned with how to care for her children yet continue to work. Upon visiting Wedad the night of that birth, Abboud remarked that "the new baby was not taken care of but bundled up and thrown on a chair." Said was found weak and in bed; she talked with Abboud about how to place her two youngest children somewhere, "pay for their board and go to work."[99] That newborn died from pneumonia months later. In contrast, Abboud was able to scale back to part-time work once she became a mother. As mentioned, she went on to have a significant career and left behind a written legacy in archival material and in her obituary. The Saids' legacies, in contrast, are difficult to trace. Further information about the Said family members is sparse beyond the institute's case file.

The case files concerning the Saids and many others demonstrate how the discursive and material circumstances of gendered and sexual norms were intertwined with labor and class in the Syrian American community. As social welfare reformers, in particular, engaged with Syrian immigrant families, they participated in the management and sometimes pathologization of many Syrian laboring practices, particularly those of women in the peddling economy. The Saids were not peddlers themselves, but what little subsistence they gathered came through the peddling economy: they were owners of a boardinghouse that Wedad managed. Because social reformers also included upper-class Syrian women, like Karam (later Abboud), an aspect of this work—discursively and materially—was a form of community self-policing. An important caveat to this point, which need not negate the presence of community self-policing, is that forms of connection and collective welfare were evident in Karam's case notes as well.

· · ·

When it came to the choices they made to sustain themselves and their families, Syrian women were often in a double bind. In Syrian families whose men peddled and women stayed at home, the adapted living arrangements and support systems that women developed were suspect. When Syrian women were peddlers themselves (or when they held other jobs working outside the home), they were often cast as negligent mothers who depended on the state, because they put their children in state care in order to work. Social workers' concern about peddling by Syrians was a concern at once about gender and about sexual normalcy, as well as about racial belonging, particularly in Boston, where so many women in the Syrian community peddled.

Despite these pressures, in her extensive research on Syrian immigrants, Naff found that "few women succeeded without the help of one or more women. The earnings of wives, mothers, daughters, and sisters, their sacrifices and labor, staved off poverty and failure in many cases and in many more cases enabled the family to improve and accelerate economic and social positions."[100] A Syrian woman's work outside the home or in addition to unpaid domestic labor often tipped the balance in favor of the family's financial health—but it also increased the chances that the woman would become a target of American social reform scrutiny and of community self-policing, which at times overlapped, as in the case of Karam. When the men of the family peddled and the women worked together to support their families in the men's absence—as often was the case—the family's adapted living arrangements were viewed as a dangerous disruption of the American family unit, as "aberrations from the normal family economy."[101] These kinds of arrangements were enough to cause the Industrial Commission on Immigration to take note, in a report about the New York Syrian neighborhood in 1901: "It is not extraordinary to find 6 to 8 women making their headquarters in such a garret, their husbands away peddling and their children in institutions."[102] That one succinct sentence pathologized the Syrian family in three respects: the neglect of patriarchal duty in men's absence, the abnormality of women in their economy of support for one another, and the dependency of children in benefiting from state welfare.

The Syrian immigrant family was monitored and disciplined in particular through the discursive and material attention paid to Syrian women's labor. Many Syrian immigrant families were quite entrepreneurial and resourceful. Every able member of the family was working or contributing to the father's or mother's work in whatever ways they could; they turned homes into places of business by running boardinghouses or by making laces or other items for peddlers to sell from within their homes. Yet this entrepreneurialism was frequently not condoned or celebrated by the social worker, because it was not embedded within a properly heteronormative family economy that preserved the private space as sexually reproductive and nonentrepreneurial. Here, public and private spaces, and selves, not only were linked through business but were also coterminous. We also see that Syrians themselves were quite divided about peddling and women's role in it (explored further in the next chapter). Community gossip was a potent mechanism of self-policing, particularly in relation to the actions of women and girls.

3

Wandering in Diaspora

The Syrian American Elite and Sexual Normativity

In her 1985 book on early Syrian American experiences, Alixa Naff notes that the Syrian American intelligentsia was particularly concerned with social issues in diaspora. These issues were an interconnected set of economic, gendered, sexual, and kinship concerns: "how to channel the social and economic energies of the young and adventurous away from the 'subversive and immoral' and onto an upward economic path; how to reconcile the widening economic role of women with the traditional restraints; how to protect the sanctity of the family; and how to uphold the honor and integrity of Syrians."[1] Many of these concerns manifested themselves in conversations about marriage among Syrian migrants, and the economic role of women figured centrally in these. When it came to women doing paid work, many elite Syrian Americans, as represented in the Syrian American press, focused on women peddlers, whose presence in public spaces—unsupervised and unaccompanied by men—threatened the idealized Syrian American identity that these migrants were crafting.[2]

The concern that women's laboring practices in diaspora would affect their reputations intensified in the pages of the Syrian American press at the turn of the century. Arab Americans who wrote for or to these periodicals claimed that peddling marred women's reputations and, by extension, the entire Syrian community. They specifically claimed a link between peddling and women's (aberrant) sexuality. Over almost thirty years, the same arguments about peddling recurred across the pages of the Syrian American press. Those arguments were the following: Women who migrate alone to peddle in the United States are shameful and should be stopped. Peddling (for women) leads to degrading behaviors, including sex work; it thus tarnishes the reputations of all Syrians. Peddling teaches Syrians to deceive their customers, which is especially harmful behavior for women and girls. Men whose wives or daughters peddle while they stay at home or hang out in coffee shops have abandoned their patriarchal duties.

The debates about peddling in the pages of the Syrian American press, particularly about "women wanderers," index an elite migrant community's concerns about the parameters of normative Syrian sexuality as refracted through white and middle-class American ideals. The term "wandering" (*tajul*) often appeared in discussions about peddling in the Syrian American press, sometimes more frequently than the word for "peddling" itself (*kasha*, which also refers to the box or pack). "Wandering" is notable for its connotation of aimlessness and perhaps license or unguided and unrestrained movement, and it may reflect a diminished value placed on the work of women peddlers. This conversation was highly binary and interconnected, often involving men speaking about women's laboring choices, and women speaking to men about their duties as husbands. The idea of a normative Syrian sexuality in the late nineteenth century depended on properly laboring, binary-gendered individuals. This normativity was of course greatly inflected by class and had already been disrupted, particularly in Mount Lebanon, by the booming silk economy and the increased presence of peasant girls in silk factories.[3] In addition, the extensive scholarship on the Nahda—that is, the "awakening," a literary and cultural movement in the late-nineteenth- and early-twentieth-century Ottoman Empire—has shown the extent to which upper-class conversations on modernity and national identity also frequently appeared in conversations about gender.[4] But migration and peddling further changed the actual practices of sexuality and gender among Syrians, as well as the ideas that circulated about them. These discussions thus took place at a time when the grounds of Syrian sexual normalcy were already shifting as a result of changes in the Levantine economy, the Nahda, and transatlantic migration.

As in many other immigrant communities, migration changed marriage patterns for Syrians. Syrians in diaspora gradually shifted from endogamous cousin- or village-based marriage to exogamous marriage practices. Once marrying from within one's kinship circle was not readily possible, these exogamous practices largely sought to preserve marriage within one's religious sect.[5] Once in diaspora, Syrians who could not easily marry among their kin often sought another Syrian of the same religious background for a spouse. However, interreligious marriages were not uncommon.

The conversations among elite Syrian migrants in the press show how they navigated both Syrian and white American classed and gendered norms, which become especially clear in discussions about women's sexuality. Simultaneously, such discussions showed that those Syrian norms were being contested by women peddlers and were themselves the result of revisions stemming from Nahda-era cultural change. Gender was a central axis on which Nahda debates about modernity and national identity turned, while explicit discourses of sexuality virtually disappeared.[6] The question of women's rights primarily concerned the duties and responsibilities of women, women's labor outside the home, women's education, and women's contact with the general public.

The small Arab population in the United States was relatively prolific when it came to periodical publications. From 1892 to 1930, some fifty Arabic-language newspapers were in circulation—for a population of no more than two hundred thousand, many of whom were not literate.[7] These periodicals were sources of information on US customs and culture, Syrian and Ottoman affairs, gossip and social news, and prominent individuals in the community, and they were places where newly arrived immigrants could place notices in search of family or friends.[8] For Syrian immigrants, they were also sites of activism regarding their homelands, repositories for articulations of race and ethnicity, venues for retaining Arabic-language practices in diaspora, and forums to work out ideas of national and transnational identity and belonging.[9]

This chapter examines the discursive perspectives regarding women's peddling found in several Syrian American newspapers. I discuss here those periodicals most referenced in this chapter and indicate the religious affiliation of each newspaper's founders and editors. However, in not all cases was the paper's readership of the same affiliation. The first newspaper was *Kawkab America* (Star of America), founded in 1892 in New York City by brothers Ibrahim and Najib Arbeely (Greek Orthodox). It ran as a weekly first and then as a daily in its final two years. *Al-Hoda* (The Guidance) was *Kawkab*'s main competition. Founded in 1898 by Naoum Mokarzel (Maronite), whose brother Salloum would later become its editor, *Al-Hoda* was the longest-running Syrian American periodical, ceasing publication in 1972. *Meraat-ul-Gharb* (Mirror of the West) was founded in 1899 by Najib Diab (Greek Orthodox), who had previously edited *Kawkab America*. Diab was an Arab nationalist, and his publication lasted until 1961. *Al-Kalimat* (The Word) was started as a biweekly periodical in 1905 by Greek Orthodox bishop (and later saint) Rafael Hawaweeny. *Al-Bayan* (The Explanation) was founded in 1911 by Sulayman Baddur and Abbas Abi Shaqra (both Druze). Their publication tended to represent Druze and Muslim perspectives. Other publications discussed herein include *Al-Wafa'* (The Fulfillment), based in Lawrence, Massachusetts, where Syrian factory workers were numerous; *Al-Jami'a* (The League), published by Farah Antoun first in Cairo and later in New York City; and *Al-Akhlaq* (The Manners), published by Yaqoub Rufail, which often addressed issues of gender.

Readership statistics are difficult to compile for these publications, in part because their editors made hyperbolic claims about their circulation. For instance, *Kawkab America* claimed to have 150,000 subscribers at one point, yet in 1894 it listed a circulation of between 400 and 800 households. *Al-Hoda* claimed that it was distributed in forty different countries; this number cannot be substantiated, but the paper did run ads from Syrian companies in Latin America.[10]

Despite their promises to the contrary, the narrators of the published pieces examined in this chapter are generally unreliable. Many pieces were written anonymously, or the author's name was omitted—but how intentional this was is unclear. These unsigned articles could have also been written by the paper's editor or could have appeared as a result of the author's having purchased space in the paper.[11]

Given this unreliability, the lack of information about these authors, and the uncertainty about these papers' circulation and reach, I am using newspapers as a way to index the discursive reality among wealthier, literate, and elite Syrian migrants regarding women, sexuality, and labor in diaspora. These newspapers also functioned as a mode of community self-policing (discussed in chapter 2) through the publication of social news and as a written record of *kalam al-nas* (what will the people say?). According to Naff, "Many of [these newspapers'] readers were also contributors. Ordinary immigrants asked questions, voiced opinions, and reflected their growing aspirations."[12] But characterizing the readership and authorship of these periodicals as "ordinary" masks clear class markers which indicate that their perspectives, particularly with regard to peddling, were not necessarily those of the common Syrian peasant migrant. Furthermore, this characterization itself indicates class differences among early Syrian migrants in the United States. We can see this in particular when we realize that peddling women were largely not represented in these perspectives, and certainly not with their own voices. They were the targets of criticism, but they did not represent themselves. Nor do we hear from men whose wives or daughters peddled and who might have defended this labor arrangement. At any rate, although these newspapers each had different audiences and emphases, with disagreements between editors of rival newspapers even landing in the courts,[13] at least one thing seemed to unite them: a concern with women's labor, and particularly with women's peddling, in diaspora.

These public discussions about gender, labor, and marriage exposed further shifts in Syrian communities relating to sexuality and gender. Could men trust women to uphold the family reputation (and, for many, the Syrian reputation writ large)? Could women count on men to live up to their patriarchal responsibilities? Were any new understandings of Syrian gender normalcy possible, related specifically to heterosexual marriage? Such questions were brought into relief as literate Syrians discussed the prevalence of women peddlers in the United States. The middle- to upper-class marriage contract was essentially put on trial as Syrian migrants debated whether and how well men and women were upholding their matrimonial promises as they wandered through this diasporic countryside.[14]

SYRIAN HONOR AND WOMEN'S SEXUALITY

Syrians referenced peddling frequently in the Syrian American press at the turn of the twentieth century. Some instances were practical, such as a how-to guide for new migrants who were looking to get started in peddling.[15] In 1898, Salloum Mokarzel warned readers of *Al-Hoda* about American customs for visiting someone, giving explicit instructions as to the etiquette of approaching someone in their home in the United States. For instance, one must not enter a home without knocking first. Knock softly, not loudly. Understand that someone could have a legitimate reason to refuse entry. Do not look through a peephole or keyhole to see inside. And ask forgiveness for your potential intrusion. These tips would have been particularly important for peddlers approaching a stranger's door.[16] But, while some references to peddling centered on such practical advice, other authors decried the moral degradation of peddling: for example, it made Syrians hyperfocused on accruing wealth to the exclusion of other values, and it encouraged them to become proficient in the ways of deception.

In 1898, one Syrian wrote a satirical poem, published in *Al-Hoda*, that claimed, "Every time the [peddling] box opens, it cheats the buyer." Here, peddling was depicted as the cause of many people's riches and just as many others' misery.[17] In 1904, *Al-Hoda* solicited essays about the so-called backwardness of Syrians and how to remedy it. Peddling figured prominently in the reader responses. Ibrahim Arbeely questioned why Syrians were not educating their "sons, daughters, and women" by sending them to public schools "like other immigrant groups." Instead, they were out peddling, where they would "use every method to deceive and lie. . . . They would swear [to Americans] that they are selling them [the goods] at the price they were purchased with, that they are committed to returning to their homeland or entering divinity schools or raising their brothers or supporting their sisters and mothers. And all of those are lies on top of lies." Arbeely criticized men who bragged about how cunning their children were and how much money their family members earned. He pleaded, "The annihilation and prevention of peddling, as previously mentioned, is necessary, and particularly among women."[18] As it happened, this moral degradation turned on a specifically gendered axis—the tactics that Syrians learned in peddling were believed to be particularly harmful to women and girls.

In 1895, the editor of *Kawkab America*, Najib Arbeely, wrote of complaints about "the number of Syrian women who leave their husbands and come to America with the intent of traveling around and subsisting on buying and selling among its people."[19] Arbeely warned that US immigration officials would stop women from entering the United States on their own, but he implored Syrians to themselves stop women. Specifically, he and a committee of men called on newspaper editors and religious leaders to prevent such women from immigrating to the United States without a husband or family member. Early federal immigration legislation created classes of individuals deemed undesirable for immigration, in sets of laws that revealed how gender, sexuality, class, and race were intimately connected in the white US imagination, particularly with regard to women.[20] These included the earliest of such laws, the Page Act (1875), which banned criminals, Chinese laborers, and women thought to engage in sex work, particularly those coming from Asian countries; the Chinese Exclusion Act (1882), which solidified opposition to Chinese immigration for ten years initially; and another 1882 measure to deny entry to those liable to become a public charge. The "liable to become a public charge" provision was strengthened in 1891, when polygamists were added to the list of excluded classes of immigrants.

Unmarried women were often viewed as liable to become dependent on the state and risked being denied entry or deported if found to be so categorized. Indeed, deportation records reflect this unease with Syrian migrant women's economic autonomy and transgression of US marriage customs. One woman, Malake Sultan, was deported in 1914 because, though having declared herself a widow, she was accused of having left her husband and child in Syria, as well as having sexual relationships with several men besides her husband. Another Syrian woman, Zahia Antony, was married but posed as the wife of another man to come to the United States via Canada. Antony worked and successfully supported herself as a peddler, but she was deported in 1910 on the grounds that she was likely to become a public charge, pointing to the perception that peddling was not a real job.[21] Interestingly, these cases materialized as a result of *transnational* Syrian community self-policing. The family or community members of these women in Syria were disgruntled with the women's lives in diaspora. They then complained to the Bureau of Immigration and entreated that agency to investigate the women, leading to their deportations. Syrian community self-policing thus had the capacity to collaborate with the carceral policies of the US state.

The criticisms of women's solo migration and peddling were most frequently directed at women themselves. An 1893 letter published in *Kawkab America* decried the participation of Syrian women in the peddling trade. Its author, a surgeon named Najib Tannous Abdou, did not mince words when criticizing the prevalence of women peddlers: "The loss of the East's honor and reputation in the eyes of Westerners who once thought it a paradise and praised its people's life, and you see them now cursing the East's water and sons." Tannous went on to specify that this tarnished image was due to Syrian women peddlers who "cheat, lie, and deceive" and who travel long distances and "enter men's spaces," where they are "subjected to humiliating experiences." Americans judged Syrians based on appearances, Tannous argued. Thus, Syrians should be very careful to consider how their actions and manners appeared to those not familiar with Syrian customs. Tannous also argued that all Syrians should move into professions other than peddling.[22]

For some elite Syrians, then, to peddle was to lie and deceive; for women, this was a question of honor. Shame, humiliation, and dishonor were frequently invoked in relation to peddling women, and these concepts were used to link peddling with women's sexuality. The conversations about peddling women in the press displayed "middle-class fears of [women's] sexuality run rampant."[23] This discourse conflated the economic independence that some women experienced in diaspora with sexual freedom. In 1903, Ilyas Nasif wrote in *Al-Hoda* of witnessing the hardships that peddling women endured. He recounted that one day, while he was talking with a group of men gathered in a hotel lobby, a Syrian woman entered carrying a heavy peddling pack. Exhausted, she set her goods down and said, "I will sell these men products for 4 or 5 dollars and I do not care if they laugh at me or mock me." She displayed her products while the men began to laugh and poke fun at her.

> Some of them bought small materials. Others asked her if she would allow them to have one kiss if they were to buy something from her. One man even asked her if he could tie her stockings for her, another asked her to demonstrate how women tie their stockings, etc. Their only intention was to pass the time and to have fun. The Syrian woman would respond to each one of them kindly and cheerfully, [saying] that she would look into his request after he had bought [something] from her, because her standing did not assist her in behaving otherwise. The Syrian woman responded to each of them with warm smiles, she cared for all of their matters after they bought.[24]

Nasif explained in his article that he left and then returned to the same spot hours later, where the presumably non-Syrian men were "still talking about the Syrian woman in the ugliest words possible" and berating Syrians for their barbarity and ill treatment of women. In Nasif's view, these men took advantage of the Syrian peddler's desperation and, as a result, her honor. By extension, the honor of Syrian men was violated as well.[25]

In 1898, Yusuf Shihadeh wrote in *Al-Ayyam* chastising "ill-mannered peddlers who have entered the honorable homes of Americans and have caused a lot of dishonor for the Syrian name." The author told of one Syrian girl who sold sewing materials. She entered the home of an American woman and displayed her products. When the woman apologized because she was not interested, "the mighty Syrian girl was angered by this and began to curse the American woman. She released any and all of the terrible words that she knew. Due to the tone of her voice, the American woman was able to tell that the Syrian girl was cursing at her." To get rid of the girl, the American woman recommended one of her friends as a potential customer. This friend knew some Arabic, and the American woman wrote to her to warn her about the Syrian girl. The same scene then played out at the home of the second woman, who understood that the Syrian girl was cursing her when she was not interested in many of her products. According to Shihadeh, the two women claimed to have published a piece on their experience in an American newspaper, "warning other Americans of Syrian peddlers and asking them to be cautious when they let them enter their homes."[26]

Ten years later, the editors of *Al-Wafa'* wrote in a similar fashion about women peddlers and "the consequences of the Syrian woman holding the wallet [an expression that meant peddling] and wandering from city to city to sell." They relayed a story told by a peddling man who went to an American customer to whom he had sold before. His customer, a woman, asked him about a Syrian woman peddler and mentioned her by name. The man knew the woman but feigned ignorance in order to hear the American woman's opinion of her. According to the American woman, the Syrian woman had told her that her husband "was once wealthy and of the elite," but she took to peddling after his business failed and their young children at home were in need. The peddling man knew this was not the Syrian woman's actual circumstances. He called the peddling woman who created false narratives to sell products "a thief and a liar at the same time" and said that such stories prove the "degradation and humiliation" of Syrian women peddlers in general. The editors continued, "The woman that carries her purse or wallet in her hand or over her shoulder [that is, who peddles], also carries the reasons for degrading her status and value."[27]

Here the *Al-Wafa'* editors described a chorus of outcries against dishonest and corrupt Syrian women peddlers. They seemed to repeat arguments that had come before, aware of their redundancy and exasperated by their ineffectiveness. They railed against the women themselves, their husbands, and the larger community that had failed to stop these women despite myriad newspaper publications against them. The editors defended peddling as useful and even respectable when men did it—"when it is necessary for trade"—but, conversely, as the thing that "marks a girl with dishonor, whenever she carries her purse." The editorial concluded with three recommendations for Syrian women. encouraging them to work in factories, where they could be properly surveilled; to work in stores where their parents or family members worked; or, best yet, to stay at home. The *Al-Wafa'* editors concluded, "We are in more need of dignity and good reputation than we are of the wealth made through the path of humiliation and degradation."[28]

In this regard, much of this published criticism against women peddlers invoked their dishonor, humiliation, and degradation. In particular, the term "honor" (*sharaf*) allowed a writer to talk about sex, and specifically women's sexuality, without directly articulating it. Although the concept of honor has become epistemologically loaded in Arab contexts based on Eurocentric understandings of Arab family systems, it figures centrally in these peddling debates in the Arab press, and it is thus essential for understanding how ideas of women's sexuality circulated to constrain women's laboring choices in diaspora.[29] In writing about women peddlers in 1906, 'Afifa Karam singled out women who lived alone without their fathers, brothers, or husbands. An early Arab American feminist, Karam wrote prolifically about women's issues for *Al-Hoda*, often addressing women themselves. However, in this 1906 essay, Karam decided to speak directly to men "because the leash of women is in their hands." As a feminist writer, Karam was primarily concerned with women's education, well-being, and betterment.[30] In her piece, she appealed to men through an argument of naturalized gender essentialism, which considered that women were weak and needed men to protect them. She claimed that Syrian men's failures to protect Syrian women put them in situations as peddlers that required them to compromise their sexual integrity: "She [the woman peddler] was not created to take insults for him, to wander trading while he goes from one place to another accompanied by laziness. She was not created to trade for him, sometimes [trading] with her honor and modesty, while he sits idly and with disgrace. She was not created to carry, on his behalf, all kinds of burdens and struggles while he does not carry anything when that is what he was created for."[31] The mention of trading "with her honor" enabled Karam to signal that women peddlers were put in situations in which they might be forced to engage in sexual activity for profit. Karam also used this opportunity to air her grievance that what Syrians valued was changing in diaspora. People were concerned no longer with "where were you and what did you do, but rather [with] what did you bring and how much did you make."[32] She chided those men who sent their wives "to sell and wander."

Layyah Barakat was more explicit in her 1911 condemnation of certain forms of women's labor in diaspora. She urged Syrian women to find respectable work: "By work, I do not mean knocking on doors bearing bags and cases because that is not considered honorable work. In fact, it is often dangerous for good, simple-hearted naïve girls who have been exposed to evil and whoredom as a result of knocking on doors. I have heard painful stories in this regard which I cannot repeat on the pages of a newspaper."[33] Perhaps the stridency of Barakat's message reflected the era in which she was writing. As fewer people peddled and more found work and lives that were less transient, "the tone of the opposition to women's work grew more strident."[34]

SYRIAN HONOR AND RACIALIZED NATURALIZATION

In the Syrian diaspora in the early twentieth-century United States, the concept of honor was imbued with complex meaning. As a matter of gendered sexual propriety, honor was tied to the very categories of desirable and undesirable immigrants delineated by the US government. These categories were ideological, sexual, and racialized, particularly with regard to non-Christian immigrants. In 1907, after the Alabama congressman John Burnett spoke against Syrians as "the most undesirable" of immigrants, a Birmingham medical doctor, H. A. Elkourie, wrote to his local newspaper twice to defend Syrians' fitness for citizenship. He sought in particular to distance Syrians from "prostitutes and anarchists," who were excluded from the categories of desirable immigrants welcome in the United States. To be sure, Elkourie's was a racial argument, but he did not use terms of color, nor did he define Syrians in opposition to Black or Asian populations, as elite Syrians later did explicitly.[35]

This imbrication of gender, sexuality, and race also depended on discourses of religious difference. After polygamists were added to the list of undesirables in 1891, anti-Muslim racism was "translated into" US immigration law.[36] For instance, while Syria and the rest of the Ottoman Empire remained eligible for immigration after being excluded from the 1907 "Asiatic Barred Zone,"

Turkish Muslims in particular began to be denied admittance to the United States because of their professed Muslim faith. Despite the indigenous Middle Eastern origins of Christianity, Syrians in the United States found themselves in an ideological terrain that privileged certain kinds of Europeans above others and held Europeanness to be synonymous with Christianity. This ideology presented an opportunity for Syrian Christians to argue for religious sameness with and, by extension, racial-cultural proximity to white Americans.[37] Syrian Muslim immigrants faced the additional risk of deportation or denial of entry because of laws that targeted Muslims based on the association of Islam with polygamy, regardless of an individual's actual beliefs or practices.[38] Syrian Muslims and Druze were thus always at risk in this legal system. Although Syrian Christians and to some extent Syrian Jews may have been legally able to access this proximity to whiteness, their everyday experiences remained precarious.[39] Some Americans associated all Syrians with Islam and thus with a racialized difference, regardless of their actual religion. And, to some extent, because of the cultural dominance of Islam in the region and the mixed nature of religious and social life in Greater Syria, this association with Islam was true.

This question of Syrian honor thus also became a matter of Syrian whiteness and, for many, Syrian Christianity. The defense of Syrian whiteness was articulated in increasingly explicit racial terms in relation to US citizenship. As Syrian immigrants petitioned US courts for naturalized citizenship, they made legal arguments in support of their whiteness that circulated in these same publications and were linked with some Syrian elite leaders. For example, Naoum Mokarzel, the editor of *Al-Hoda*, also founded the Syrian American Association in 1909. This organization, with Mokarzel as president, went on to aid in the defense of George Dow's 1913 federal petition for citizenship through an argument for Syrian whiteness that also hinged upon Syrian Christianity.[40] When Dow's initial petition was denied, *Al-Hoda* printed a fundraising appeal from the Syrian Society for National Defense. In reference to the Dow case, the organization's secretary, Najib Al-Sarghani, wrote, "We have found ourselves at the center of an attack on the Syrian honor."[41] Dow's case would eventually be decided in his favor in the US Supreme Court, which ended the federal adjudication of Syrian whiteness with regard to citizenship.

Sarah Gualtieri has analyzed how these claims to whiteness on behalf of the Syrian community moved from initially being couched in terms of civilizational and religious likeness to Europeans to also explicitly claiming that a white identity meant "not Black" and "not Asian."[42] Indeed, in the Dow case in which the Supreme Court ultimately decided in the Syrians' favor, the argument linked Christianity to ethnological classifications of race and whiteness as central to Syrian identity. The argument also used the legal precedent of European Jews' naturalization rights and linked Syrians to them through ethnological classifications of the Semite.[43] These Syrian petitioners used their proximity to Jews, even as the assumed Christian identity of Syrian immigrants played a significant role in adjudicating their whiteness.

Representing whiteness through Christianity is apparent in these claims of Syrian petitioners, who offered evidence both in terms of their religious identifications as Christians and the historical geography of Syria and the life of Jesus. Judges in these Syrian naturalization cases often viewed "Arab" as synonymous with "Muslim," at a time when the latter was an unequivocally nonwhite racial category.[44] They also voiced concern about ancestral mixing between Syrian Christians and Muslims and thus the lack of purity in Syrian Christian claims to whiteness.[45] But these were concerns of miscegenation, which is a specific racial *and sexual* anxiety. Thus, claiming an authentic Christian identity as grounds for naturalization appealed not only to an ethnoreligious distinction from Muslims but also to a heteronormative and thus hetero-reproductive purity. As Junaid Rana has shown, the category of "Muslim" as historically constructed by Europeans has depended on "a racial logic that crosses the cultural categories of nation, religion, ethnicity, and sexuality."[46] Race is a concept of heterosexual embodiment, in which bodies are categorized and systematized according to difference; heterosexuality, then, is "the means of ensuring, but also the site of endangering, the reproduction of these differences."[47] Thus, claiming or gaining proximity to whiteness demands normativity in other aspects of self and, in particular, sexuality. This was the case both in how elite Christian Syrians articulated whiteness for themselves and in how they distanced themselves from their Muslim counterparts.[48]

The naturalization process at this time, though primarily about racial fitness for citizenship, was thus also a question of sexual fitness and worked within an "economy of desire" in which the state "selects its own objects of desire and produces them as citizens."[49] The naturalized subject was presumed to be a sexually reproductive one. This imagined immigrant was one who desired the United States and would sexually reproduce and raise future citizens in the nation's likeness.[50] Syrian honor was thus a matter of sexual, gendered, classed, religious, and racial respectability. When elite Syrian Americans made appeals for women to stop peddling because it was degrading; when they argued that Syrians should be able to naturalize because they were similar to Europeans and white Americans; when Syrian American Christians distanced themselves from Islam or made anti-Muslim statements—in all these cases, the arguments revealed a burgeoning ideology of Syrian American respectability politics rooted in white American heteronormative ideals. Tracing this use of honor in debates about both women's peddling and Syrian naturalization further illuminates the coconstitutive relationship between race and sexuality in the Syrian American diaspora. This analysis also provides historicist corroboration that, rather than merely being a culturally delineated concept, honor was an affective category that contained a range of Syrians' anxieties about race, sexual and gendered normativity, and modernity—anxieties that were refracted through and shaped by American white supremacist and heteronormative politics.

MEN'S PROBLEMS: THE *AL-HODA* ROW
OVER WOMEN PEDDLERS

One *Al-Hoda* article published in 1903, and a series of ensuing responses, provides a microcosm of these arguments linking women peddlers with declining Syrian honor and patriarchal failure. The author, Yusuf Al-Zaʿni Batruni, was a peddler himself and spoke from his peddling experience, as well as from his conversations with other Syrians. He was unflinching in his assessment that women peddlers made things more difficult for everyone, but in particular for Syrian men: "The source of all problems come from the peddling woman." He acknowledged that some might bristle at his opinion of women peddlers but said that his were "hurtful but true words." Batruni advocated for a federal ban prohibiting women from crossing state lines to peddle. He continued, "The honor and dignity of the Syrian man can be returned after peddling has been stripped from the hands of the women that have been the source of this dishonor and shame." Batruni was ostensibly motivated by his patriotism and his desire to "[protect] the Syrian name." But for him, Syrian honor and men's honor were the same. While he directed most of his consternation at women, Batruni circuitously lobbed his criticisms at the husbands of peddling women: "lazy men whose livelihood is dependent on their wives."[51] If women were banned from peddling, Batruni claimed, this ban would force their husbands to do the peddling work themselves instead, thus restoring honor to Syrian men, Syrian women, and the Syrian reputation writ large.

Al-Hoda published several responses, including two follow-up pieces from Batruni himself. Unsurprisingly, ʿAfifa Karam was one of those who responded. An incessant champion of women's education, Karam praised Batruni's calls for reforms and then quickly pivoted. She turned Batruni's argument against women's peddling into one for women's literacy: "You, oh virtuous, should take it from me that there are only 5 percent who are well behaved among the immigrant women, so how can we hope to reform the illiterate who cannot read?"[52] This pivot extended more broadly to become a critique that Syrians were not reading newspapers or books. Of course, Karam had much to say about women peddlers as well: "There are many who peddle either because their husbands push them to work, or because they don't have a man, and they remain righteous and [therefore] undeserving of the scholars' anger."[53] Karam agreed that some women peddlers indeed ruined the Syrian name: "These women, as you have said, who themselves made the American [man] despise them and mark them with depravity, and who almost even managed to carry the germs of their disease to healthy bodies, for you rarely find an American man who sees the Syrian woman as pure."[54] It is unclear if Karam was referring here to the literal spread of disease (for instance, sexually transmitted infections, because women peddlers were linked with sex work) or to a figurative spread that degraded Syrian standing and morality—or to both. Karam was pointed in her critique of such women, who she claimed did not think about the future or their reputations in the United States but only about returning to a home where no one would ask about their actions abroad.[55]

The perspectives of women peddlers themselves were largely absent from these conversations. However, the visibility and contributions of their labor could not be entirely erased. A third article published in response to Batruni, written by Amin Silbi, features Silbi's discussion of Batruni's article with two women peddlers. Rebuking the claim that peddling marred the Syrian reputation, the women claimed that "the popularity of the Syrian name, from start to finish, is from peddling." They suggested that women peddled only because their husbands realized that they themselves could not succeed at it but their wives could. For them, this practice was not a source of shame but rather a reflection of practicality, utility, and recognition of their husbands' labor for the family: "The woman's peddling is not for the reasons claimed by the author, but done out of necessity, in order to help her husband whose hard work she has lived off of for many years. If she helps him for two or three years, there is neither shame on her or him."[56] Essentially, these women argued that they were proud of helping their families in this way when needed. The younger of the two women also took Batruni to task for his claim that he criticized women out of the pride he had in his Syrian community. She countered that Batruni's "words come from severe anger, and not from patriotic zeal, because he who is protective of the Syrian name, and especially of the gentle sex, should not be publicizing his words of ridicule and scorn across all corners of the world."[57] The two women, like others, maintained that women who migrated alone to peddle were in the minority. Instead of shaming and complaining, they suggested, men should look for ways to help those women who had no other options for income.

Silbi, who conveyed these women's words, wrote at the beginning of the piece that, when he had begun talking to them, he was "hopeful that they would quit this profession." But, unfortunately for those who shared his perspective, these comments from women peddlers showed that they were steadfast in defending it. Their perspectives seem to respond to the overwhelming print discourse that ignored women's own agency in decisions regarding migration and labor. The lack of perspectives from women peddlers and from others who might defend women's peddling work only reinforced the idea that women peddlers were either lost souls corrupted by their work and unfamiliar diasporic environments, or else unwitting pawns of their inept husbands.

When Batruni responded a few weeks later, he returned to his initial argument that 75 percent of women peddlers earn their money through "indecent actions" and that 25 percent of them were "moral and pure."[58] To those who defended single women peddlers who had no other options, Batruni reminded them that women could work in textile factories or as seamstresses with less stain on their character. He refuted those who objected to his essay and thanked those who supported his efforts. In a second response, Batruni focused on speaking directly to the men whose wives peddled, appealing to a naturalized division of gendered labor endowed by God: "We know that the man was created to work, and since the beginning of his existence on Earth, God said to him, by the sweat of your face, you shall eat your bread. But the men who are in good and complete health," yet stay at home, "killing time and playing with the children, and send their wives to peddle; they have lost their honor and are nothing but vile, and now eat from the woman's hard work, drinking her sweat and livelihood."[59]

The voices of women were present within these debates about women's peddling, but they rarely reflected the perspectives of women who actually peddled. Given the relatively low literacy rates of the Arab American population at this time and the fact that the subscriptions to these periodicals did not include the entire community, we can take these perspectives as only partial, and particularly as representing sectors of the social elite of the early Arab American community.[60] This likelihood does not mean that these ideas did not reach nonliterate audiences, as newspapers would also have been read aloud in groups. But it is difficult to tell in what ways such arguments reached and influenced women peddlers themselves.

In many of these pieces, peddling as a potential source of women's empowerment (because of the income it provided) was critiqued as an example of men's declining power. In this way, the object of scrutiny moved away from women and (back) to men. Although peddling was clearly a "women's issue," these discussions about peddling often orbited men, either by speaking directly to them rather than to women or by centering men's feelings and men's reputations.[61] This raises the question: Was some animosity directed at women peddlers because of a sense of frustration on the part of male peddlers who felt they could not compete with women's peddling successes?

PATRIARCHAL FAILURE AND SYRIAN SEXUAL NORMATIVITY IN FLUX

The heated discussion about women wanderers reflects the discomfort that elite Syrian Americans felt about the changes in norms that coincided with immigration, particularly related to marriage practices. Syrians who migrated experienced broad shifts in marriage patterns, such as the move from familial or village-based (endogamous) marriage practices to religious-based preferences, the tenuous nature of transatlantic marriages, bigamy, and Syrians in diaspora not marrying at all. Akram Khater even suggests that some Syrian women migrated for the sole purpose of securing a spouse, because women who remained in Syria were overburdened with family responsibilities and subject to gossip when they remained unmarried.[62] As much as the proliferation of these topics may indicate that marriage was a priority for many Syrians, archival evidence also suggests that for others it was not. Some elders of this generation, when interviewed in the 1960s, recalled a variety of ideas in relation to being single, many of which were contrary to the assumption that "the state of being single was both unnatural and deplorable."[63] These included the views that being single was common among Syrians in the United States, that there was no pressure for women to get married, and that there was no shame in not marrying.[64]

These peddling critiques implicated husbands and fathers in patriarchal failure when women immigrated alone to the United States and began peddling. One response was to chastise men for their role in the crisis of women peddlers. 'Afifa Karam's previously discussed 1906 editorial implored men not to send women alone to the United States, where they would surely end up peddling, be subjected to insults, and potentially engage in sex work. Here, Karam criticized men whose wives worked as peddlers. They failed to uphold their patriarchal responsibilities, and their economic burden thus fell to their wives. The *kasha* (peddling box) that women carried became a symbol for all the "burdens and struggles" that husbands had neglected to carry for their wives.[65]

Married women who peddled were most especially an indictment of their husbands, and these husbands were thus popular targets for those who deplored women wanderers. Such a husband failed to provide adequately for his family and led his wife and daughters into moral decay. The 1908 editorial in *Al-Wafa'* discussed earlier bemoaned Syrian women peddlers for spinning dramatic tales about their lives to "[steal] the emotions" of their customers. The editor continued, "How many a girl whose ears were not accustomed in her family home to hearing anything but virtuous words, heard [while peddling] words that hurt the ears and the morals, and how many a girl whose eyes have only seen the good and pure, has [then] seen then the ugly and corrupt."[66] The writer was equally displeased with Syrian husbands who spent their time gambling and drinking while their wives peddled. These women would then come home from peddling, the editorial claimed, and give their earnings to "their lazy, despicable, and dishonorable men."[67] Even so, the editorial quickly pivoted back to place blame on Syrian women for the ills of peddling.

Women writers were steadfast in their criticisms of Syrian men who were linked to women's peddling work, both those in diaspora and those back in Syria. One particularly incisive critique was lodged by Zubayda Butrus Sa'b in 1904 when she wrote that husbands were sending their wives to the United States to peddle and send money back home for the husbands to enjoy. "But the blame, all the blame, is on her husband, who thinks his wife is a slave of his, whom he can dispose of in whichever way he chooses, and so he sends her to America to make him money. And [then] she comes and finds more humiliation than she can bear, for she asks for death a thousand times during the day as she carries the peddling box on her head."[68] Sa'b understood married women peddlers to be exploited workers who served their husbands' sole economic gain. According to these perspectives, women were finding themselves in a situation outside what was expected for them in marriage. In this context, the extensive discussions about marriage published in the same periodicals highlight that the very understanding of what was normative in Syrian sexuality was shifting.

When elite Syrians criticized women's peddling, they frequently cited a failure of Syrian patriarchy. That is, they blamed men for not upholding their patriarchal duty to provide for and protect the women in their families and claimed that, as a result, these women were either forced to peddle or were exposed to the dangers of peddling because they knew no better (i.e., a man did not correct them).

FREEDOM, SEX, AND MONEY: A QUESTION OF VALUES

These critical discussions about marriage emphasized some fraught consequences of migration. Discussions about Syrian values regarding money, family, marriage, freedom, and sexuality were abundant in the pages of the early Syrian American press. The last two—freedom and sexuality—were frequently linked in the Syrian press, as the changes in sexual norms wrought by migration and peddling were referenced particularly through a discourse of excessive freedom. Any consensus, if indeed one had ever existed, on the values of Syrians was shaken by transatlantic dispersal.

The preoccupation with values was often signaled in the ways writers criticized Syrian migrants' focus on money, and this criticism was often routed through the work of peddling. In one satirical story about life in the United States, a Syrian immigrant envies his educated, elite counterparts (who engage in nontransient work). The peddler-to-proprietor trope unfolds slowly here, as the immigrant moves from peddling to opening a fruit stand and later a dry goods store.[69] Yet, all the while, he still desires to be in the inner circle of the Syrian elite and moves to New York to open a store. Once in New York, he remarks that his "biggest greed" was not so much for the money he sought as for the company of these elite Syrians. "Doesn't money open the door to everything?" he asked. Indeed, the author is sure that "money opens the doors to their homes . . . money is everything!"[70]

Another writer lamented this focus on money and its effects on Syrian American matchmaking. Amin Silbi wrote in *Al-Hoda* in 1902 that families were frequently more concerned with money—how much the husband would make and how large the dowry was—than with the potential groom's character and manners. In these situations, married women often ended up peddling. A woman would know no more about her future husband than these financial details; and "as soon as the girl settles in his house, and he has a hold on her," according to Silbi, the man sends his new wife out to work, to at least recover the cost of the dowry he gave her father. Silbi urged Syrian parents and their daughters to think about a man's manners and his family of origin, rather than money and appearances: "In this way, we will no longer see many women selling in a degrading state, because the man who honors his woman will find it easier to withstand poverty and the roughness of living, rather than expose her to insult and force her to work in professions unsuitable for women. May the intelligent pay attention to this matter in the country of freedom and independence."[71]

Nearly twenty years later, Victoria Tannous wrote about the way that work plagued Syrians in Syria and in diaspora, but in different ways. "Life will end but work will not" was the saying passed down to her from her mother, aunts, and neighbors in Syria. Tannous said she immigrated to the United States "to escape the work" but instead found "an endless routine of work that does not stop."[72] Whereas in Syria, a woman working outside the home was a source of shame, Tannous claimed, in diaspora men and women, young and old, married and unmarried, all left their houses daily for the drudgery of work. To be sure, Tannous writes here through an idealized lens, describing what she had expected life in the United States to be like, certainly one of relative economic ease. "In America," Tannous wrote "this mentality has flipped. The Syrian man in America believes that his own employment is a source of shame. In fact, he believes that it is one of his wife's duties to earn a living for herself and her children, and even to provide for him. I know many who are of this kind. They spend their days in coffee shops with the excuse that they cannot find work, and their wives carry the burden of working either in fabric or as peddlers."[73] Tannous also argued that the reverse—those men who prevented their daughters from working because of "tradition"—was wrong too. "Every family that has a hardworking, self-sufficient girl who does not rely on her father or brother has the right to be proud of her. It is the lazy girl who believes that working brings her dishonor who becomes a burden on her family."[74] Essentially, Tannous advocated for unmarried women to learn some skill to become self-sufficient, which she would then cease performing once she married: "Working for an unmarried girl is an honor and a shame for a married woman." Tannous argued that the married woman who worked outside the home enabled a lazy husband, leading him "to despise her and view her only as an object to be used to please his needs, and not as his wife and life partner."[75]

In 1904, *Al-Hoda* editor Naoum Mokarzel invited women to write on issues pertaining to them for the newspaper. "He who thinks that restraining the woman is advantageous for the nation, protective of morality, and honorable for the family, is either oppressive or unwise,"[76] he wrote. "Research on women demands a woman's pen." Mokarzel lamented the attention paid to women's bodies and appearance in neglect of their character and intellect. He pointed out what he saw as a hypocrisy particular to Syrian Americans: "What is strange is that in our diasporas, we cast an ugly freedom on the woman to explore the forests and the wilderness, to go into the cities and roam the villages, while weighed down by her load. But we constrain her otherwise, for we do not allow her to give a speech as a speaker or do research as a writer."[77] Here Mokarzel juxtaposed the freedom given to women who peddle with the freedom denied women in matters of literacy and public intellectualism.

In the Syrian American press, freedom was a salient trope and a frequent topic of discussion, as Syrians considered the differences between living under Ottoman rule and living in the United States. But freedom could present a peculiar problem for Syrians living in diaspora. According to Iskandar Atallah, writing in *Al-Kalimat* in 1909, this freedom was, for Syrian migrants, "like putting the sunlight in their eyes, which can surely incinerate them."[78] Atallah described how "this excessive freedom" led specifically to bigamy in the Syrian migrant population, whose men would leave wives in the homeland and marry again in the United States. He noted that some families of betrothed women in Syria were being instructed to make sure migrant men were not already married in the United States, and he praised this caution. He also urged Syrian migrant men to have letters of certification attesting to their unmarried status when they traveled back to Syria to find brides.

Druze Syrian migrants also wrestled with migration and marriage. A series of articles in *Al-Bayan* in 1914 debated the possibilities and pitfalls of Druze women joining men in the United States. The numbers of Druze who migrated to the United States were especially low in comparison to their Christian counterparts, but those of Druze women were minuscule. As in other Syrian communities, Druze religious leaders became concerned about the effect of this migration on marriage, children, and the reproduction and maintenance of Druze religious and communal practices. According to oral history interviews, these leaders required early Druze migrants to sign an oath vowing that they would return to their wives and fiancées within two years or release them from marriage.[79]

The predominant tone of these articles in *Al-Bayan* sided against the immigration of Druze women. All of the writers agreed that migration was harmful for Druze women. Where they differed was in whether it was more harmful for Druze women to be in the United States or for them to be without men in Syria. In the fourth article of this five-part series, the writer Amin Abu Isma'il argued against this immigration because for Druze women to stay in the homeland would motivate Druze men to return rather than staying in the United States permanently. Isma'il also argued that what prevented women from migrating was not religion but morality. For immigrants to protect the "family's morals" was impossible, Isma'il claimed, when a woman has "absolute freedom" and her husband is forced to be absent due to his work. The bottom line? "Absolute freedom brings about immorality," and the United States is a country of "freedom, modernization, and immorality."[80]

Others argued that while Druze men and women were not meant to be separated (which was the one argument in favor of Druze women's migration), the United States was a land of dishonor and corruption for women that would further disperse the Druze population and prevent them from having a single place to call home. This could "lead to [their] extinction."[81] These pieces were inflected by the questions of Druze nationalism and the role of women's reproductive capacities, biologically and socially, in nationalist ideology. Druze women's immigration posed an existential threat in which women's exposure to the kind of freedom available in the United States would lead them to abandon their traditions and moral habits. Druze women's immigration would, ironically, cause the community to lose its specificity as Druze as members dispersed and assimilated into other communities.[82]

In the last article in the *Al-Bayan* series, As'ad Husayn Abu 'Ali wondered what would become of the Druze woman without familial support in diaspora: "And what would the supporters of women's immigration say if something were to occur that forces the woman to divorce from her husband while in diaspora, or if her husband dies and she is left without an ally or provider and was the mother of children who cannot provide for themselves; what would the result be then? And what shall that poor woman do to get the necessary sustenance for her and her children?" The only choice for survival, in these cases, was peddling. Abu 'Ali went on to remark that the trials of peddling were well known among the Druze, including "the struggles and bootlicking and other things that it includes that are inappropriate to mention."[83] Peddling was particularly harmful, the author argued, because Druze children were left alone while a widowed or single Druze mother peddled. The children would thus stop being raised "in the manner appropriate to human society," preventing their integration into Druze society writ large: "Their return [to the homeland] will become impossible." The tone of these pieces is both highly chauvinistic and incredibly urgent: "[Women's immigration] will be the fatal blow for the Druze sect," Abu 'Ali wrote, "and in less than tens of years, the sect will be nothing but a trace."[84] Questions of lineage, cultural knowledge and inheritance, and community religious identity loomed large. The migration of Druze women, to a land where Druze religious and cultural practices were not recognized or valued, threatened their ability to properly reproduce the Druze nation.

One satirical short story about modern marriage among American Syrians took these worries of changing Syrian values to an extreme. "Marriage on the Latest Fashion Trend" claimed that women were so free in the United States that they could experiment wildly with heterosexual marriage arrangements. In the story, Um Tannous and Abu Tannous are the mother and father of three daughters who live in the United States. Um Tannous travels from Syria to visit them, and each visit with a daughter reveals new ways that this "country of trendiness" has wreaked havoc on Syrian marriage and gender norms. First, Um Tannous visits her oldest daughter in New York, who has three children. Um Tannous inquires as to the whereabouts of her son-in-law, who has not come to greet her. Her daughter informs her that she divorced her husband and is now looking for another to help raise her children. The daughter normalizes divorce in the United States, saying that divorce was the "trend" as well as a right that belonged to both women and men. She then goes on to list the numbers of divorced women that she knows. None of this consoles Um Tannous, of course, and she continues to think about this "trend" into the night. The next morning, the story says, "she woke up terrified, because she dreamed that Abu Tannous had come to America to divorce her and follow the trends like his daughter."[85]

Um Tannous then visits her next-oldest daughter in Jersey City, New Jersey. She is introduced to her daughter's husband, an older man in his sixties who greets her respectfully. Soon after, a man closer to her daughter's age enters the house, and she learns that this is her daughter's lover. "These words fell on Um Tannous's head like a bolt of lightning," the story explains, "and she wished that the ship had sunk with her on it, before she had reached America and heard this news."[86] That night Um Tannous has another dream; in this one, her husband comes to the United States to follow this trend of taking a younger lover.

Finally, Um Tannous returns to New York to visit her youngest daughter. After she spends time at this daughter's home, her daughter announces that she is waiting for her husband. This announcement surprises Um Tannous, who has believed her daughter to be unmarried. It surprises her more because this husband has also not been home since her arrival. Her daughter explains, "Mom, I am not married based on the trend like my sisters, I am married on the 'latest trend.'" She then goes on to reference Fannie Hurst, the early-twentieth-century American feminist whose unconventional marriage was publicized widely by the US press. This daughter explains that she and her husband live in separate residences, like Fannie Hurst and her spouse, and that their marriage follows several of Hurst's "conditions." In addition to living separately, these conditions include eating breakfast together only twice a week, letting any children choose which parent they are named after, and having the freedom to spend their time separately as they choose. Perhaps crucial for the debates over women's peddling, another condition expressed by the daughter concerns the right not to have marriage impede one's work: "Marriage has nothing to do with daily work, for if the wife was a writer for example, she has the right to continue in her job after she is married, and marriage should not stand in her way in this regard."[87]

Um Tannous spends a total of three months in the United States and ruminates daily on these developments. Increasingly, she regrets her decision to send her daughters abroad and to come herself: "At times, she would curse the day she came to this country. At other times, she would blame herself for allowing her daughters to travel alone to the country of trends, and they had been, before their travel, amongst the girls whose virtuous behavior was an example to follow."[88] The short story closes with this self-flagellating mother's lament as a warning to those who would send their daughters to the land of "trends."[89]

Freedom appeared to be a specifically gendered and sexualized danger. For women, freedom meant wandering alone, engaging in sex work, getting a divorce, or forming unconventional marriages. Freedom for men lead to bigamist marriages, the breaking of patriarchal responsibilities, and diminished patriarchal power. Freedom from the Ottoman regime was welcome for many Syrians. But freedom in the United States was also one of (relatively) unrestricted movement, and it had sexual repercussions—repercussions of sexual excess—that Syrians had to guard against. Moreover, all of these sexual and gendered consequences stemmed from the problem of distance from Syrian communities and their authoritative structures, a distance that migration and peddling enabled and exacerbated. Given the intensity of the connection between peddling and aberrant sexuality in the minds of the American public, as demonstrated in chapter 1, we might expect some preoccupation with that association to pop up in the pages of the Syrian American press as well. In relation to peddling, however, this connection was rare. The media focus was decidedly on women peddlers. The more seldom mentions of men's sexuality emerged through this discourse of too much freedom.

These class-bound conversations show just how normative Syrian sexuality was sutured to properly laboring men and women. Peddling and migration disrupted that system dramatically. Women peddlers' perspectives were largely absent from these conversations, but their labor and visibility in the American diaspora provided a focus for the disquiet that elite Syrian Americans felt. An almost unanimous chorus of opinion urged Syrian women to cease peddling, and those who did peddle were accused of engaging in sex work as part of their trade. The discourse of honor used to police women's labor had significant connections to the racial discourse used to press for Syrian naturalization in the same publications. The husbands of women peddlers, presumed to be profiting from their wives' harmful labor, were subject to critiques that castigated them for leading their wives down the path of dishonor.

All of these details point to a kind of perverted freedom that Syrians experienced in the United States: Syrians worshipped money, women lost their sense of propriety and virtue, and the specific patriarchal and gendered arrangement within heterosexual, monogamous marriage was threatened. These conversations were embedded in larger anxieties about assimilation and cultural authenticity, in which questions of freedom were indistinguishable from questions of modernity. Lisa Lowe writes that the concept of modernity is the history of "liberal forms monopolizing the meaning of freedom for the human and denying it to others placed at a distance from the human."[90] The print discourse about peddling and morality, along with other oral forms of community self-policing discussed in chapter 2, shaped the ideas about this perverted freedom that were specific to the Syrian diaspora. These ideas represent the complexities of broader anxieties about assimilation, including both the racialized desire to be seen as respectable and American and the desire to maintain cultural distinctiveness, as demonstrated most clearly in the discussion of Druze women's migration. Sexuality and gender became unsurprising yet consequential focal points of these anxieties.

4

The Possibilities of Peddling

Imagining Homosocial and Homoerotic Pleasure in Arab America

If we have inherited a colonial white heteronormative way of seeing and knowing, then we must retrain ourselves to confront and rearrange a mind-set that privileges certain relationships.

—EMMA PÉREZ, "QUEERING THE BORDERLANDS: THE CHALLENGES OF EXCAVATING THE INVISIBLE AND UNHEARD"

In his 1962 interview with Alixa Naff, Elias Lebos discussed some of the characteristics of his Syrian peddling community: "In our community, we kept our traditions: eating, singing, drinking, and enjoying ourselves." Lebos went on to describe some of the living conditions for peddlers, people of all genders and marital statuses, up to twenty of whom might sleep in the same room together. In Lebos's telling, these circumstances seemed to aid the traditions he talked of, rather than simply marking a hardship or even a disruption of those practices. "We used to cook together and enjoy life and laugh," he recalled. "We'd join together and share expenses and the cooking, our traditional meals. Men did it, of course, but women too. We spent great evenings together. People then were more full of affection for each other than these days."[1] Francis Slay, in an interview conducted by Naff the same year, also talked about affection as part of these traditions, but in particular between men. Slay discussed how his father would kiss his sons and brothers and how he was always sure to kiss his own adult son and son-in-law. Naff remarked to him, "There seems to be a special quality about the Lebanese men," and Slay responded, "Honey, let me tell you . . . It's not a put-on. What it is, is a showing of love." In contrast, Naff suggested that "a lot of men are very uncomfortable with that kind of thing."[2]

Evoked in these interviews are ways of being and relating to one another that these immigrants understood to be constitutive of their cultural practices and of what made them who they were, be that Syrian, Lebanese, Arab, or some other

102

regional or village-based identification. Given that the oral history interview tends to encourage the interviewee to think back on their past, these statements also cement a loss of these intimate practices at the moment they are evoked, a melancholic reference to assimilation under white supremacy. To invoke "culture" here is not to refer to an unchanging and ahistorical set of practices and characteristics.[3] Rather, the very traditions mentioned were shaped through peddling practices in diaspora. Here, the dynamics of gender shifted and allowed all Syrians to labor together in the creation of these communal meals. Notably, as Syrian immigrants and their descendants gained proximity to whiteness, many of their distinctly regional or local cultural practices were called into question with regard to their compatibility with American life, posing a potential threat to that privileged proximity. Slay's exchange with Naff about the loss of men's homosocial affection indicates that not only were cultural practices incompatible with whiteness but more intimate ways of being were incompatible as well. What other kinds of intimate affections and pleasures, then, threatened "Syrian whiteness"?

Coverage of Syrian communities in the US press offers a starting point for identifying some of the aspects that fell outside white and middle-class acceptability. In 1902, the small Syrian community in La Crosse, Wisconsin, came under scrutiny for what the local newspaper described as "midnight orgies" that "shake the rattle-trap dwellings and which can be heard in the dead of the night for several blocks." These so-called orgies were apparently distressing nearby white citizens.[4] What this newspaper described was a party held when long-distance peddlers returned from their peddling trips. As a member of that community explained decades later, men would gather to tell stories of their travels and drink, and the women would cook and talk together in the kitchen. There would also be lots of singing and dancing. Attendees would start late at night and draw down the shades, which perhaps contributed to whites' speculation about these soirees.[5]

By turning first to those practices and intimacies that attracted white supremacist scrutiny, we can also begin to ask what meaning these threatened practices held for Syrian migrants. The queer ecology of peddling is a useful site for this exploration because of the opportunities it provided for intimacy among peddlers, who were often of the same gender, as well as among those whose work supported the peddling economy in other ways.

That peddling was difficult and dangerous work is well documented. Peddlers were robbed on the road; they were subject to the whims of the elements, particularly when they could not find shelter at night; long-distance peddling could be a lonely and physically grueling experience; and numerous peddlers were assaulted or murdered while peddling, as discussed in chapter 1. More generally, transient workers were targeted by immigration restrictions, property ownership and voting laws, and police campaigns in the first half of the twentieth century.[6] Earlier chapters have also outlined the discursive violence enacted through the ideas that circulated about peddlers and Syrians immigrants: for example, they were manipulative, distrustful, lazy, and subservient; their work was a ruse for begging; the men involved were ineffective and sexually deviant, and they abandoned their duties toward the family; and the women were irreverent, failed mothers who persisted in breaking the conventions for proper women.

The practices and ways of being that endangered Syrians by shifting them closer to nonwhiteness (specifically peddling practices that crossed gendered and sexual norms of the white American middle class) were not exclusively sites of violence; they were also sites of pleasure. What were these possibilities for pleasure in the queer ecology of peddling? Peddlers could, for example, experience different landscapes and meet new people in the course of their travels. Peddlers who traveled together formed bonds with one another, as did the women who stayed home while men left to peddle. And women peddlers were able to experience a level of independence—in economics and mobility—that they may not have enjoyed otherwise. Arab American historiography has largely addressed pleasure in ways that reify heteronormativity and obscure how Arab familial and community structures were incompatible with US white supremacy. But peddling provided an avenue for infinite homosocial intimacies. As men peddled together, as women stayed home together, and as other women peddled together, homosocial bonds were not only inevitable but were constitutive of early Syrian American culture.

In an interview with Naff, one woman, Budelia, described growing up around other Syrian immigrant women. Budelia's mother had peddled before and after her husband's death, up until her own death at the age of seventy. Her mother's cousin, another Syrian woman, told Budelia's mother where to go and helped her find a supply of items to sell. Budelia remembered that women would visit together while sewing and crocheting items for peddlers to sell, especially embroidered pillowcases with "fringe and rickrack" and dust caps with wide ribbons. She recalled "women crocheting together while eating big beautiful tomatoes, beefsteak tomatoes, and peppers from the garden, and grapes and apples from a big bowl; hands and mouths moving at the same time."[7] The sensuousness of this language is a reminder that memory is embodied; it is a somatic experience. That sensory experience of a homosocial space also allows us to remember the slippages between homosociality and homoeroticism, or what Gayatri Gopinath calls the "latent homoeroticism of female homosocial space."[8] Gopinath writes, "It is often in moments of what appears to be extreme gender conformity, and in spaces that seem particularly fortified against queer incursions—such as the domestic arena—that queer female desire emerges in ways that are most disruptive of dominant masculinist scripts of community and nation."[9] This remembering—in Naff's interview with Budelia and in my labor to place it in a lineage of queer Arab American history—is sensuous knowledge.[10]

This chapter asks how we can account for the intimacies enabled by the queer ecology of the peddling economy, particularly those intimacies that ran counter to the mandates of white, middle-class heteronormativity. I use historical-grounded imagining to examine the homosocial and homoerotic pleasures apparent in a number of photographs selected from the Faris and Yamna Naff Arab American Collection (housed at the Smithsonian Institution's National Museum of American History). My discussion in this chapter focuses especially on a number of photographs that I believe were included in these archival materials because they lend themselves to a normative sexual and gendered reading—that is, because they can be interpreted as evidence that Syrian Americans fit within US heteronormative standards. Yet this heteronormative reading is not the exclusive meaning that we can glean from these images. In particular, the photographs examined in this chapter allow us to focus on the pleasure related to the peddling economy: the pleasures experienced in the act of peddling, the pleasures among peddlers while not at work, and the pleasures that others in the peddling economy experienced in their work together.

THEORIZING PLEASURE: EROTICS AND INTIMACIES

To understand how pleasure functions within and through these photographs, a working definition of "pleasure" is necessary. But pleasure is a subjective experience. Something that elicits pleasure for one person maybe be unpleasant for another; the experience of physical pain is a prime example of this. The variety of reasons and ways that people experience pleasure works against giving a singular definition of pleasure. A more feasible, and more productive, approach is to understand what links all of these varied experiences of pleasure.

First, pleasure is an affective and corporeal experience, one that touches not only the emotions and sensations that we recognize as our feelings, but also physical sensations in the rest of the body that may feel good but might be unarticulated or unnoticed. Second, pleasure occurs in relation to something else: to a physical sensation, to a thought or memory, to another person. Pleasure is thus relational as well as corporeal. Third, pleasure contains both erotic and intimate elements, two concepts that center the sensory and corporeal as well as the relational, respectively, in issues of power. Not all intimacies are pleasurable, but I understand pleasure as necessarily having an element of intimacy. In this section, I critically examine intimacy and erotics in order to ground my understanding of pleasure in the queer ecology of Syrian peddling.

Intimacy can be pleasurable or unpleasant or can involve multiple configurations of both. Intimacy, particularly as documented in Middle East and North Africa studies scholarship, is both interactive and intersubjective, and the study of intimacy reveals that the links between structural forces (such as the state, religion, and kinship networks) and the particular ways that norms of intimacy are mediated and change historically.[11] Lisa Lowe outlines three types of intimacy that aid in understanding how power (specifically racialized, colonial power) works through relationships: spatial proximity, sexual and affective intimacy, and constellations of contact among people who are situated differently in terms of power.[12] The different environments and landscapes encountered while peddling were intimate experiences; they forced Syrians to think about their relationship to the lands they traveled and the power of those lands over them, especially regarding terrain, climate, and weather. Peddlers' encounters with their customers—whether friendly, hostile, or ambivalent—were also intimate, as Syrians (and their customers) had to negotiate power-laden differences of language, race, culture, gender, and sometimes religion. Peddlers in the course of their work also confronted state power in the form of local regulations that sought to restrict movement, public appearance, and sales (such as peddling licenses, vagrancy laws, and the "ugly laws" discussed in chapter 2). The bonds formed among peddlers while on the road—among siblings, cousins, friends, or others—were intimate bonds; and the new relationships that peddling enabled, specifically friendships and sexual relationships that may not have been possible within the Syrian settlements, were also intimate.

Lowe cautions against the uncritical acceptance of sexual and affective intimacies as belonging to the realm of the private, because doing so is part of the "biopolitics through which the colonial powers administered the enslaved and colonized and sought to indoctrinate the newly freed into [Eurocentric] Christian marriage and family."[13] The example of peddling intimacies that were affective and sexual can illuminate the constructed nature of that confinement, because these intimacies occurred during the course of work or were enabled by particular laboring practices.

These theories of intimacy and power link forms of contact and relationship that are commonly understood to be individual with systemic and macro levels of dominance. Audre Lorde's theory of the erotic is rooted in a different framework, but it is also one that connects the individual with the systemic—specifically, the power that queer women of color have in their lives in relation to one another and to their own experiences, feelings, and desires. Used in conjunction with theorizations of intimacy, Lorde's radical reenvisioning of the erotic further clarifies how peddling practices were sites of powerful possibility for homosocial and homoerotic pleasure. For Lorde, the erotic is not singularly about the sexual but more broadly about the sensual and the sensory as well. Lorde's theory of the erotic allows for an articulation of work in the peddling economy as a set of laboring practices that also contained a sensuality and physicality of relationship to one's work, world, and surroundings. Lorde calls this the act of "sharing deeply any pursuit with another person."[14]

I understand these erotics as a form of interdependence, as it functioned in the queer ecology of the Syrian peddling economy. The historical-grounded imagining of photos that I demonstrate in this chapter is important for reminding us that stories of race are always simultaneously stories of gendered, sexual, and classed legibility or illegibility. Specifically, the status of Syrian migrants' racial position hinged not only on whom they were positioned in relation to and where, but also on how Syrian migrants were understood as gendered, sexual, and classed beings—that is, whether they were understood as such in normative or nonnormative ways according to white, middle-class, heteronormative standards. An analysis of pleasure that accounts for its erotic (corporeal) and intimate (relational) elements is essential for understanding this process for Syrians, because we can then clarify that their affective lives had significant potential to unsettle both normative white American ideals of personhood and the elite Syrian American response. Lorde says that the erotic is "the power of our unexpressed or unrecognized feeling."[15] Thus the verbal articulation of erotic feelings, desire, friendship, or care—let alone the claim to a sexual identity—is not a requirement for theorizing about the existence of erotic pleasure in peddling and making visible the possibilities of homoerotics.

Syrians adapted to peddling practices in ways that maintained the system of interdependence, care, and companionship that they valued. Syrians who peddled together experienced this kind of interdependence; they relied on one another for safety, food, shelter, and companionship on the road. The Syrian women who did not peddle but worked from home while male relatives were away combined households with other women to consolidate childcare, cooking, and cleaning—and, again, for companionship. Those who stayed home spent days preparing for the return of long-distance peddlers by readying rooms, harvesting crops, procuring ingredients, and making large quantities of Arab foods.[16]

Based on interviews with Syrian Americans from this early community, Naff poignantly described the joy in these reunions and the rest that peddlers could find in the Syrian settlements:

> It was in the settlements that peddlers revived their spirit and reveled in a sense of belonging. Here they rediscovered continuity with the past; *values, which often seemed out of place elsewhere, were validated.* It was here that life's vitality, numbed by the frustrations of the road, was restored; here people of their own kind spoke the same language, laughed at the same humor, called their names, and bantered in familiar accents. Here, they bathed, perhaps for the first time in weeks, and savored tastes they had craved. *Emotions, pent up on the road, poured forth in the settlements.*[17]

We could interpret this description as one that builds a homogeneous and essentializing portrait of the Syrian community, in which all members felt complete just by belonging, with no differences in power to complicate these feelings. Instead of this interpretation, which does have merit, I focus on Naff's articulation of the cultural validation felt within the community and of the affective release. I argue that the Syrian values viewed as "out of place" were precisely the ones I mention above—interdependence, companionship, and care—as being at odds with normative American ideals of independence, individualism, and self-sufficiency. This argument complicates the recuperative positioning of peddlers as pioneers, given that the settler colonial pioneer embodies those normative American ideals. The emotions that were "pent up on the road" and finally released when peddlers returned home could also be understood as Lorde's "unexpressed or unrecognized feeling." Thus, this validation and this release had power that conflicted with the disciplinary economy of heteronormative white supremacy in which Syrian Americans lived. This theoretical framework of pleasure is particularly pertinent for thinking about the queer ecology of peddling, wherein Syrian migrants traveled together, braved unknown and sometimes hostile geographies together, and came home and rejoiced together.

HOMOSOCIALITY, HOMOEROTICS, AND SYRIAN AMERICAN COMMUNITIES

Diasporic communities in which homosociality was normative have often been places where homoeroticism also existed. Scholars such as Gayatri Gopinath have documented the numerous slippages between homosociality and homoeroticism, particularly between women.[18] A reckoning with same-gender desire and sex in Arab American history is essential for combating the intertwined effects of white supremacy, Orientalism, and the "metanarrative of modernity" under which Syrians toiled.[19] The apparent absence of identifiable homosexual Syrians from this time period should not preclude us from knowing that these desires and sexual acts existed in the early Syrian American community. Historians of sexuality have long chronicled the obstacles in finding archival evidence of queer subjects. In addition, the identification of historical subjects as "queer," "homosexual," "gay," "bisexual," or "lesbian"—whether through sexual practices, aesthetics, or expressions of interiority that resemble identity—is an endeavor frustrated by the particularities of how these ways of being have developed in culturally, economically, regionally, and nationally specific contexts. Middle East and North Africa studies scholars have also long examined the existence of sexual practices, regimes, and ways of being that do not fit within the modern Eurocentric model of the heterosexual-homosexual binary. This examination includes the effects of colonialism on those ways of being, as well as the efficacy and effects of various practices of naming sexuality that conform to a neoliberal and cosmopolitan legibility framework. Nor do Middle East and North Africa studies scholars of sexuality agree what this history of colonialism and imperialism should then mean for contemporary sexual and bodily autonomy.[20]

These histories are varied and dynamic in the North American context as well. For instance, historian John Howard has shown that in rural spaces, where most of these peddlers operated, queer sexual practices followed trajectories of circulation and mobility, in contrast to the congregation more commonly found in urban areas.[21] The bars, boardinghouses, train stations, and cars through which Syrian peddlers and other transient workers passed were what Nayan Shah calls "queer sexual publics": they were semiprivate spaces in which same-gender sexual encounters were possible and frequent, even as they were heavily policed at the same time.[22]

In describing the small Syrian settlements that developed along peddling routes, Naff explains that living in crowded quarters was a new experience for those who came to the United States from villages: "In the settlement, one might share a tight space not only with relatives or fellow villagers but with strangers. Consequently, the settlement provided opportunities for new relationships not usually available in the village."[23] This insight is given within the context of Naff's discussion of marriage norms, but we cannot be sure that marriages were the only relationships that grew out of these new circumstances. What kinds of relationships were these, and how were they different? Were these marriages or friendships or intimate relationships that blurred boundaries between the sexual and the platonic? Were they welcome changes, or did they chafe against the expectations of certain boundaries? And what of sexual violence? One of Naff's interlocutors described a house in Spring Valley, Illinois, where Syrian peddlers stayed when they came through town: "about two dozen at a time—both men and women, husbands and wives, single men and single women—slept there on the floor, two or three families to one room."[24] Presumably, children were present as well.

The opportunities for various relationships would have been abundant in a place with intimate and novel mixing of people, but what of other possibilities that may not have been imagined in heteronormative historical frameworks? What of nighttime explorations between eager friends? Or of the unwelcome advances from an older peddler upon a child? Imagining these possibilities removes the impetus to characterize a particular historical situation as positive or negative; instead it allows for the complexity of those situations and the possible unintelligibility of historical experience interpreted in our present moment, particularly with regard to sexuality and gender. This practice of historical-grounded imagining also creates space for the differences in community opinions about various relationships and intimacies, for the wide variation in participants' experiences of those relationships and intimacies, and for the reality of sexual violence and abuse also present in intimate encounters enabled by migration and the peddling economy.

Although all of the images in the Naff collection can have multiple meanings, the images I present here are particularly fruitful for thinking about the apparent lack of same-gender pleasure in the constructed narrative about early Arab American communities. Put another way, homosociality and homoeroticism function as present absences, traces of nonnormative connections that have been occluded within Arab American collections. I thus think about and with these photographs as "socially salient objects" in order to illustrate queer traces in Arab American history.[25]

The queerness here lies in several domains: in the possibility, which includes the reality, of homoerotic desire (homoerotic relationships and sexual acts were possible among peddlers on the road and among women who stayed home); in the impossibility of banishing from the archive nonnormative desires and intimacies (not limited to homoerotic intimacies); and in a methodological practice of "queer looking" and "queer feeling." In this last regard, I am influenced by Kara Keeling's work in Black queer studies, visual studies, and affect, which asks us to track our awareness and responsiveness to things from the past, particularly through noticing things that are felt and perceived yet may be unrecognizable to "our current common senses."[26] Thus, as I produce knowledge about these photographs in the Naff Collection, I am looking not for a nonnormative sexuality or gender as an identity but for pleasures that can be sensed as queer—pleasures that were used to bolster the notion of Arabs' cultural and racial differences from normative ways of being, particularly in relation to white American cultural norms (in the context of this immigration) and to European cultural norms (in the context of colonialism and imperialism). I propose that the queer pleasures imagined and produced through this practice might allow us to undermine the racial, classed, and heteronormative assimilationist model readily encountered in archived personal collections.

PHOTOGRAPHY AND THE STAGING OF ARAB AMERICAN HETERONORMATIVITY

The Faris and Yamna Naff Arab American Collection at the Smithsonian Institution's National Museum of American History was created by historian Alixa Naff over the course of her career. While it is known especially for extensive oral histories conducted with first- and second-generation Arab Americans from this older immigrant community, the collection also has more than two thousand photographs donated by Arab Americans from their personal family collections. Altogether, the Naff Collection contains abundant evidence of Syrians at work. The numerous accounts of laboring practices and photos of Syrians in front of their businesses, in factories, and on the road as peddlers make clear that this collection is an archive as much of labor as of the Arab American community's entrepreneurial contributions. These objects provide a framework of Syrians as proper laborers in ways that ready them for inclusion in the American nation.

When I first encountered these photographs as someone not yet familiar with studies of visual culture, I was particularly drawn to how they seem to stand as unmediated evidence of historical acts and how they recuperate the Arab family as a normative American unit. For instance, Syrian immigrants were pioneer peddlers with families depending upon them, using horses and carriages as well as packs on their backs and motorized vehicles. Syrian families owned and operated groceries, general stores, restaurants, and ice cream shops. Syrian families enjoyed time at the beach, drove cars, and had formal family portraits taken. One can interpret a thread of familial normativity that runs throughout these images, perhaps even more so because items in the collection are arranged by the families who donated those materials. Marianne Hirsch calls this the "familial gaze": the conventions and ideologies through which family members see themselves.[27]

Among these images, formal family portraits and images of Syrians at work predominate. Through their visual representation of heteronormative family structures and proper laboring practices, these photographs make a case for the respectability of the early Arab American community.[28] Sprinkled among this collection are other photographs—outdoor images, some posed and some candid—in which men or women are socializing together. These largely gender-segregated photographic spaces illuminate the homosocial bonds of Arab families and communities, and of Syrian peddlers in particular. Although they reflect the collection's focus on the United States (most of the photographs were taken of Arab Americans in the United States or abroad), the photographs span the reaches of the Levantine diaspora, including South America, Southwest Asia, North Africa, and other regions in North America. I focus my analysis on roughly eighty of these photographs and, in this chapter, give particular attention to a handful of them.

A photograph is a "certificate of presence" that invokes "an existential connection between 'the necessarily real thing which has been placed before the lens' and the photographic image."[29] Although heavily mediated by social processes of power, photographs function as the ultimate proof signifying "the real" or the authentic.[30] They are thus curated as essential items in the creation of archival collections. The idea that photographs are truth in representation continues to frame the way many of us think about photography. Walter Benjamin's proclamation that photography was "the first truly revolutionary means of reproduction" gestured toward the liberatory possibilities of this apparatus, one in which the knowledge produced from photographs could be democratic and multiple.[31] But this medium also seemed to harness the real and make it far more accessible than visual art forms had done previously, allowing that real image to pose as a representative image, even as mass production radically distanced the photo from its own contextual reality. Therein lies the contradictory nature of photography: photographic images, specifically portraits, can be both radically self-representative and essentializing, both honorific and repressive.[32] These paradoxes have been articulated as scholars have grappled with the expansive possibilities and varied meanings of photography—as an apparatus, as a visual archive, as text (what photographs mean), and as a pedagogical tool (what photographs do).

As an apparatus, the camera allowed a more rapid process of recording an image, as well as a closer resemblance to the actual figure or person in the image, than did mediums like painting or drawing. Because of the belief in the objectivity of Eurocentric science, the scientific processes used in photography lent support to the idea that photographs are unmediated representations of the real. Photographs thus function as visual documentation, always already existing as part of a terrain of biopolitical knowledge. Specifically, portraiture was used to establish the notion of a "knowable interiority" based on physical manifestations of the body—most frequently through immutable phenotypical traits of skin color, facial features, and head size, but also in material markers of class such as dress and decor.[33]

Photography was thus employed in creating a white, middle-class identity through the nineteenth century, while it was also implicated in eugenicist projects that pathologized nonwhiteness, poverty, criminality, and disability.[34] As mediated through these labored frameworks of representation, photographic archives are sites through which "narratives of national belonging and exclusion are produced."[35]

Photography first arrived in Southwest Asia and North Africa via colonial practices. European and American anthropologists, missionaries, and government officials produced photographs of the landscape and of the indigenous inhabitants which buttressed Orientalist ideas that Arabs were uncivilized and exotic. Photographs of Arabs either rendered them as part of the land's natural topography or highlighted their racial and cultural difference from Europeans and Euro-Americans. Harnessing the power of the camera's perceived documentarian capacity, these photographs also presented an image of Arabs as being anachronistic in comparison to Euro-American modernity.[36] Eurocentric photography of Arabs also depicts—as Sarah Graham-Brown writes of early Middle Eastern photography—"costume, particularly the costume of women," in a way that "became a form of visual identification for Westerners of races, 'types' and ethnic groups, and contributed to the imagery of the picturesque, the exotic, and the erotic."[37] European mythology cast the head covering of Middle Eastern and North African women (of all religions) and the space of the harem as modes of patriarchal control, in contrast to the supposed freedom of European women. European male sexual fantasy was central to this mythology because veiling and seclusion within the harem blocked male colonizers' access to Middle Eastern and North African women's bodies (but also provided an opportunity for women to gaze without being fully seen).[38] Still, Orientalist paintings tried to offer Westerners "a stolen glance," a peek inside the blocked view of the harem.[39]

Photography built on this Orientalist tradition, making nudity and various stages of undress a prominent feature in early Western photography of Middle Eastern women.[40] Americans, too, participated in this Eurocentric imaging of the Middle East and North Africa, and particularly of the regions' women inhabitants. For instance, the bodies, movements, and dress of Arab women dancers at the 1893 Chicago World's Fair became a focal point of white American fascination and revulsion. The photographic legacy of these dancers crystalized them as "mythological figures through which to trace contemporaneous US engagements with the disorienting processes of modernization and expansionism."[41]

Toward the end of the nineteenth century, cameras became accessible to the Arab upper class through the production and circulation of "press and shoot" Kodak cameras. These cameras were first available in the Ottoman Empire in 1888 and were mass-produced in simpler and cheaper form (such as Kodak's Brownie cameras) beginning in 1900.[42] These cameras greatly enabled family photography practices that did not rely on a formal studio or a professional photographer. Upper-class Arabs in particular used photography as a means to claim modernity, delineate national and class identities,[43] and establish a site for resisting the Orientalist framework that had been imposed on them. Photography was also configured as a medium "that would make visible the social aspirations of the family."[44] Thus the visual portrayal of proper family structures, class status, and a national Arab identity was central to these images.[45]

As the camera became more accessible and families were able to take photographs themselves rather than in a formal studio, other domestic intimacies could be visualized. The portraiture that documented family respectability continued to exist alongside these newer forms of domestic, amateur photography. Photography thus emerged as a site through which oppositional images could be produced. Because the advent of photography worked in tandem with European and American white supremacist and colonialist ideologies, photography has often been used to counteract those damaging reproductions. As access to photography spread across class lines, it further enabled the oppressed to have ownership of and to participate in making images of themselves.[46]

Within the Naff collection photographs, I paid attention to any images of peddlers and other Syrians engaging in laboring activities. These photographs include peddlers pictured with their peddling packs, a horse and buggy (see figure 3), or a motorized vehicle. Some peddling photographs show peddlers with their goods spread out in front of customers while the customers also pose for the camera. Other photographs show Syrians standing inside or in front of their brick-and-mortar stores: groceries, dry goods stores, dress shops, restaurants. Most photographs of peddlers show adult men, and the majority of the photos of Syrians at work show men working. This overrepresentation of laboring men connects to Eurocentric gendered and classed delineations of separate private and public spheres. Here, Syrian men appear in their apparently rightful place, working outside the home, so that their wives remain home and care for children.

Figure 4 exemplifies this vision of the proper labor of Syrian immigrants. It shows the interior of Joseph Grocery & Meats, an Arab-owned store in Drumright, Oklahoma. The picture is dated circa 1916–25. Pictured, from left to right, are Chic Fogaley, proprietor Henry Joseph, and George Elias. This photo is the image of the respectable Syrian American capitalist: the owner and operator of a business, one with a physical and permanent storefront. Such photographs, through their explicit framing and staging as well as their inclusion in a national ethnic archive, enact an affective equation with white, middle-class Americans; they "[naturalize] claims of sameness through an appearance of familiarity."[47] Nothing visual indicates a deviation from white American masculinity. Understood in this way, these photographs are building blocks of the Arab American inclusion narrative, which says that Arab Americans are, and have been, worthy of belonging in the (white) American national family.

Women and children also show up in photographs of family businesses, usually as they pose with their male relatives inside or in front of their stores (see figure 5).

FIGURE 3. Peddlers near Louisville, Kentucky, at the turn of the twentieth century. Faris and Yamna Naff Arab American Collection, Archives Center, National Museum of American History, Smithsonian Institution, Series 2, Box 67.

Only the rare photograph features child peddlers or women working in a factory setting, despite the statistical prominence of the latter.[48] Photos of women working threatened to contradict the respectability of the men-at-work photos. Yet such photos could also demonstrate the liberation of Syrian women within the context of their migration to the United States. Despite the numbers of Syrian women who peddled, they are rarely pictured in ways that connect them to that work (with peddling packs or displaying their wares, for instance.)

In studying these photography archives, I also noted the plethora of photographs of leisure. For instance, photographs from the 1910s through 1940s depict Syrian Americans showing off their cars: posing in front of, on the hoods of, or inside their vehicles (see figures 6 and 7). Figure 7 also provides another instance through which to index the active curation of Syrian American modernity in the Naff archive. This image, dated around 1919, shows a woman driving a car, with another woman next to her and three children in the back seat. The image bears a notation on the reverse: "Independent woman, drove her own car." Many of the Naff archive photographs have two sets of notations, one belonging presumably to those who donated the images and the second to Naff herself, who wrote notes and added details as people handed these images over to her. Based on a comparison of the handwriting to other photographs' notations, these words appear to be Naff's editorial voice. The image itself offers a glimpse of how Syrian immigrant life could be multiply interpreted. In this case, the Western dress

FIGURE 4. Interior of Joseph Grocery & Meats, Drumright, Oklahoma, circa 1916–25. Faris and Yamna Naff Arab American Collection, Archives Center, National Museum of American History, Smithsonian Institution, Series 2, Box 64.

FIGURE 5. Interior of dry goods store, Oklahoma, circa 1915–16. Faris and Yamna Naff Arab American Collection, Archives Center, National Museum of American History, Smithsonian Institution, Series 2, Box 64.

FIGURE 6. Girl and young woman posing with car, Detroit, 1942. Faris and Yamna Naff Arab American Collection, Archives Center, National Museum of American History, Smithsonian Institution, Series 2, Box 72.

FIGURE 7. "Independent woman, drove her own car," circa 1919. Faris and Yamna Naff Arab American Collection, Archives Center, National Museum of American History, Smithsonian Institution, Series 2, Box 64.

and hairstyles, as well as the use of the automobile, might signal that these Syrians were engaging with sartorial and technological registers of modernity. Yet, as discussed in chapters 2 and 3, the presence of Syrian women in public spaces, particularly without men, clashed with those same Eurocentric registers, which produced a gendered and classed distinction between public and private domains. Naff's notation functions as a palimpsest of these historical engagements with discourses of modernity.[49] Her recasting of the driver as an "independent woman" hints at the instrumentalization of women's lives in this history, as well as Naff's own feminist consciousness.

In addition to Syrians with automobiles, some photos marked special occasions and holidays when young Syrian women wore furs and pin-curled their hair, and Syrian men dressed in their finest suits. Other photos of gatherings showed events such as lamb slaughter in preparation for large community meals and family picnics. A number of photographs marked moments of rest and pleasure during peddling trips, moments in which peddlers toured landmarks of the area they were visiting or dipped weary feet into a stream or a lake. Although informal family gatherings and lamb slaughters do not automatically fall into this categorization, displays of leisure time are often demonstrations of class status and upward class mobility. The photos of cars and of Syrians posing in fine outfits are evidence of a claim to a normative class identity (that is, a middle-class identity).

Closely related to the leisure-time photographs as a marker of class, the numerous formal studio portraits in the collection registered a family's or individual's class status or class aspirations. The studio portrait visually describes its subject and inscribes within it a social identity; "it is also a commodity, a luxury, an adornment, ownership of which confers status."[50] These photographs include young children in matching outfits, men in suits and top hats or *tarabish*,[51] and women in fine dresses and hats. For example, figure 8 shows a Syrian family whose members were maternal relatives of the person who donated the photograph. The photo is undated, but the family's dress and hairstyles date it to the early 1930s. The nuclear family emerges in this image, with the father and mother seated at the same level and the two children nestled protectively between them. The backdrop indicates it is a studio portrait, a particular marker of middle-class status or middle-class aspiration. The family's clothing also points to financial well-being; note the children's matching outfits and their shoes. This photo is typical of posed family portraits included in the Naff Collection. They represent the Arab American family as a productive unit, a corporation,[52] and portray its members as productive individuals, worthy of belonging in the national US family. The configuration of these families, and the identities of the people included in the photos, affords rich sites of meaning related to competing spheres of kinship, nationalism, and modernity.

In the Arab context, particularly toward the end of the nineteenth and the beginning of the twentieth century, the bourgeois family was the symbol of this modernity in portraiture. The bourgeois family portrayed the father as the "productive head" of the family and the mother as the "reproductive base."[53] Many photographs showed the fathers standing while mothers and children were seated or at least positioned at a lower sight level than the father. A man's wearing of a tarboosh signified that he was educated and part of the Arab elite, while Western clothing aligned the upper-class Arab family with modernity. The bourgeois family portrait included only one set of parents and children—that is, just two generations—thus severing the full extent of Arab familial intimacies from the frame. The bourgeois family thus excluded grandparents, aunts and uncles, and cousins— "those who [were] peripheral to the modern vision of self and family."[54] These portraits of the bourgeois family, however, did not simply replace representations of the "extended" family (the term "extended" is itself a construction that signals a marginalization of certain forms of kinship). For instance, figure 8 features one set of parents and their children. The photo showed the donor's relatives in the extended family, and not the donor of the picture themselves. Presumably, when asked to offer things that were important to the history of their family and migration, this donor included a studio portrait of extended family members. The inclusion of this photograph signals the tension in this transition from conceptualizing the family in more expansive and indigenous terms to depicting the family using the Eurocentric bourgeois model. The family was another axis upon which racialized conceptions of modernity turned.

FIGURE 8. Studio portrait of parents and children, circa 1930–34. Faris and Yamna Naff Arab American Collection, Archives Center, National Museum of American History, Smithsonian Institution, Series 2, Box 72.

FIGURE 9. Studio portrait of large family, circa 1920–24. Faris and Yamna Naff Arab American Collection, Archives Center, National Museum of American History, Smithsonian Institution, Series 2, Box 68.

FIGURE 10. Family gathering at unknown beach location, circa 1935–39. Author's personal collection.

FIGURE 11. Group photo after a large family dinner at Christmastime, Louisville, Kentucky, circa 1960–66. Author's personal collection.

In the Naff Collection, the later the photographs go into the twentieth century, the less visible the bourgeois family structure becomes, with the father standing as the head and the mother and children as the base. Later family portraits might be more identified as modeling the nuclear family, showing the mother and father as one unit and the children as the fruitful products of their labor. Julia Hirsch writes that this kind of family photograph, whether formal or amateur, represents the family in three ways: "as a state whose ties are rooted in property; . . . as a spiritual assembly which is based on moral values; and . . . as a bond of feeling which stems from instinct and passion."[55] Most often, Hirsch says, the father symbolizes the family as state and spiritual assembly, and the mother is the emotional bond.[56] Many of the family photographs in the Naff archives, especially family portraits, fall into these representations of the bourgeois or nuclear family model, in which the family is bounded, unified, and properly reproductive.

Still, a few formal family portraits exceed the bounds of the bourgeois or nuclear family, such as figure 9. These images often show three generations and adult siblings, along with a married couple and their children, or they show multiple related married couples and their children. Still staged in a formal portrait studio, they are markers of class status, but they gesture toward an Arab, Syrian, or other indigenous frame for modernity. Figures 10 and 11, which are not part of the Naff

Collection, are historical images of Arab America and provide a useful counterpoint to these family portraits. Figure 10, undated but probably from the 1930s, shows a group of twenty-five adults and children gathered on a rocky beach and posing for a group photo. Figure 11, from circa 1960–66, shows a Christmastime gathering of more than forty people, adults and children, posed around a train of dinner tables inside someone's home. Both are photos of Arab American families—my own ancestors and relatives, to be precise.

Images like these, showing an entire or extended Arab family grouped informally or even in formal studio portraits, serve as fissures in the narrative of Arab familial normalcy (Arab modernity) and gesture toward the expansive affective ties of the Arab family. I am reminded of two competing anecdotes about Arab American life from this history. One, from a government report on immigration in 1901, says, "Unlike the padrone system, the Syrian immigrants bring with them the primitive clan organization of the family, so that it is not strange that a score, or even a hundred, may claim relationship."[57] Government officials were particularly concerned about contract labor systems among immigrants, often referred to as "padrone" systems because of their strong association with Italian immigrants, but these comments also echo concerns about the "coolie" labor system among Chinese and some other Asian immigrants. This language indicates an anxiety about the large kinship networks that animated Syrian life, their incommensurability with Eurocentric norms of family relationships, and their assumed threat to white, US-born labor. The second anecdote, from the interview with Francis Slay, opens this chapter; Slay discussed the importance of maintaining bonds of love and affection within a family, what he called "the teaching to love another." He remarked about the frequency with which his family gathered: "We have all of our family over to the house; I have my brothers and sisters over all the time, not once a year, but summer, spring, fall, all the time together; I just had 65 [family members] over [at] my house."[58]

In these anecdotes and photographs, we find an insistence that the bonds of cousins and grandparents and aunts and uncles are just as significant as those of parents and children. Indeed, the Arabic language has many terms that can be used to describe a family, suggesting the importance of family as an organizing unit of Arab societies and the different units and scales of family relations.[59] These archival artifacts challenge the rise of the nuclear family model. They also form pictorial evidence of an Arab "intimate selving" that prioritizes connectivity through networks of biological kin over the "bounded, autonomous, and separate self" that has been universalized in Eurocentric models of human development.[60]

American photography has also been linked to the disciplining of immigrant populations. A small handful of photos in the Naff collection connect to that disciplinary practice. Photography was central to the development and implementation of US immigration policy, particularly regarding Chinese and Asian exclusion. Chinese women migrants were the first to be issued photographic identification cards at the border, followed by almost all Chinese and Chinese-descended people, those crossing the US-Mexico border, and all other immigrants in the early twentieth century.[61] Family photographs also became evidence of Asian immigrants' whiteness and Americanness when the state sought to strip them of their naturalized citizenship. These photographs included shots of the inside of defendants' homes to show that "we live just like American people."[62] As a result of these and other measures of anti-Asian state violence, Asian Americans have a long history of using photography to produce evidence of their own civility, a requirement of US citizenship.[63] The Naff Collection contains a small selection of photos that represent the state or of the state's gaze. These were passport and naturalization photographs, portraits of enlisted Arab Americans in military uniform, and photos that Arab American service members took while on tour.

A QUEER ARAB AMERICAN IMAGINING

To account for pleasure and power in these photographs, I track my own pleasure in looking at them, and I imagine the possible pleasures of the individuals captured within their frames. Following scholarship on photography and affect, I center the idea that affective response to (not just pleasure in) visuality carries important meaning and builds on the foundations of materialist visual culture scholarship, without reproducing a binary of "thinking" versus "feeling."[64] Here, I also think of Gayatri Gopinath's work, which shows how "the visual serves as a portal to other senses and affects."[65] My tracking of pleasure also follows Roland Barthes's assertion that "the image launches desire beyond what it permits us to see."[66] Barthes refers here specifically to the "punctum" of a photograph, a fundamentally affective response that one adds to an image. Whereas the "studium" of a photograph is "that very wide field of unconcerned desire" that registers, for instance, whether one likes or dislikes an image, the punctum spurs the spectator of a photograph to imbue that image with something more. For Barthes, the punctum is "what I add to the photograph and *what is nonetheless already there*."[67] Finally, in thinking of the physicality of photographs, as well as our embodied senses of photographs when they are in our possession, I am indebted to Tina Campt's theorization of "haptic images." Rather than referring singularly to the tactile, Campt says that haptic images accrue three senses of touch: "an indexical touch, a physical touch, and an affective touch."[68]

Using these photographs, I conceptualize the queer ecology of peddling through an attention to pleasure for the people pictured in them and for me as a queer Arab American spectator. I consider the tropes surrounding US immigration stories, Arab cultures, and the people who provided the material forces for those tropes, and I imagine other possibilities of what the archival traces they left behind might mean.

The photographs in the following discussion were donated to the Naff Collection by two of the subjects within them: Nazha and Budelia, whose recollections of homosocial gatherings are discussed at the beginning of this chapter. Nazha and Budelia (also known as Bud) were cousins and are shown together in two of the photos. Also pictured are Daher (Nazha's husband), two men named George and Khalil, Bud's mother, and several other, unnamed people. Nazha and Bud were both interlocutors of Alixa Naff and were also interviewed for her research. Given the known relationships among some of the people in these photographs, I proceed with Emma Pérez's caution to "confront and rearrange" the privileging of certain relationships (and our assumptions about those relationships) and to imagine other possibilities stemming from the intimacies created in and by these images.[69]

The first photograph, figure 12, was dated to the early 1920s and shows Daher and another man, named Khalil. A notation on the back of the photo tells us that the two men are "friends and fellow peddlers of oriental rugs and imported laces and linens singing in Ottawa [Illinois]." The caption offers a "redirected look" that opens further possibilities for meaning here.[70] That they are "friends" tells us that their bond is intentional, willing, and nonfamilial. The indication that they are "fellow peddlers" may mean that they peddled together, perhaps procuring items from the same supplier, dividing up routes, and providing mutual protection and companionship on the road. The two men sit together, gesturing and, it appears to me, laughing, but the notation indicates that they are singing. I wonder which song this might have been. An American tune? An Arabic folk song? The latter is unlikely given the sheet music they hold in their hands. A wedding ring is visible on each man's left hand; and in the far-right edge of the frame lie two hats, ostensibly belonging to the subjects of the photograph. Because they are not wearing their suit jackets, the scene feels casual. It is possible that this photograph was taken during a peddling trip. In the focal point of the image, the men's postures are animated, and their gazes are fixed on the booklet that one of the men holds, rather than being directed at the camera. This suggests that this is a candid shot. However, the synchronicity of their poses—the right arm of each man bent at the same angle, their index fingers pointed simultaneously in exclamation—could indicate that the photograph is staged or could simply point to rhythmic movements that accompanied their singing.

But the bottom half of the photograph may tell a different story. Daher's leg is draped over Khalil's, as if he is approaching sitting on the lap of his friend. And somewhat obscured at the top of the photo, we can make out the image of this same man's arm wrapped around the body of his friend, and his hand is curled into his friend's hair. Curling, not curled—it feels active, as if it is happening now. In executing this embrace, Daher is in the midst of a grin, his eyes nearing shut, while Khalil's mouth is open, carrying the song. Their closeness resembles what Glen Mimura has called "frontier homosociality," the ease and casual intimacy born by the sharing of domestic and leisure responsibilities in the absence of women.[71]

The second photograph (figure 13) pictures Daher on the right and another man, named George. The picture is undated, but notes indicate that it was taken in Canton, Ohio, where Daher and Nazha lived at the time. Based on the time frame indicated for these photos, the earliest it could have been taken is the early 1920s. What I notice first about this photograph is the way that their figures dominate and

FIGURE 12. "Friends and fellow peddlers" Daher and Khalil singing together, 1920s. Faris and Yamna Naff Arab American Collection, Archives Center, National Museum of American History, Smithsonian Institution, Series 2, Box 72.

FIGURE 13. Peddlers George and Daher on steps in front of house, 1920s. Faris and Yamna Naff Arab American Collection, Archives Center, National Museum of American History, Smithsonian Institution, Series 2, Box 72.

fill the frame. The two men are outdoors, in front of a house, and their positions indicate a candid nature—the uneven height of the two men as they are placed in the frame, the movement of the Daher's arm upward or downward, the grasp of George's arm around the neck of his fellow peddler. Candid, but not casual, the two are dressed in three-piece suits. Whereas the previous photograph suggests animation and movement, the figures in this image are largely still, perhaps also suggesting hesitation and awkwardness. The rigidity of the two figures might be also reinforced by the suggestion of the house behind them and by the ways in which domestic space was often a space of regulation with regard to sexuality.[72] Daher's gaze is directed toward the photographer, and George's gaze is slightly below the lens of the camera. The look of both is one of interruption. But what strikes me about this photograph is the intimacy it also relays. There is a faint, blurred, almost imperceptible boundary in between the two. The close proximity of their bodies—they are literally pressed against each other—suggests an unclear delineation between where one man's body ends and the other begins. While the tone of the previous photograph is jovial and flirtatious, the enmeshed bodies and intense stares of the second photograph suggest a more serious tone.

Daher is also pictured in the third photo (figure 14), a blurry image of him with five other unnamed men. Taken in 1920 in Petoskey, Michigan, the picture shows the five men standing behind Daher in a line staggered by their differing heights. The second man from the left sinks even lower; he is embracing Daher, who awkwardly squats and reaches his arms backward to join in the embrace. Daher's eyes are closed or cast downward. The unnamed men are dressed in suit jackets and ties, save for Daher, who wears dark pants and a button-down shirt. Among the others, some wear hats, and all but one have soft smiles on their faces. The notation on the back of the photo describes this scene: "drunk & happy, Daher horsing around with brother and fellow immigrant peddlers." These photographs and Nazha's interviews provide evidence that Petoskey—a coastal resort town off Lake Michigan—was on Daher's peddling route. Potentially, the first and the last photographs discussed here were taken during the course of peddling trips, blurring the distinction between work and leisure.[73]

As I look at these photographs, the possibilities of what life as a peddler may have enabled loom large. The impetus of movement, of circulation, prompted a reorienting of relationships for those Syrians who had not previously led nomadic lives. I imagine what it might feel like, in my own body, to be in such proximity to someone else, a friend, a family member, a lover, who also shared this migratory experience—an experience of migration different from the transatlantic one that had already taken place. I imagine the feel of a loved one's hair curled in my fingers, the pulse and vibrations quickened from singing in unison, the warmth generated from the movement of two bodies, from the length of our bodies joined together. I imagine feeling grateful for my companion, for someone to be at ease with after a week of walking, of making the pitch over and over again, of separation from those of whom I make part.

FIGURE 14. Daher with five other men peddlers, Petoskey, Michigan, 1920. Faris and Yamna Naff Arab American Collection, Archives Center, National Museum of American History, Smithsonian Institution, Series 2, Box 72.

Once this past week, I feared for my life when the husband of a customer took offense at something I did—I'm not sure what—and got his shotgun. This was not the first time, but it does not get easier with repetition. You were too far away to intervene, but you heard the commotion. Although my cheeks were burning from embarrassment and anger at these people who are so quick to assume the worst about us, I was able to ignore those feelings and feign humble apology in order to defuse the situation. For hours after, I thought I would break down, but your hand on my back steadied me as we walked, reminded me that I was not alone in this life. I cannot tell my wife; she has too much to worry about while I'm gone, but at least there is someone who understands me without having to speak about it. For you, I am grateful.

Finally out of danger and off duty, here, we take off our jackets, worn so that customers see that we are respectable, so that wives and daughters do not fear our strangeness. Here we take off our hats, finally feeling the full warmth of the sun before it sets. Soon, ties will be loosened, sleeves rolled up, and perhaps belts unbuckled, after the abundance of dinner. Soon we will tend to our families, but for now the time is just ours, for joy and rest with someone who knows what my everyday is like.

The next two photos (figures 15 and 16) were also taken in Canton, Ohio, and depict Nazha and Bud. The relationship between these two is known in one sense: they are cousins. This fact neither substantiates nor invalidates any claim of erotics or intimacy between them. First, although we know the familial relation between them, we do not know the substance of that relationship. Second, intimate and sexual connections between cousins were common, particularly through the endogamous marriage system that was prevalent in Syrian communities.[74]

Taken outdoors like the first two photographs discussed here, both photos are clearly staged. In the figure 15 photo, donated by Nazha, the two women are pictured standing in front of a house. There is a great distance between the photographer and the women. At first glance, the women are diminutive, overshadowed by the house behind them and sent to the background by the expanse of lawn in front of them. But their poses are aggressive in the frame, as if they have made themselves take up more space to compensate for their smallness in the photograph itself. Julianne Hirsh has offered that "the simplest way of suggesting spatial mastery outdoors is to show a housefront or a stoop, symbolic pieces of territory."[75] Bud juts her leg out from behind the bushes, extending it long and angled out from her body; and Nazha is placing her arm upward against the trellis, above her cousin. They gaze directly at the camera, but in ways that subtly mitigate that directness. Nazha has turned her face toward the side, while still keeping her eyes toward the camera's lens. Bud faces the camera completely but angles her head downward, in a move that feigns a kind of coyness—an attitude her eyes betray. The punctum here shifts constantly. It is Bud standing behind—no in—the bushes. And, or maybe instead, it is Nazha's hand poised above Bud's head. It is the odd, long distance between the photographer and the photographed. The women are partially hidden by the foliage around them, as if to keep something from the camera's eye, as if to suggest that there is something for themselves, between them-

FIGURE 15. Cousins Budelia and Nazha, Canton, Ohio, 1920s. Faris and Yamna Naff Arab American Collection, Archives Center, National Museum of American History, Smithsonian Institution, Series 2, Box 72.

FIGURE 16. Budelia and Nazha in front of store, 1923 or 1924. Faris and Yamna Naff Arab American Collection, Archives Center, National Museum of American History, Smithsonian Institution, Series 2, Box 74.

selves, that they have deemed beyond the view of this photographic gaze. The distance between them and the photographer also achieves this. Their stances and gazes—particularly those of Bud, on the left—are assertive. The tilts of their heads acknowledge the norms of decorum that they are supposed to uphold as women; the position behind the bushes defiantly blocks the complete access of the photographic (and audience's) gaze. This interruption of the gaze both invites curiosity and speculation—my curiosity and speculation—and refuses any full knowing. The photograph forces me, as a desiring consumer of the photographic image and as an Arab American scholar of Arab American history, to grapple with the unknown and the unknowable.

In the figure 16 photo, Bud and Nazha appear with a storefront in the background. They have some space between them, and they are connected by a loose interlacing of their fingers. Bud, on the left, is dressed in dark colors with long sleeves and a wide lace collar. Her face is solemn, but she is perhaps beginning to smile or being photographed mid-sentence. In contrast, Nazha is in a light-colored dress with short sleeves and a broad smile. Not all of the writing on the back of the photo is legible, but it indicates that the photograph was taken in 1923 or 1924 on Bud's "first trip" to Canton, presumably to visit her cousin.

The first photo was donated by Nazha; the second, by Bud. They wear the same dresses and hairstyles in both photos, offering the possibility that these images were taken during the same visit. One kept one photo, and the other kept the other. The physicality of these images as objects is striking; both photographs show the marks of attachment. The edges of both photos are worn with creases, and one has been torn. When I contrast them with the images of Daher and other male peddlers, I am struck by the evidence of how much these two images of Nazha and Bud have been touched, kept in pockets or wallets, and stored within reach to gaze at or to show others. The reciprocity of attachment to each woman's photograph here provides some hint of the bonds between the two, this touching evidence perhaps suggesting longing, fondness, or regret.

Budelia was born in 1903 in Rachaya Al-Wadi—a town in the southern Beqaa Valley of present-day Lebanon—and came to the United States with her parents when she was one year old. She lived in Spring Valley, Illinois, which was then a hub for Syrian peddlers. Bud's mother, pictured in the next photo (figure 17) and discussed at the beginning of this chapter, was a peddler and was related to Naff. After her mother was widowed, Bud was raised in a home with her mother and two maternal uncles, who were also single. Most of the images that Bud donated show her and other women and girls. Aside from her uncles' presence, Bud's life may have been surrounded by women, like those standing with her mother in the photo. In her interview with Naff, she noted that because she was an unmarried girl and woman, a lot was forbidden to her. Her uncles were very attentive to her activities and to those with whom she associated. This life of women—if indeed her photographic legacy is representative of such—may also have been a

FIGURE 17. Budelia's mother and five other women peddlers, World War I era. Faris and Yamna Naff Arab American Collection, Archives Center, National Museum of American History, Smithsonian Institution, Series 2, Box 74.

protective one. Equally so, it may have been a pleasurable one, as Bud's recollection of women eating and crocheting together may indicate. This life with women was both homosocial and homoerotic. It is echoed in the photo in figure 17, in which Bud's mother is grouped in an embrace with a number of other women; and it echoes in Bud's memories of kitchen spaces of work, joy, and sensuous connection among women.

Nazha's own life as a peddler took her throughout the Midwest. She donated to the archive many images of her and Daher taken on their peddling trips. But unlike Nazha, Bud was not a peddler. She completed a grade-school education and then went on to work in a garter factory and in department store sales. Bud seemed a private person and did not want to disclose much about her personal life to Naff. Naff's notes say that Bud told her, mid-interview, that "she didn't want too much of her personal life in this," whereupon Naff reassured her that she should only tell what she was comfortable revealing.

Bud had another means of evading the direct probing of the historian-cum-ethnographer: she would not sit for an interview on her own but rather acted as intermediary for Naff with other women. She mediated Naff's access to at least three other women interlocutors. On one hand, this information from the historical record makes me concerned about the ethics of centering my analysis on someone who valued so intensely her privacy (even just looking at photographs of her, even by way of an imagining). On the other hand, this detail returns me to the first photograph of Bud and Nazha (figure 15). Together they form an image of inherent privacy, a blocking of view, perhaps mirroring the ways that Bud controlled access to information about her own life. Making meaning out of this mediated access cannot be an endeavor of certainty. I am reminded of Stephanie Rogerson's remarks upon looking at a picture of her great-aunt's lover: "My sense is that I both know her and that she is unknowable to me."[76] Martha Vicinus's ruminations on lesbian history also present the possibility that "perhaps this was not a failure to know, but a refusal to know."[77]

Because these histories, this imaginary, and this research are not separate from me as the author, I am also compelled to analyze my relationship to this archive and these photographs. What am I asking these photographs to do, and what does it mean for the subjects that they have been immortalized in this visual form? I acknowledge that, as I looked through these photographs, I wanted to find evidence of queer desires and intimacies in the early Arab American community, particularly ones that would be legible as such today. Despite this desire, I cannot name any individuals in the photographs I discuss as queer subjects, and I have proceeded with caution regarding the information about these individuals in the historical record. I long hesitated about researching their actual lives and identities beyond these images, because doing so would shift the focus back to the impetus to name, categorize, and identify in ways tightly linked to state power. In some cases, the historical record would frame these individuals as explicitly heterosexual. Regardless, the disciplinary regime of heteronormative white supremacy (and its imbrications with discourses of modernity) affected, and continue to affect, entire Arab American communities irrespective of actual sexual identity, desire, or behavior.

Patricia Holland writes that "snapshots contribute to the present-day historical consciousness in which our awareness of ourselves is embedded."[78] As pictures that were part of a family collection, the photographs I discuss in this chapter are part of the historical memory of that particular family. Yet as images that were also included in the Naff Collection—photographs taken from the family album and placed in a national ethnic archive—the images have become part of the historical memory of the Arab American community. As a result, they are implicated in a larger narrative of assimilation and belonging; they have been put to use for perhaps different purposes than those of the family. But the relationship between the individual and the family, and between the individual and the community, does not dissipate with the transfer of images from the family album to the ethnic archive. By asking after my own relationship to these photographs and to this analysis, my intention here is to center the way that family photographs "can operate at this junction between personal memory and social history, between public myth and personal unconscious."[79]

I read these photographs of Syrians who participated in the peddling economy to imagine the intimate bonds that were created through the migratory experiences of peddling, as well as the relationship of other family and community members to the queer ecology of peddling. Specifically, I see each image as providing an archival trace of the homosociality and homoeroticism of Syrian migrant peddling communities. A danger lies in this analysis and this imagining. The danger lies not necessarily in its homoerotic subversiveness but rather in the central problematic of the photograph itself: the naturalized relationship between the photograph and the real thing or person it displays. This relationship persists stubbornly in the face of the many attempts to sever it. Considering what I desire to do with these photographs and what I try to do even against that desire, my direct reference to them, and to the archive in which they reside, will always call us back to wondering about the real: the "real" identities of the subjects within, the "real" relationships between them, the "real" desires, dreams, and fears that their lives contained. Despite this nagging desire for definitive answers to questions of who, what, when, where, and how, we must also come to terms with the finite and ultimate limits of the historical record. State and family documents will never contain all of the answers we seek as inheritors of these legacies. As gender-segregated images of Arabs, these images can also be read in a way that reinforces the Orientalist stereotypes of heterosexism and patriarchal norms in Arab cultures. Yet doing so forecloses the reality—not just the possibility—that these were spaces wherein homosociality and homoeroticism were constitutive of Arab American identities in the late nineteenth and early twentieth centuries. There is pleasure in my relationship to these photographs—in the knowledge that they cannot be fully consumed by heteronormativity, and even that their apparent normativity enables my pleasure. This pleasure lies in imagining the homoerotics and homosociality among the photographs' subjects, as well as in knowing that those intimacies can never be fully eradicated from the historical record.

Conclusion

Alixa Naff and the Parenthetical Syrian American Lesbian

The research and legacy of Alixa Naff is threaded throughout this book, providing invaluable source material, as well as bearing the brunt of some of my critique of Arab American scholars who recuperated the peddler as a respectable figure. Eulogized as the "mother" and "grande dame" of Arab American studies, Naff had an incalculable impact on the field.[1] Her archival collection remains a centerpiece of early Arab American primary source materials. This collection, which Naff donated to the Smithsonian in 1984, contains 500 artifacts, 450 oral history interviews, and more than 2,000 photographs, as well as the personal papers of individuals and organizations, magazine and newsletter clippings, and a wealth of other manuscripts and publications on Arab Americans. Naff procured the bulk of its contents in the course of conducting oral history interviews with first- and second-generation Syrian Americans from this early history.

These oral histories are most prominently featured in Naff's book, *Becoming American: The Early Arab Immigrant Experience*, which also provides the most comprehensive social history of the Syrian American peddling experience. *Becoming American* is at once Naff's scholarly intervention and a community narrative. The tensions between these narrative pulls are evident throughout her book, as well as in the primary source materials that inform it. Some of those tensions—particularly between presenting a respectable story of the Arab immigrant as modern and probing the more complex, disconcerting, and even violent dimensions of existing as an Arab in the United States—I have explored here in *Possible Histories*. The queer ecology of Syrian American peddling is one site through which those tensions are abundantly visible.

Throughout the journey to produce this book, I "found" an Arab American queer subject in only one instance. More concrete than a rumor, archivally speaking, the evidence, as provided by Naff and examined here by me, nonetheless feels like a whisper.

By the summer of 1962, Naff had a bachelor's degree from the University of California, Los Angeles, and took off to travel the United States and Canada in her blue Volkswagen Beetle.[2] She was "armed with a history degree . . . , a tape recorder, and a grant from the university's Folklore Department."[3] During that summer, Naff interviewed eighty-seven first- and second-generation Syrian Americans and Syrian Canadians in sixteen communities about their life histories. Almost two decades later, after she completed a PhD in history, a National Endowment for the Humanities grant allowed Naff to expand this endeavor into a major project, which formed the basis for her book.

In one of these 1962 interviews, Naff sat down with her half sister, Wedad Frenn, who had come to the United States from Rachaya Al-Wadi in 1921, when she was six years old. Wedad's father was a peddler, and Wedad and her mother learned to embroider pillowcases and make dust caps for him to sell. Around 1930, the family moved to Fort Wayne, Indiana, and opened a grocery store. Fort Wayne was a peddling hub where her father had many friends who were, like him, also from Rachaya. Thus, although most of the family was unhappy in Fort Wayne, Wedad's father enjoyed this place with its familiar faces. Naff's interview notes from this session contain (to my knowledge) the single instance of an Arab American lesbian from this history. Naff wrote that Wedad's father—who was also Naff's father—often gathered in the store with his old peddling friends and retold old stories—and she says that "especially one woman (a Lesbian) kept the group together—like a leader—she was very respected."[4] Given that the anxieties regarding peddler sexuality, and queerness specifically, were most visible in discussions of Syrian peddling men, the mention of a lesbian who was hanging out with her old, male peddling buddies—and was their "leader" to boot—is striking.

Because these were Naff's notes and not transcripts, I cross-referenced them with audio from Naff's interview with her half sister. Both the interview notes and the interview were in English. I wanted to see if the recording gave any indication of how Naff gleaned this parenthetical knowledge. In the recording, Naff and Wedad indeed discussed how Wedad's father liked to gather with this group of people. Wedad said that there was "one particular woman that used to really keep them going. She [clears throat] was everybody's friend. She was in their clique. [Naff speaking; audio unclear] Hmm? Of course, Dad enjoyed the association there, but not the rest of us."[5] From there, the interview continued with no further mention of this woman or any clue as to how Naff might have determined that she was a lesbian.

Both promise and excitement lie in this bit of archival material, as do confusion and doubt. Was this information gossip, or was it something that the person in question embraced and shared with others? Given the half-sibling relationship between Naff and Wedad, and given Naff's intimate knowledge of Syrian American communities, it is plausible that Naff had other knowledge of this woman, beyond what was shared in this interview. Naff was raised in the same family as Wedad; and Faris Naff, Wedad's father, who spent time with this person, was also Naff's father. Alixa Naff had lived in Fort Wayne for a few months during this time, so she may have known this woman directly. Perhaps in the indecipherable moment where Naff speaks, she is confirming the identity of the woman in question. I am also intrigued by the capitalization of "Lesbian" here and—given her propensity to use both Arabic and English in her notes—by Naff's use of the English word rather than attempting any equivalent in Arabic. In this pre-Stonewall moment in 1962 in the United States, was Naff signaling (or revealing) here her knowledge of the burgeoning gay liberation and lesbian feminist movements? Was Naff naming "Lesbian" as an identity in its own right and purposely avoiding Arabic or English terms that were derogatory? Without further evidentiary recourse, we are, of course, left only to imagine these things.

Throughout *Possible Histories*, I show how gossip, as a form of community self-policing, disciplined Syrian immigrants and their descendants to uphold norms of white heteropatriarchy as evidence of their modernity. In contrast to this power of gossip and to the rumor about my great-grandfather with which I open this book, Naff's parenthetical Lesbian can serve as a refutation and resignification of community self-policing. As a woman who remained unmarried all her life, pursuing a social and professional path that contrasted with those of many of her peers, Naff herself surely experienced the disciplinary mechanisms of *kalam al-nas* (what will the people say?). Even though this anecdote is minimized within the archival collection, Naff offers here the promise of a place for queer Arab Americans and others whose desires and intimate lives did not accord with the disciplinary mechanisms of white heteronormativity. This place lives on within the community record, rather than through the internalized shame of rumor.

A queer affective method of historical-grounded imagining is vital to the work that we need to do for historical knowledge production. This imaginative practice pushes the limitations of how historical records have been produced and curated and how historical evidence has been defined. It helps us recognize those limitations, because imagining beyond these boundaries enables us to see what the historical records do not tell us. To imagine critically and historically, however, does not fully redress these archival limitations. I hope I have shown through this book that such knowledge is fundamentally partial and incomplete. But, even so, in this case, it is no longer formed through heteronormativity and its imbrication with white supremacy and Eurocentric discourses of modernity. Rather than attempting to complete that knowledge or be satisfied with filling in the gaps, we must think expansively; we must go beyond traditional disciplinary boundaries and the separations between the imaginative and the scholarly. Such thinking depends on shrinking the facile boundaries between truth and fiction, particularly through the identification and uses of narrative in historical knowledge production.

I also hope to have shown that this queer affective method of historical-grounded imagining is both situated and embodied. To imagine beyond the evidence of archives forces an acknowledgment of a relationship between the researcher and the historical past and its actors. To be sure, this relationship is always present, but historical-grounded imagining brings it to the surface. When I engage in historicist scholarship, I bring my own desires and body into the research project, and that has to be negotiated. For scholars who understand themselves as disconnected personally from their research or from the communities they study, that negotiation is often suppressed—but it is present nonetheless, even as those scholars present themselves and their research as objective. A situated and embodied imagining is produced through one's own presence in the world. How else do we conceive of these possibilities but through our own imagination, grounded in our mediated experiences of the world and our limited knowledge of the past?

Dina Georgis identifies the story as a method of social inquiry in which "we narrate the past, seek and transmit knowledge, and imagine our future."[6] I argue that, whereas Georgis focuses on works of fiction, these elements are always present in scholarly narratives of history as well. Georgis is interested in "the invisible matter of history" that is "unspeakable, hard to name, and queer because [it is] dangerous and disruptive."[7] We can see efforts to articulate the "unspeakable matter" of these early Syrian American imbrications with white supremacy and the discourses of modernity through several recent works of fiction, including Ismail Khalidi's unpublished play "Dead Are My People," Cheryl Reid's novel *As Good as True* (2018), and Zeyn Joukhader's novel *The Thirty Names of Night* (2020). Joukhader's novel is especially significant for its explorations of the many ways migration and the queer ecology of peddling opened new possibilities for queer sexual encounters and living beyond the gender binary. These works of fiction remind me of Georgis's provocation that "in fiction, history is granted the space to mourn."[8] Rather than taking this remark as a call to abandon the work of history for fiction, I draw on this provocation as a way to push at the boundaries of historical knowledge making. *Possible Histories* meditates broadly on the queer possibilities of Arab American history. It serves as an incomplete and partial invitation to ask what further possibilities of our history exist.

INTRODUCTION

1. Shadid, *Crusading Doctor*.

2. "The Peddler of Rugs," *Vici (OK) Beacon*, July 4, 1940.

3. Shadid, *Doctors of Today and Tomorrow*. This is especially remarkable considering that there were seven candidates in the first election and ten in the second.

4. Bald, *Bengali Harlem*; Hoganson, *Consumers' Imperium*.

5. Stockton, "Ethnic Archetypes and the Arab Image," 135.

6. Somerville, *Queering the Color Line*; Somerville, "Queer," 199.

7. Section 2169 of the *Revised Statutes* (1878) stipulated that any immigrant seeking naturalization must be considered either a "free white person" or a person "of African nativity or African descent." Only one petitioner claimed naturalization rights through African heritage. See *In re Cruz*, 23 F. Supp. 774 (1938). The case that ultimately determined naturalization rights for Syrians was *Dow v. United States*, 226 Fed. 147 (1915).

8. See Haney López, *White by Law*; Gualtieri, *Between Arab and White*; Jacobsen, *Whiteness of a Different Color*; Maghbouleh, *The Limits of Whiteness*.

9. Armenians were also granted naturalization rights. While there were no Iranian petitioners in this period, Iranians appeared in court arguments as a hinge on which others' arguments for whiteness turned. See Craver, "On the Boundary of White"; and Maghbouleh, *The Limits of Whiteness*, 17–24.

10. Furumoto and Goldberg, "Boundaries of the Racial State," 85.

11. Gualtieri, *Between Arab and White*, 130.

12. Halaby, "Dr. Michael Shadid and the Debate over Identity in 'The Syrian World.'"

13. Unless otherwise stated, I use "American" throughout this book to refer to hegemonic articulations of who was suited for US citizenship and belonging, most notably through the interrelated logics of whiteness, upward class mobility, and cisgender heteronormativity.

This usage is not to erase the multiple claims to Americanness throughout this history, including those of Syrian migrants, but to underscore that the category of "American" itself was mobilized by marshaling structures of power and oppression that were foundational to the US state.

14. Birla, *Stages of Capital*, 2.

15. Jarmakani, *Imagining Arab Womanhood*, 64.

16. Gualtieri, *Between Arab and White*.

17. Important examples of feminist analyses and scholarship on women in Arab American history include Gualtieri, *Between Arab and White*; Naff, *Becoming American*; Shakir, *Bint Arab*; and Saylor, "Subversive Sisterhood." Most contemporary studies in Arab American scholarship largely ignore sexuality; exceptions include Cable, "An Uprising at the Perfect Moment"; Jarmakani, *An Imperialist Love Story*; Naber, *Arab America*; Shomali, "Scheherazade"; and Shomali, *Between Banat*.

18. Fay, "Old Roots—New Soil," in Zogby, *Taking Root, Bearing Fruit*, 1:21.

19. On the associations between transience and sexual nonnormativity, see Canaday, *The Straight State*; and Shah, *Stranger Intimacies*. Another instance in which Arabness has been understood in both racialized and sexualized terms is through the figure of the sheikh. Alternately racialized by his queer gender or sexuality or sexualized by his racial difference, the sheikh character has been both racially and sexually ambiguous in film and literature since the 1920s. See Somerville, *Queering the Color Line*, 149–56; and Jarmakani, *An Imperialist Love Story*, 155–88.

20. Gualtieri, *Between Arab and White*; Samhan, "Not Quite White"; Maghbouleh, *The Limits of Whiteness*, 5; and Tehranian, *Whitewashed*, 37.

21. Pérez, *The Decolonial Imaginary*, 20.

22. Lowe, "History Hesitant," 90–91.

23. Karem Albrecht, "Why Arab American History Needs Queer of Color Critique."

24. See Jasbir Puar's concept of homonationalism in *Terrorist Assemblages*.

25. Naber, *Arab America*, 6.

26. Abdulhadi, "Sexualities and the Social Order in Arab and Muslim Communities," 470.

27. Jarmakani, *Imagining Arab Womanhood*, 3.

28. Jarmakani, 7.

29. The categorization "Arab migration" is fraught and complicated by a number of factors, including the self-identification of Arab as a culturally, historically, and politically contingent practice; the anti-Blackness in non-Black Arab communities; and the exclusion from Arab migration history of the forced migration of enslaved West African Muslims who spoke Arabic. See Hassoun, "Class and Color among Arab Americans."

30. Gualtieri, *Arab Routes*; Cainkar, "Palestinian Women in the United States."

31. For a fuller discussion of these discrepancies, see Gualtieri, *Between Arab and White*, 45–46.

32. Majaj, "Arab Americans and the Meanings of Race," 321.

33. Gualtieri, *Between Arab and White*, 24–29.

34. Gualtieri, 28.

35. Gualtieri, 29.

36. Naff, *Becoming American*, 150–51.

37. Bald, *Bengali Harlem*.

38. Naff, *Becoming American*, 130.

39. Naff.

40. Naff, 178. Like their male counterparts, the vast majority of Syrian women peddlers were Christians. This is in part proportional to the overall demographics of the Syrian immigrant community in the first half of the twentieth century. Naff suggests that the absence of Muslim and Druze women peddlers reflects the timing of their migration during the decline of Syrian peddlers' heyday toward the end of the first decade of the twentieth century, and to the conservatism regarding women in those religious traditions. However, two things should be taken into account regarding this assertion. First, there is documentation of at least one Syrian Muslim woman peddler, who lived in the sizable Syrian Muslim community in North Dakota in the early 1900s. Second, Syrian Christian women peddlers were far from universally sanctioned, as discussed in chapters 2 and 3. Some Syrian Jews from this period were also peddlers, but it is unclear if women were among their ranks.

41. Gualtieri, *Between Arab and White*, 143–45.

42. Berman, *American Arabesque*, 180.

43. Kayal and Kayal, *The Syrian-Lebanese in America*, 91.

44. Canaday, *The Straight State*.

45. Fahrenthold, "Ladies Aid as Labor History"; Shakir, *Bint Arab*; Stiffler, "A Brief History of Arab Immigrant Textile Production."

46. Gualtieri, *Between Arab and White*, 137.

47. Naff, *Becoming American*, 233; Gualtieri, *Between Arab and White*, 137.

48. Naff, *Becoming American*, 233.

49. Canaday, *The Straight State*; Shah, "Between 'Oriental Depravity' and 'Natural Degenerates'"; Shah, *Stranger Intimacy*. While Canaday's work elucidates how these concerns of sexual deviance centered on same-sex sexuality among white men, homosexual acts between white and nonwhite men also triggered disciplinary actions. Nayan Shah's work documents the sexual encounters between South Asian migrant workers and white men during this period—encounters that did not surface in community collections but were recorded in the arrest records of many of these men.

50. Naff, *Becoming American*, 164.

51. Jacobs, *Strangers in the West*, 15–25.

52. Naff, *Becoming American*; Shakir, *Bint Arab*. While it is important to note that both Alixa Naff and Evelyn Shakir wrote women into the histories of the early Arab American community, these significant scholarly contributions are still predicated on the compulsory heterosexuality and binary cisnormativity of Arab American women and girls.

53. Pérez, *The Decolonial Imaginary*, 6–7.

54. Arondekar, *For the Record*, 7. See also Arondekar, "In the Absence of Reliable Ghosts."

55. Lowe, "History Hesitant," 93.

56. Hartman, "Venus in Two Acts," 2, 11.

57. Hartman, *Wayward Lives, Beautiful Experiments*, xiv.

58. Hartman, xv.

59. Kunzel, "The Power of Queer History," 1560–61.

60. Kunzel, 1563–67.

61. Kunzel, 1580.

62. Gopinath, *Impossible Desires*, 22; Manalansan, "The 'Stuff' of Archives."

63. Arondekar et al., "Queering Archives," 219.

64. Al-Kassim, "Psychoanalysis and the Postcolonial Genealogy of Queer Theory," 345.

65. Jacob, "The Middle East," 347.

66. Ferguson, *Aberrations in Black*, 4.

67. Manalansan, "Messing Up Sex," 1287.

68. Tompkins, "Intersections of Race, Gender, and Sexuality," 173.

69. Shah, "Queer of Color Estrangement and Belonging," 262.

70. Here I'm indebted to Cathy Cohen's foundational critique that white queer theory failed to fully account for the normalizing forces of hegemonic sexuality. See Cohen, "Punks, Bulldaggers, and Welfare Queens."

71. In the context of Middle Eastern and North African sexual genealogies, see Abu-Khalil, "A Note on the Study of Homosexuality"; Amer, "Medieval Arab Lesbians and Lesbian-Like Women"; Babayan and Najmabadi, *Islamicate Sexualities*; Najmabadi, *Women with Mustaches and Men without Beards*; and El-Rouayheb, "Before Homosexuality in the Arab-Islamic World." See also the special issues of *Journal of Middle East Women's Studies* 7, no. 3 (2011); and *International Journal of Middle East Studies* 45, no. 2 (2013).

72. Macharia, "belated: interruption," 561; Macharia, "On Being Area-Studied."

73. Macharia, "On Being Area-Studied," 186.

74. Arondekar and Patel, "Area Impossible," 152.

75. Amin, "Haunted by the 1990s," 289.

76. Mikdashi and Puar, "Queer Theory and Permanent War," 216.

77. On diasporic connections that do not trace the route of diaspora back to a nation, see Alfaro-Velcamp, *So Far from Allah, So Close to Mexico*; and Gualtieri, *Arab Routes*.

78. See Bawardi, *The Making of Arab Americans*.

79. Gopinath, *Unruly Visions*, 5.

80. On queer theory and diaspora, see, among others, Eng, "Out Here and Over There"; and Gopinath, *Impossible Desires*.

81. Gopinath, *Unruly Visions*, 29.

82. Shomali, "Dancing Queens," 137.

83. Steet, *Veils and Daggers*, 57.

84. Regina Kunzel, quoted in Arondekar et al., "Queering Archives," 230.

85. Amin, *Disturbing Attachments*, 5–8.

86. Amin, "Haunted by the 1990s," 290 (emphasis in the original).

1. TRAVELER, PEDDLER, STRANGER, SYRIAN: QUEER PROVOCATIONS AND SEXUAL THREATS

Epigraph: Dresbach, "The Syrian Peddler," 314–15.

1. I am indebted to Sarah Ensor for her generative meditation on this aspect of my research.

2. Amin, "Haunted by the 1990s."

3. Moloney, *National Insecurities*, 132.

4. Louis L. Interview Notes, Faris and Yamna Naff Arab American Collection, Archives Center, National Museum of American History, Smithsonian Institution (hereafter Naff Collection), accessed May 23, 2022, at Arab American National Museum, https://aanm.contentdm.oclc.org/digital/collection/p16806coll10/id/103/rec/3.

5. Louis L. Interview Notes, Naff Collection.

6. For instance, in Naff's interview notes, she asks the sister of the person she was interviewing if she found things difficult living in the United States. Naff writes: "She was also reluctant to speak. Her husband, brother, nephew, and his wife were present. She was also reluctant to say anything that might appear derogatory about her country or the US and asked to turn tape recorder off so she could rehearse her statements." In a set of notes regarding a different interlocutor, Naff writes, "She was very conscious of being taped and put the best coloring on everything." Such hesitancy could also stem from a desire not to speak disparagingly about one's situation in front of family or to avoid saying something that could be perceived as critical of the state. See Essa and Mary M. Interview Notes and Alice A. Interview Notes, Naff Collection.

7. Essa and Mary M. Interview Notes, Naff Collection, accessed May 23, 2022, at Arab American National Museum, https://aanm.contentdm.oclc.org/digital/collection /p16806coll10/id/106/rec/3.

8. Alice A. Interview Notes, Naff Collection.

9. Aryain and Pate, *From Syria to Seminole*, 54–55.

10. "It Looks like Murder: A Missing Peddler's Pack and Blood Stains Found near Plymouth," *Philadelphia Inquirer*, November 10, 1891.

11. "Syrian Peddler Disappears," *Baltimore Sun*, May 24, 1903.

12. "Peddler Murdered," *Nashville American*, July 27, 1906, 7.

13. "Death Sentence," *Highland Recorder* (Monterey, VA), January 26, 1906.

14. "Believe Nadir Was Murdered: Further Mystery Surrounds the Death of the Syrian Peddler," *Morning Olympian-Tribune* (Olympia, WA), November 15, 1893, 1.

15. "Head Severed by Ax: Syrian Peddler Killed by Negroes—Motive Robbery," *Tensas Gazette* (St. Joseph, LA), November 5, 1909.

16. "Masters of Mendicants: Syrian Arabs Infesting the Cities," *New York Times*, February 21, 1888; "'Sanctified' Arab Tramps: Wretched Maronite Beggars Infesting This Country," *New York Times*, May 25, 1890, 17.

17. "New Arrivals from Syria," *New York Times*, August 8, 1885, 8.

18. "With Fear: People of South Louisville Look on Syrians," *Louisville (KY) Courier-Journal*, December 5, 1902, 6.

19. "The Definition of a Peddler," *Fort Worth Gazette*, April 26, 1890, 5.

20. "Retail Merchants Aroused," *Oklahoma Leader* (Guthrie), February 27, 1908.

21. Naff, *Becoming American*, 174.

22. "Syrians Grabbing the Business of El Paso," *El Paso Herald*, July 22, 1912, 5.

23. Editorial, *Beaver (OK) Herald*, March 18, 1909.

24. Tompkins, "'You Make Me Feel Right Quare,'" 54. Tompkins builds upon Cheryl Harris's concept of "whiteness as property." See Harris, "Whiteness as Property."

25. Birla, *Stages of Capital*, 3. See pages 2–12 for an extended discussion of vernacular capitalism. I use this framework provisionally, understanding that Syrians were not indigenous capitalists in the context of the United States.

26. Abu-Laban and Suleiman, *Arab Americans*, 2; Haddad, "The Woman's Role in the Socialization of Syrian-Americans in Chicago," 90; Naff, *Becoming American*.

27. Hooglund, "Introduction," in Hoogland, *Taking Root*, 2:4.

28. Naff, *Becoming American*, 46.

29. Naff, 130.

30. Naff, 169, 145–46.

31. Naff, 15–16.

32. Schechla, "The Mohameds in Mississippi," in Hooglund, *Taking Root*, 2:43–44.

33. Conklin and Faires, "'Colored' and Catholic," 78.

34. John, "Arabic-Speaking Immigration to the El Paso Area," 108.

35. "Congress to Tackle the Immigration Problem," *Los Angeles Herald*, January 9, 1898, 18.

36. Zirbel, "Amulets, Fortune-Telling, and Magic."

37. "'Syrian Prophet' Pays $50 Fine on Assault Charge," *Washington Times*, February 20, 1918, 16.

38. "Burned Her Home to Get Even with Her," *Herald-Republican* (Salt Lake City), August 21, 1910, 3.

39. "Lone Irishman Tries Lynching," *Okeene (OK) Eagle*, April 28, 1905, 6; "Lone Irishman Tries Lynching," *Jonesboro (AR) Weekly Sun*, April 12, 1905, 2.

40. Tompkins, "'You Make Me Feel Right Quare,'" 54.

41. "Special to Daily Leader," *Guthrie (OK) Daily Leader*, August 6, 1903, http://chroniclingamerica.loc.gov/lccn/sn86063952/1903-08-06/ed-1/seq-6/.

42. Ting, "Bachelor Society."

43. Naff Collection, Series 2, Box 68.

44. Gualtieri, *Between Arab and White*, 137.

45. This experience could easily have been a white supremacist response that simply assumed a relationality among all Arabs.

46. The alternate transliterated spelling of an Arabic name here could indicate that this was a different family, but not necessarily.

47. Jacobs, *Strangers No More*, 158–61.

48. Hartman, "Venus in Two Acts," 8.

49. Indian Territory was a US-defined region inside the Louisiana Purchase territory, but the region shifted and decreased in size every time a new state was created. It ceased to exist altogether after Oklahoma became a state in 1907.

50. Carter, *Oklahoma!*

51. Carter, 85.

52. Carter, 189.

53. Carter, 189.

54. See Carter, *Oklahoma!*; Kirle, "Reconciliation, Resolution, and the Political Role of *Oklahoma!*"; Most, "We Know We Belong to the Land"; and Most, *Making Americans*.

55. Kollin, *Captivating Westerns*, 136.

56. On the historical interrelation of anti-Jewish and anti-Muslim racial concepts, as well as articulations of Jews and Arabs, see Rana, "The Story of Islamophobia."

57. The assumption of the Europeanness of Jewry is intended here. Neither Rodgers and Hammerstein nor scholars who have studied Ali Hakim consider the existence of Persian or other Southwest Asian Jews, despite evidence of peddlers among the small populations of Syrian and Yemeni Jews in the United States. Because the peddler is never allowed to have been both Jewish and Persian, or Jewish and Syrian, this analysis reiterates the ontological privileging of Ashkenazi Jews within Jewish studies. It also sets Jewish legibility against Arab and Southwest Asian legibility, as if the two cannot exist simultaneously.

58. To say that Arab Jews have a right to belong in the Middle East and North Africa outside Israel should not discount the documented histories of anti-Semitism that Arab

and other Middle Eastern Jews have faced. The Israeli state also fomented anti-Semitism in some places in the Middle East and North Africa in order to encourage Jewish immigration to the newly formed territory. See Shohat, "Dislocated Identities."

59. Canaday, *The Straight State.*

60. Chang, *The Color of the Land*, 129.

61. Chang, 189.

62. See, for example, Miranda, "Extermination of the 'Joyas'"; Driskill et al., "Introduction," in *Queer Indigenous Studies*; Simpson, *As We Have Always Done.*

63. Brown, *Stoking the Fire*, 121.

64. Cited in Rich, "Oklahoma Was Never Really O.K."

65. Brown, *Stoking the Fire*, 16.

66. Riggs, *Green Grow the Lilacs*, in *The Cherokee Night and Other Plays*, 2–105.

67. Riggs, 33.

68. Riggs, 33.

69. Riggs, 34.

70. Riggs, 34.

71. Riggs, 36.

72. Hoganson, *Consumers' Imperium.*

73. Hoganson, 52–53.

74. Hoganson, 14.

75. Bald, *Bengali Harlem*, 46.

76. Riggs, *Green Grow the Lilacs*, 34.

77. Riggs, *Knives from Syria.*

78. One could also argue that, in light of their small role and the characters' anonymity, Syrians are not primarily those to whom Riggs wanted to give voice. Perhaps both assessments are true.

79. Caldwell, "The Syrian-Lebanese in Oklahoma," 39, 33.

80. Braunlich, *Haunted by Home*, 16; Hakim et al., "Annie Abdo." At least three other families claim that their ancestor was the basis for the Syrian peddler character in Riggs's plays (phone interview with Kristin Shamas, scholar of Syrian and Lebanese history of Oklahoma, October 17, 2019).

81. "Play of Prairies Is Given at Ford's by Theater Guild," *Baltimore Sun*, January 13, 1931, 9.

82. Katherine T. Von Blon, "Guild Play Primitive in Power: Wild Enthusiasm Greets 'Green Grow the Lilacs' at Pasadena Community," *Los Angeles Times*, July 1, 1932, A11.

83. "And Now Lynn Riggs: After Several Ventures in the Theatre, He Arrives with 'Green Grow the Lilacs,'" *New York Times*, February 1, 1931, 109.

84. Chang, *The Color of the Land*, 6.

85. Chang, 76.

86. Weaver, *That the People Might Live*, 99.

87. Weaver, 99.

88. Chang, *The Color of the Land*, 191.

89. Carter, *Oklahoma!*; Most, "'We Know We Belong to the Land'"; Kirle, "Reconciliation, Resolution, and the Political Role of *Oklahoma!*"

90. Aikin, "Was Jud Jewish?"; Most, "'We Know We Belong to the Land.'"

91. Riggs, *Green Grow the Lilacs*, 34.

92. Carter, *Oklahoma!* 100.

93. This joke was not original to *Oklahoma!* A similar joke about Filipino Muslims figured in a political cartoon more than four decades earlier, during the Philippine-American War. See Mendoza, *Metroimperial Intimacies*, 132.

94. Rodgers and Hammerstein, *Oklahoma!* 26.

95. Rodgers and Hammerstein, 32.

96. Carter, *Oklahoma!* 201.

97. See the discussion of these fears and discourses in Jarmakani, *An Imperialist Love Story*, 167–74. Jarmakani cites Garber, *Vested Interests*, 304–10; and Studlar, "Discourses of Gender and Ethnicity."

98. Berman, *American Arabesque*, 179–84; Karem Albrecht, "An Archive of Difference," 134–35.

99. Caton, "The Sheik," 113–14.

100. Shah, *Stranger Intimacy*, 62.

101. Kirle, "Reconciliation, Resolution, and the Political Role of *Oklahoma!*" 265.

102. Most, "'We Know We Belong to the Land,'" 77.

103. Most, 81.

104. Canaday, *The Straight State*, 134.

105. Canaday, 137–38.

106. Pollack-Pelzner, "The Hidden History of '*Oklahoma!*'"

107. Kollin, *Captivating Westerns*, 127.

108. Rodgers and Hammerstein, *Oklahoma!* 78.

109. Canaday, *The Straight State*, 98.

110. Toth, "Birmingham," 34; Peterson, "Houston," 62; Toth, "Jacksonville," 68.

2. "A WOMAN WITHOUT LIMITS": SYRIAN WOMEN IN THE PEDDLING ECONOMY

1. Haddad, "Timthal al-Huriyya."

2. Haddad, 180.

3. Haddad, 181.

4. Saylor, "Subversive Sisterhood," 9.

5. The threat or fear of gossip comes in the form of *kalam al-nas*, loosely translated as "what will the people say," in which "the people" refers to other Arabs. For a contemporary understanding of how "what will the people say" functions to police the behaviors and bodies of women and girls, see Naber, *Arab America*, 1–9.

6. Traub, *Thinking Sex with the Early Moderns*, 17. Traub goes on to assert that maintaining an analysis of gender alongside sexuality "also stems from a historical sense that queer studies misrecognizes its own conditions of emergence when it categorically rejects affiliation with feminism in the name of analytically separating sexuality from gender" (18).

7. Khater, *Inventing Home*.

8. Khater, 32.

9. Afif Tannous Interview Notes, Naff Collection, Series 3, Box 83, Folder 20. Regarding her 1980 interview with Afif Tannous, Naff noted: "In commenting about the Damascenes in the US who were proud to say they didn't peddle, informant states that the reason for this is that the 'majority of the farmers [in Syria] were serfs until 1960s when internal revolution took place and land reform was established.' 'Syria,' he added, 'was a landlord country.'

Therefore, especially during the time of Greater Syria, the Damascenes were proud of saying that they were from Damascus, because Damascus was the center of power. To be a Damascene is to belong to a city of a country where the farmers are serfs. Therefore being a farmer is embarrassing for some families. The only people who were proud of being farmers were the Lebanese villagers because they were independent."

10. Naber, *Arab America*, 71–73.

11. Tannous, "Acculturation of an Arab-Syrian Community," 270.

12. Tannous, 266–67.

13. Tannous, 267.

14. Tannous, 271 (emphasis in original).

15. Haddad, "Timthal al-Huriyya," 180.

16. Hitti, *The Syrians in America*, 58.

17. Hagopian, "Institutional Development of the Arab-American Community of Boston," 69.

18. Haddad, "The Woman's Role in the Socialization of Syrian-Americans in Chicago," 90–91.

19. Ong, *Buddha Is Hiding*, 11.

20. Tice, *Tales of Wayward Girls and Immoral Women*, 112.

21. Naff, *Becoming American*, 144. Naff notes that an absence of six months to a year, as well as longer trips back to Greater Syria, was not uncommon for long-distance peddlers, who were mostly men.

22. Khater, *Inventing Home*, 87.

23. International Institutes were originally founded in the 1920s through the Young Women's Christian Association (YWCA) specifically to address the needs of new immigrant populations. They often had "nationality secretaries"—a first- or second-generation American from an immigrant community who was bilingual and acted as both social worker and community liaison. International Institutes could be found throughout urban areas in the United States, and they eventually formed their own federation separate from the YWCA. International Institutes frequently held galas and pageants that celebrated the different national cultures of the immigrants they served, but they remained at their core organizations that sought to normalize and assimilate immigrants. These sites of celebration became sites of consumption for white, native-born Americans and sites of discipline, rather than liberation, for immigrants.

24. "A Precious Syrian Sister," *New York Sun*, May 23, 1888.

25. For instance, one Syrian American woman peddled as a child with her father because her presence enabled him more easily to find lodging at night (Interview with Elizabeth Beshara, Naff Collection, Series 3, Box 79, Folder 6). See also Younis and Kayal, *The Coming of the Arabic-Speaking People to the United States*, 169.

26. "Syrian Peddlers: Eastern Women Trained from Childhood to Carry Heavy Weights," *Detroit Free Press*, September 10, 1911.

27. "Syrian Peddlers."

28. Louise Seymour Houghton, "Syrians in the United States: Sources and Settlement," *The Survey* (New York), July 1, 1911; Houghton, "Syrians in the United States: Business Activities," *The Survey*, August 5, 1911; Houghton, "Syrians in the United States: Intellectual and Social Status," *The Survey*, September 2, 1911; Houghton, "Syrians in the United States: The Syrian as an American Citizen," *The Survey*, October 7, 1911.

29. Interview with Nicola Shamiyyi, Naff Collection, Series 3, Box 88, Folder 5.

30. Naff, *Becoming American*, 178.

31. Hourani, "'Aqlah Brice Al Shidyaq," 52–55.

32. Al Shidyaq, "Sitta 'Aqlah."

33. Naff, *Becoming American*, 178, 230.

34. Houghton, "Syrians in the United States: Business Activities," 648.

35. Associated Charities of Boston, *Annual Report*, 1899, 57.

36. Associated Charities of Boston (1899), 57.

37. Associated Charities of Boston (1899), 60; Associated Charities of Boston, *Annual Report*, 1905, 41. Akram Khater argues that Syrian men were not as keen as some other immigrants to work in factories, because their identities were closely tied to working the land. In this light, peddling may have been something that approximated or kept them closer to their desired vocations. See Khater, *Inventing Home*, 33.

38. Houghton, "Syrians in the United States: Business Activities," 650.

39. Schweik, *The Ugly Laws*.

40. Schweik, 3.

41. Schweik, 144.

42. Schweik, 145.

43. Schweik, 193.

44. Schweik, 146.

45. Naff, *Becoming American*, 166.

46. Schweik, *The Ugly Laws*, 178.

47. Schweik, 212.

48. Houghton, "Syrians in the United States: Intellectual and Social Status," 799.

49. Y. M. Karekin, "Armenians Not Peddlers" (letter to the editor), *The Survey*, September 9, 1911, 841 (emphasis added).

50. Canaday, *The Straight State*, 26.

51. Fraser and Gordon, "A Genealogy of Dependency," 320.

52. Fraser and Gordon, 319.

53. Associated Charities of Boston, *Annual Report*, 1899, 58.

54. C., "Syrians in Boston" (letter to the editor), *The Survey*, October 29, 1911, 1088.

55. C., "Syrians in Boston."

56. Tice, *Tales of Wayward Girls and Immoral Women*, 111; Kunzel, *Fallen Women, Problem Girls*, 58.

57. Canaday, *The Straight State*, 127; Kunzel, *Fallen Women, Problem Girls*; Tice, *Tales of Wayward Girls and Immoral Women*.

58. Shakir, *Bint Arab*, 38; Khater, "Like Pure Gold," 66–67.

59. Dina Dahbany-Miraglia, "Random Thoughts on the Position of Women among Early Arab Immigrants" (unpublished manuscript, Center for Migration Studies, Staten Island, NY, n.d.), Group II, Box 5, Folder 149, Syrian American Archival Collection; Khater, "Like Pure Gold," 92–93.

60. Houghton, "Syrians in the United States: Intellectual and Social Status," 799.

61. Tinsley, *Thiefing Sugar*, 9.

62. Canaday, *The Straight State*, 12.

63. Interview with Mary Agemy, Naff Collection, Series 3, Box 88, Folder 5.

64. Naff, *Becoming American*, 174.

65. "Syrian Woman Arrested; Told Hard Luck Story," *Atlanta Constitution* (1881–1945), May 16, 1910.

66. "Infant in a Cesspool," *Scranton (PA) Tribune*, September 6, 1900 (morning edition), 5.

67. "Mrs. Mary Tamar Is under Arrest," *Scranton (PA) Tribune*, September 7, 1900 (morning edition), 5.

68. Adele Linda Younis, "The Coming of the Arabic-Speaking People to the United States," PhD diss., Boston University, 1961, cited in Cory, "The Women from the Levant," 21–31.

69. "Nursery for Syrian Babies: It Is to Be Founded in Lower New York by the Syrian Woman's Union, a Charitable Society," *New York Times*, March 19, 1899.

70. Litia Namoura, "The Dances of the Exotic East," Naff Collection, cited in Cory, "The Women from the Levant," 130.

71. US House of Representatives, *Reports of the Industrial Commission on Immigration ... and on Education*," vol. 15 (Washington, DC: Government Printing Office, 1901), 443.

72. Schechla, "Dabkeh in the Delta," 32.

73. Schechla, "Dabkeh in the Delta," 33; Interview with Abe Abraham, Naff Collection, Series 3, Box, 88, Folder 5.

74. Moloney, *National Insecurities*; Luibhéid, *Entry Denied*.

75. Kunzel, *Fallen Women, Problem Girls*; Mink, "The Lady and the Tramp"; Tice, *Tales of Wayward Girls and Immoral Women*.

76. Mink, "The Lady and the Tramp," 93–94.

77. Mink, 103.

78. National Conference of Social Work, *Proceedings*" (1915), 594.

79. National Conference of Social Work, 54, 55.

80. Khater, *Inventing Home*, 80; Khater, "Like Pure Gold," 92.

81. International Institutes sometimes had a first- or second-generation American from an immigrant community who was bilingual and acted as both social worker and community liaison. For more information on International Institutes, see Mohl, "Cultural Pluralism in Immigrant Education."

82. International Institute of Boston, Massachusetts Records, Box 13, Folder 256, General/Multiethnic Collection, Immigration History Research Center Archives, University of Minnesota, Minneapolis (hereafter cited as G/MC IHRCA). According to the IHRCA's use guidelines, the names of International Institute clients have been changed to protect privacy. Victoria Karam (later Victoria Abboud) is the real name of the social worker.

83. The case file notes do not say how she was financially able to do this.

84. International Institute of Boston, Massachusetts Records, Box 13, Folder 256, G/MC IHRCA.

85. International Institute of Boston, Massachusetts Records, Box 13, Folder 315, G/MC IHRCA.

86. International Institute of Boston, Massachusetts Records, Box 14, Folder 398, G/MC IHRCA.

87. International Institute of Boston, Massachusetts Records, Box 15, Folder 579, G/MC IHRCA.

88. Spivak, "Subaltern Studies: Deconstructing Historiography," in *In Other Worlds*, 211, 214.

89. Potter, "Queer Hoover," 360.

90. Shah, *Stranger Intimacy*, 41.

91. Interview with Elizabeth Beshara Notes, Series 3, Box 79, Folder 6, Naff Collection.

92. Canaday, *The Straight State*, 12.

93. International Institute of Boston, Massachusetts Records, Box 13, Folder 256, G/MC IHRCA.

94. International Institute of Boston, Massachusetts Records, Box 13, Folder 256, G/MC IHRCA.

95. International Institute of Boston, Massachusetts Records, Box 13, Folder 256, G/MC IHRCA.

96. International Institute of Boston, Massachusetts Records, Box 13, Folder 256, G/MC IHRCA.

97. Cory, "The Women from the Levant," 111.

98. Amy E. Nevala, "Victoria Karam Abboud, 98; Social Worker Aided Children, Immigrants," *Chicago Tribune*, September 27, 2001; Cynthia Scheider, "Victoria Karem Abboud," *William G. Abdalah Memorial Library Newsletter* (September 1990).

99. International Institute of Boston, Massachusetts Records, Box 13, Folder 256, G/MC IHRCA.

100. Naff, *Becoming American*, 178.

101. Gualtieri, *Between Arab and White*, 144 (citing Ferguson, *Aberrations in Black*, 14–16; and Shah, *Contagious Divides*, 13–15).

102. Gualtieri, *Between Arab and White*, 144. Original "Reports of the Industrial Commission," vol. 15 (1901), p. 444.

3. WANDERING IN DIASPORA: THE SYRIAN AMERICAN ELITE AND SEXUAL NORMATIVITY

1. Naff, *Becoming American*, 234.

2. Not all elite Syrian Americans agreed completely about the idealized identity in relation to Syrianness and Americanness. These conversations overlapped with conversations about modernity taking place in Ottoman Syria. But even in disagreement, they were united by a concerted push for gendered and sexual respectability.

3. Khater, *Inventing Home*, 20–33.

4. The Nahda centered primarily on Egypt, Lebanon, and Syria. Khater, *Inventing Home*; Zachs and Halevi, *Gendering Culture in Greater Syria*.

5. Naff, *Becoming American*, 235–36; Khater, *Inventing Home*, 64–65; Gualtieri, *Between Arab and White*, 139.

6. Zachs and Halevi, *Gendering Culture in Greater Syria*; Ze'evi, *Producing Desire*.

7. Naff, "The Arabic-Language Press," 6. Population estimates for Syrians in the United States are not entirely accurate given the US government's divergent naming practices. This ratio of literate population to numbers of publications likely also explains why many of these periodicals did not survive for long.

8. Naff, 4.

9. See Bawardi, *The Making of Arab Americans*; Fahrenthold, "Transnational Modes and Media"; Fahrenthold, *Between the Ottomans and the Entente*, 15; Gualtieri, *Between Arab*

and White; Sawaie, "Arabic in the Melting Pot," 83–86; and Womack, "Syrian Christians and Arab-Islamic Identity."

10. Jacobs, *Strangers in the West*, 268–72.

11. Jacobs, 261–78.

12. Naff, "The Arabic-Language Press," 5.

13. Jacobs, *Strangers in the West*, 278.

14. Khater, *Inventing Home*.

15. Shabal Nasif Damus, "Hal al-Suriyyin fi Dar Hajartuhum" (The State of the Syrians in the Land of Their Migration), *Al-Jami'a*, September 21, 1907, 1.

16. Salloum Mokarzel, "Qara' al-Bab" (Knocking on the Door), *Al-Hoda*, March 22, 1898, 9, Moise A. Khayrallah Center for Lebanese Diaspora Studies Archive, North Carolina State University, Raleigh (hereafter cited as Khayrallah Center Archive).

17. Khalil Sam'an, "Al-Ma'na" (The Meaning), *Al-Hoda*, May 10, 1898, 15–18, Michael W. Suleiman Collection, Arab American National Museum, Dearborn, MI.

18. Ibrahim Arbeely, "Fi al-Mawduwa' aladhi Iftarahahu al-Khawajat Batrakiyyan Akharan 'an 'Sabab T'akhar al-Suriyyin al-Muhajirin wa-Dawa'uha'" (Decision as to the Best Essay on "The Causes and Remedies of the Backwardness of Syrians"), *Al-Hoda*, November 16, 1904, Khayrallah Center Archive.

19. Najeeb Arbeely, "Al-Muhajarat al-Suriyat" (The Syrian Immigrant Women), *Kawkab America* (June 1895): 4, Khayrallah Center Archive.

20. Luibhéid, *Entry Denied*, xii.

21. Moloney, "Women, Sexual Morality, and Economic Dependency," 111.

22. Najib Tannous Abdou, letter to the editor, *Kawkab America*, March 31, 1893, 2–3, Khayrallah Center Archive.

23. Khater, *Inventing Home*, 99.

24. Ilyas Nasif, "Al-Mar'a al-Suriyya wa-l-Kasha" (The Syrian Woman and Peddling), *Al-Hoda*, May 26, 1903, 2, Khayrallah Center Archive.

25. Nasif.

26. Yusuf Shihadeh, "Al-Ba'a al-Qalilu al-Adab" (Some Ill-Mannered Peddlers), *Al-Ayyam* 2, no. 67 (August 25, 1898): 5–6.

27. "Al-Suriyya al-Ba'i'a" (The Female Syrian Seller), *Al-Wafa'* 2, no. 131 (1908): 2, Khayrallah Center Archive.

28. "Al-Suriyya al-Ba'i'a," 4.

29. For more context on the genealogies and circulation of "honor" with regard to gender-based violence, see Abu-Lughod, "Seductions of the 'Honor Crime'"; and Olwan, *Gender Violence and the Transnational Politics of the Honor Crime.*

30. Gualtieri, "From Lebanon to Louisiana"; Saylor, "Subversive Sisterhood."

31. 'Afifa Karam, "La Tarsilu Nisa'kum ila al-Harb bi-Ghayyir Silah" (Do Not Send Your Women to War without Any Armor), *Al-Hoda*, October 17, 1906, 1, Khayrallah Center Archive.

32. Karam, "La Tarsilu," 1.

33. Layyah Barakat, "The Eastern Woman in the West," *Al-Hoda*, n.d., 1911, 19, cited in Shakir, *Bint Arab*, 41.

34. Khater, *Inventing Home*, 98.

35. Gualtieri, *Between Arab and White*, 69.

36. Moloney, *National Insecurities*, 139. Antipolygamy measures coalesced around opposition to Mormonism but also drew on anti-Muslim racism.

37. Majaj, "Arab Americans and the Meaning of Race"; Naber, *Arab America*.

38. The majority of Muslims turned away were Turkish or South Asian, but some Syrian Muslims were also denied entry. See Moloney, *National Insecurities*, 144.

39. Gualtieri, *Between Arab and White*.

40. Gualtieri, 67.

41. Gualtieri, 71. Gualtieri notes that this same language was also reflected in *Meraat-ul-Gharb*, which also covered Dow's case.

42. Gualtieri, 53, 69.

43. Gualtieri, 67–68. The interweaving of Ashkenazi and Syrian Christian processes of racialization in the United States is also evident here. European Jews, like other European petitioners, were granted naturalization rights without those petitions going to the courts. Successful Syrian petitioners thus used these links of proximity to Ashkenazim (ethnological, religious, historical-geographic, etc.) to build a case for whiteness. It would be illuminating to know where Syrian Jews fell on this grid of racial testing: Were they counted as Hebrews, as European Jews were often labeled, and thus given naturalization rights without question? Was their geographic origin in Asia enough to include them with their conationals? Unfortunately, none of these naturalization cases concerned a Syrian Jewish petitioner. This line of inquiry can also be followed through extralegal routes. In immigration scholarship, Syrian Jews are often studied with Ashkenazim in pan-Jewish work and are separated from Syrian Christians and Muslims. Conversely, many studies on the Syrian immigrant population give little attention to the Syrian Jewish community. Some instances of anti-Syrian racialization depended heavily on anti-Semitic (more specifically, anti-Ashkenazi) tropes as well.

44. Beydoun, "Between Muslim and White," 29.

45. Beydoun, 51.

46. Rana, "The Story of Islamophobia," 148.

47. Dyer, *White*, 20.

48. Gualtieri, *Between Arab and White*, 145–46. Gualtieri's work also shows evidence of anti-Muslim sentiment within the Christian Syrian American press, which linked the mistreatment of women explicitly with Muslims and the practice of polygamy.

49. Somerville, "Notes toward a Queer History of Naturalization," 661–62.

50. Somerville. In discussing the desirable immigrant, Somerville draws on Berlant, *The Queen of America Goes to Washington City*.

51. Yusuf Al-Zaʿni Batruni, "Al-Marʾa al-Suriyya wa-Kashtaha wa-Hiyya Asl Balaʾtaha" (The Syrian Woman and Peddling Which Is the Source of Her Affliction), *Al-Hoda*, July 7, 1903, 2, Khayrallah Center Archive.

52. ʿAfifa Karam, "Al-Fadilat Sahibat al-Imdaʾ" (For the Virtuous Woman Who Owns This Signature), *Al-Hoda*, July 14, 1903, Khayrallah Center Archive.

53. Karam, "Al-Fadilat."

54. Karam.

55. Karam.

56. Amin Silbi, letter to the editor, *Al-Hoda*, July 18, 1903, 2, Khayrallah Center Archive.

57. Silbi.

58. Yusuf Al-Zaʿni Batruni, "Al-Marʾa al-Suriyya wa-Kashtaha wa-Hiyya Asl Balaʾtaha" (The Syrian Woman and Peddling Which Is the Source of Her Affliction), *Al-Hoda*, July 28, 1903, 2–3, Khayrallah Center Archive.

59. Yusuf Al-Za'ni Batruni, "Al-Mar'a al-Suriyya wa-Kashtaha: Asl al-Bala' al-Rajl" (The Syrian Woman and Peddling: The Source of Her Affliction Is Men), *Al-Hoda*, August 15, 1903, 2–3.

60. Naff, *Becoming American*, 115.

61. A notable exception is 'Afifa Karam's women's publication *Majallat al-'Alam al-Jadid al-Nisa'iyya*, which catered to women readers.

62. Khater, *Inventing Home*, 67.

63. Naff, *Becoming American*, 230.

64. Interviews with Ollie Okdie (Box 83, Folder 4), Rahmy Francis (Box 80, Folder 7), Peter Solomon (Box 83, Folder 17), Adeby Coury (Box 81, Folder 13), and Zahdi Barsa (Box 81, Folder 2), Naff Collection, Series 3. Druze women in diaspora who wanted to marry might have had only non-Druze suitors to choose from.

65. Karam, "La Tarsilu," 1.

66. "Al-Suriyya al-Ba'i'a" (The Female Syrian Seller), *Al-Wafa'* 2, no. 131 (1908), n.p., Khayrallah Center Archive.

67. "Al-Suriyya al-Ba'i'a."

68. Zubayda Butrus Sa'b, "al-Muhajara Ramnaha wa-Adiraruha" (Advantages and Disadvantages of Emigration), *Al-Hoda*, November 4, 1904, n.p., Khayrallah Center Archive.

69. See also Karem Albrecht, "Narrating Arab American History," 100.

70. Barakat Tannus Adhem, "Qisati bi-'Ashrin Satar imma Akthar Qalilan" (My Story in Twenty Lines, or a Little Bit More), *Al-Sa'ih*, January 29, 1918, n.p., Michael W. Suleiman Collection.

71. Amin Silbi, letter to the editor, *Al-Hoda*, May 3, 1902, 6, Khayrallah Center Archive.

72. Victoria Tannous, "Al-Fataa al-'Amila" (The Working Girl), *Al-Akhlaq* (June 1920), Khayrallah Center Archive.

73. Tannous, "Al-Fataa al-'Amila."

74. Tannous.

75. Tannous.

76. Naoum Mokarzel, "La Tazlamuhunna" (Do Not Do Them Injustice), *Al-Hoda* (August 1904): 2, Khayrallah Center Archive.

77. Mokarzel, "La Tazlamuhunna."

78. Iskander Atallah, "al-Muhajara" (Emigration), *Al-Kalimat* 5 (1909): 348–50.

79. Naff, *Becoming American*, 90.

80. Amin Abu Isma'il, "Muhajarat al-Mar'a al-Druziyya" (The Emigration of the Druze Woman), *Al-Bayan*, March 10, 1914.

81. As'ad Husayn Abu 'Ali, "Muhajarat al-Mar'a al-Druziyya" (The Emigration of the Druze Woman), *Al-Bayan*, March 31, 1914.

82. "Al-Mar'a al-Hayaat al-Umma" (Women Are the Life of the Community), *Al-Bayan*, February 24, 1914.

83. "Al-Mar'a al-Hayaat al-Umma."

84. Abu 'Ali, "Muhajarat al-Mar'a al-Druziyya."

85. "Li-l-Muqbilin 'ala al-Zawaj" (For Those Soon to Be Married), *Al-Akhlaq* 1, no. 7 (July 1920), Khayrallah Center Archive.

86. "Li-l-Muqbilin 'ala al-Zawaj."

87. "Li-l-Muqbilin 'ala al-Zawaj."

88. "Li-l-Muqbilin 'ala al-Zawaj."

89. "Li-l-Muqbilin ʿala al-Zawaj."

90. Lowe, "History Hesitant," 89.

4. THE POSSIBILITIES OF PEDDLING: IMAGINING HOMOSOCIAL AND HOMOEROTIC PLEASURE IN ARAB AMERICA

Epigraph: Pérez, "Queering the Borderlands," 124.

1. Interview with Elias Lebos, Naff Collection, Series 3, Box 79, Folder 18.

2. Interview with Francis Slay, Naff Collection, Series 3, Box 80, Folder 14.

3. Naber, *Arab America*, 64.

4. *La Crosse Chronicle*, July 6, 1902, 1, quoted in "From *Mahatta* to 'Little Assyria': The Beginnings of a Permanent Syrian Presence in La Crosse," *Past, Present, and Future: The Magazine of the La Crosse County Historical Society* 24, no. 3 (June 2002): 5–6.

5. "From *Mahatta* to 'Little Assyria,'" 6.

6. Shah, *Stranger Intimacy*, 2.

7. Interview notes with Budelia Malooley, Naff Collection, Series 3, Box 88, Folder 5.

8. Gopinath, *Impossible Desires*, 25. See also Aghdasifar, "Rhythms of the Banal."

9. Gopinath, *Impossible Desires*, 25.

10. Gordon, *Ghostly Matters*, 60.

11. Zengin and Sehlikoglu, "Everyday Intimacies of the Middle East"; Najmabadi, *Women with Mustaches and Men without Beards*; Zeʿevi, *Producing Desire*.

12. Lowe, *The Intimacies of Four Continents*, 17–21.

13. Lowe, 195.

14. Lorde, "Uses of the Erotic," 57.

15. Lorde, 53.

16. Naff, *Becoming American*, 213–14.

17. Naff, 212 (emphases added).

18. Gopinath, *Impossible Desires*, 103.

19. Jarmakani, *Imagining Arab Womanhood*, 64.

20. On studies of sexuality and queerness in the Middle East and North Africa, see, among others, Abu-Khalil, "A Note on the Study of Homosexuality"; Amer, "Medieval Arab Lesbians and Lesbian-Like Women"; Babayan and Najmabadi, *Islamicate Sexualities*; El-Rouayheb, *Before Homosexuality in the Arab-Islamic World*; Habib, *Islam and Homosexuality*; and Massad, *Desiring Arabs*.

21. Howard, *Men Like That*.

22. Shah, "Policing Privacy," 281.

23. Naff, *Becoming American*, 206.

24. Naff, 207.

25. Edwards and Hart, *Photographs Objects Histories*, 2.

26. Kara Keeling, "Looking for M—," 567.

27. Hirsch, *Family Photographs*, xi.

28. For more on respectability and the volatile nature of showing Arab and Asian women at work, see Howell, "Picturing Women, Class, and Community in Arab Detroit"; and Kozol, "Relocating Citizenship," 231.

29. Barthes, *Camera Lucida*, 87; Tagg, *The Burden of Representation*, 1, citing Barthes.

30. Jarmakani, *Imagining Arab Womanhood*, 88–91.

31. Cadava, *Words of Light*, xviii.

32. Sekula, "The Body and the Archive," 345.

33. Smith, *American Archives*, 4.

34. Smith, *American Archives*; Sekula, "The Body and the Archive."

35. Smith, *American Archives*, 5.

36. Steet, *Veils and Daggers*, 57.

37. Graham-Brown, *Images of Women*, 118.

38. Betts, "Wanted Women, Woman's Wants."

39. Djebar, "A Forbidden Glimpse."

40. Alloula, *The Colonial Harem*. Alloula's classic work on postcards made of such photographs intricately details how this sexual fantasy was central to Orientalism and colonialism.

41. Jarmakani, *Imagining Arab Womanhood*, 64. For Jarmakani's full discussion of these photographs and the context that produced them, see pages 63–101.

42. Because of Brownie cameras' widespread popularity in middle-class and aspiring middle-class US culture, some Syrian peddlers likely carried the cameras for sale.

43. Sheehi, "A Social History of Early Arab Photography."

44. Sheehi, 191.

45. Sheehi, 179. Sheehi writes specifically about Lebanese national identity. The articulation of a national identity (whether "Arab" or nation-state specific) would have varied throughout the Arab regions of the Ottoman Empire.

46. hooks, "In Our Glory," 389.

47. Kozol, "Relocating Citizenship," 231.

48. Although images of Syrian women in factory settings can be found in other archival collections, few of them appear in the Naff Collection.

49. On the palimpsest as a concept through which to trace multiple historical processes in Arab American life, including racial exclusion and national affiliation, see Gualtieri, *Arab Routes*.

50. Tagg, *The Burden of Representation*, 37.

51. This is the plural form of "tarboosh," the word for the flat-topped brimless hat worn especially by men in the region.

52. Hirsch, *Family Photographs*, 32.

53. Sheehi, "A Social History of Early Arab Photography," 193.

54. Sheehi, 192.

55. Hirsch, *Family Photographs*, 15.

56. Hirsch, 15.

57. "Review of Special Reports," in US House of Representatives, *Reports of the Industrial Commission*, xli.

58. Interview with Francis Slay, Naff Collection, Series 3, Box 80, Folder 14.

59. Joseph, "Introduction: Family in the Arab Region," 3; and Zaatari, "Lebanon," 193, citing Zuhair Hatab, *Al-Rajul wa Tanziyym al-Usra fi Lubnan* (Beirut: Jam'iyyat Tanzym al-Usra, 1988).

60. Joseph, "Introduction: Theories and Dynamics," 1–12.

61. Pegler-Gordon, "Chinese Exclusion, Photography, and the Development of U.S. Immigration Policy"; Pegler-Gordon, *In Sight of America.*

62. Munshi, "'You Will See My Family Became So American,'" 660.

63. Phu, *Picturing Model Citizens.*

64. Brown and Phu, *Feeling Photography.* See also Gopinath, *Unruly Visions*; and Campt, *Image Matters.*

65. Gopinath, *Unruly Visions,* 12.

66. Barthes, *Camera Lucida,* 59.

67. Barthes, 55.

68. Campt, *Image Matters,* 43.

69. Pérez, "Queering the Borderlands," 124.

70. Halberstam, "Queer Faces: Photography and Subcultural Lives," 98.

71. Mimura, "A Dying West?" 708.

72. I am indebted to Retika Adhikari for this latter reading of the photograph.

73. Ibson, *Picturing Men,* 125.

74. Gualtieri, *Between Arab and White,* 169.

75. Hirsch, *Family Photographs,* 51.

76. Rogerson, "Without Words You Spoke," 13.

77. Vicinus, "Lesbian History," 59.

78. Holland, "Introduction," 10.

79. Holland, 13–14.

CONCLUSION: ALIXA NAFF AND THE PARENTHETICAL SYRIAN AMERICAN LESBIAN

1. "In Memoriam: Alixa Naff"; Samhan, "Farewell to the Grande Dame of Arab American Social History."

2. "In Memoriam: Alixa Naff," 341.

3. Samhan, "Farewell to the Grande Dame of Arab American Social History," 96.

4. Wedad F. Interview Notes, Oral Histories from the Faris and Yamna Naff Arab American Collection, Arab American National Museum, accessed June 7, 2022, http://cdm16806.contentdm.oclc.org/cdm/singleitem/collection/p16806coll10/id/90/rec/93.

5. Interview with Wedad F. (summer 1962), Oral Histories from the Faris and Yamna Naff Arab American Collection, Arab American National Museum, accessed June 7, 2022, https://aanm.contentdm.oclc.org/digital/collection/p16806coll10/id/75/rec/1.

6. Georgis, *The Better Story,* 1.

7. Georgis, 10.

8. Georgis, 11.

BIBLIOGRAPHY

ARCHIVAL COLLECTIONS

Adele L. Younis Papers. Syrian American Archival Collection. Center for Migration Studies, Staten Island, NY.

Billy Rose Theatre Division. The New York Public Library, New York, NY.

Faris and Yamna Naff Arab American Collection. National Museum of American History. Archives Center. Smithsonian Institution, Washington, DC.

International Institute of Boston Records. Immigration History Research Center Archives. University of Minnesota, Minneapolis.

International Institute of Minnesota Records. Immigration History Research Center Archives. University of Minnesota, Minneapolis.

Michael W. Suleiman Collection. Arab American National Museum, Dearborn, MI.

Moise A. Khayrallah Center for Lebanese Diaspora Studies Archive. North Carolina State University, Raleigh, NC.

Philip Khuri Hitti Papers. Immigration History Research Center Archives. University of Minnesota, Minneapolis.

Philip M. Kayal Papers. Syrian American Archival Collection. Center for Migration Studies, Staten Island, NY.

PRIMARY SOURCE NEWSPAPERS AND PERIODICALS

Atlanta Constitution
Al-Akhlaq (New York)
Al-Ayyam (New York)
Baltimore Sun
Al-Bayan (New York)

Beaver (OK) Herald
Detroit Free Press
El Paso Herald
Fort Worth Gazette
Guthrie (OK) Daily Leader
Herald-Republican (Salt Lake City)
Highland Recorder (Monterey, VA)
Al-Hoda (New York)
Al-Jami'a (Cairo, NY)
Jonesboro (AR) Weekly Sun
Al-Kalimat (New York)
Kawkab America (New York)
La Crosse (WI) Chronicle
Los Angeles Herald
Louisville (KY) Courier-Journal
Meraat-ul-Gharb (New York)
Morning Olympian-Tribune (Olympia, WA)
Nashville American
New York Sun
New York Times
Okeene (OK) Eagle
Oklahoma Leader (Guthrie, OK)
Philadelphia Inquirer
Al-Sa'ih (New York)
Scranton (PA) Tribune
The Survey (New York)
Tensas Gazette (St. Joseph, LA)
Vici (OK) Beacon
Al-Wafa' (Lawrence, MA)
Washington Times (Washington, DC)

ALL OTHER CITED SOURCES

Abdulhadi, Rabab. "Sexualities and the Social Order in Arab and Muslim Communities." In *Islam and Homosexuality*, edited by Samar Habib, 463–88. Santa Barbara, CA: Praeger, 2010.

Abdulhadi, Rabab, Evelyn Alsultany, and Nadine Naber, eds. *Arab and Arab American Feminisms: Gender, Violence, and Belonging*. Syracuse, NY: Syracuse University Press, 2011.

Abu-Khalil, As'ad. "A Note on the Study of Homosexuality in the Arab/Islamic Civilization." *Arab Studies Journal* 1, no. 2 (1993): 32–48.

Abu-Laban, Baha, and Michael W. Suleiman, eds. *Arab Americans: Continuity and Change*. Belmont, MA: Association of Arab-American University Graduates, 1989.

Abu-Lughod, Lila. "Seductions of the 'Honor Crime.'" *differences* 22, no. 1 (2011): 17–63.

Aghdasifar, Tahereh. "Rhythms of the Banal: Tracing Homosociality in Iranian Bra Shops." *Women and Performance: A Journal of Feminist Theory* 30, no. 2 (2020): 195–213.

Aikin, Roger Cushing. "Was Jud Jewish? Property, Ethnicity, and Gender in *Oklahoma!*" *Quarterly Review of Film and Video* 22, no. 3 (2005): 277–83.

Alfaro-Velcamp, Theresa. *So Far from Allah, So Close to Mexico: Middle Eastern Immigrants in Modern Mexico*. Austin: University of Texas Press, 2007.

Alloula, Malek. *The Colonial Harem*. Translated by Myrna Godzich and Wlad Godzich. Minneapolis: University of Minnesota Press, 1986.

Amer, Sahar. "Medieval Arab Lesbians and Lesbian-Like Women." *Journal of the History of Sexuality* 18, no. 2 (2009): 215–36.

Amin, Kadji. *Disturbing Attachments: Genet, Modern Pederasty, and Queer History*. Durham, NC: Duke University Press, 2017.

———. "Haunted by the 1990s: Queer Theory's Affective Histories." In *Imagining Queer Methods*, edited by Amin Ghaziani and Matt Brimm, 277–93. New York: New York University Press, 2019.

Arondekar, Anjali R. *For the Record: On Sexuality and the Colonial Archive in India*. Durham, NC: Duke University Press, 2009.

———. "In the Absence of Reliable Ghosts: Sexuality, Historiography, South Asia." *Differences* 25, no. 3 (September 1, 2014): 98–122.

Arondekar, Anjali, and Geeta Patel. "Area Impossible: Notes toward an Introduction." *GLQ: A Journal of Lesbian and Gay Studies* 22, no. 2 (2016): 151–71.

Arondekar, Anjali, Ann Cvetkovich, Christina B. Hanhardt, Regina Kunzel, Tavia Nyong'o, Juana María Rodríguez, Susan Stryker, Daniel Marshall, Kevin P. Murphy, and Zeb Tortorici. "Queering Archives: A Roundtable Discussion." *Radical History Review* 2015, no. 122 (2015): 211–31.

Aryain, Ed, and J'Nell Pate. *From Syria to Seminole: Memoir of a High Plains Merchant*. Lubbock: Texas Tech University Press, 2006.

Aswad, Barbara C. *Arabic Speaking Communities in American Cities*. Staten Island: Center for Migration Studies of New York, 1974.

Associated Charities of Boston. *Annual Report*. Boston: various publishers, 1880–1905.

Babayan, Kathryn, and Afsaneh Najmabadi, eds. *Islamicate Sexualities: Translations across Temporal Geographies of Desire*. Cambridge, MA: Harvard University Press, 2008.

Bald, Vivek. *Bengali Harlem and the Lost Histories of South Asian America*. Cambridge, MA: Harvard University Press, 2013.

Barthes, Roland. *Camera Lucida: Reflections on Photography*. New York: Macmillan, 1981.

Bawardi, Hani J. *The Making of Arab Americans: From Syrian Nationalism to U.S. Citizenship*. Austin: University of Texas Press, 2015.

Berlant, Lauren Gail. *The Queen of America Goes to Washington City: Essays on Sex and Citizenship*. Durham, NC: Duke University Press, 1997.

Berman, Jacob Rama. *American Arabesque: Arabs, Islam, and the 19th-Century Imaginary*. New York: New York University Press, 2012.

Betts, Gregory K. "Wanted Women, Woman's Wants: The Colonial Harem and Post-colonial Discourse." *Canadian Review of Comparative Literature* 22, no. 3–4 (1995): 527–55.

Beydoun, Khaled A. "Between Muslim and White: The Legal Construction of Arab American Identity." *New York University Annual Survey of American Law* 69, no. 1 (2013): 29–76.

Birla, Ritu. *Stages of Capital: Law, Culture, and Market Governance in Late Colonial India*. Durham, NC: Duke University Press, 2009.

Braunlich, Phyllis Cole. *Haunted by Home: The Life and Letters of Lynn Riggs*. Norman: University of Oklahoma Press, 2002.

Brown, Elspeth H., and Thy Phu, eds. *Feeling Photography*. Durham, NC: Duke University Press, 2014.

Brown, Kirby. *Stoking the Fire: Nationhood in Cherokee Writing, 1907–1970*. Norman: University of Oklahoma Press, 2019.

Cable, Umayyah. "An Uprising at the Perfect Moment: Palestine in the 1990s Culture Wars." *GLQ: A Journal of Lesbian and Gay Studies* 26, no. 2 (2020): 243–72.

Cadava, Eduardo. *Words of Light: Theses on the Photography of History*. Princeton, NJ: Princeton University Press, 1998.

Cainkar, Louise. "Palestinian Women in the United States: Coping with Tradition, Change, and Alienation." PhD diss., Northwestern University, 1988. ProQuest.

Caldwell, Tom Joe. "The Syrian-Lebanese in Oklahoma." PhD diss., University of Oklahoma, 1984. ProQuest.

Campt, Tina M. *Image Matters: Archive, Photography, and the Making of the African Diaspora in Europe*. Durham, NC: Duke University Press, 2012.

Canaday, Margot. *The Straight State: Sexuality and Citizenship in Twentieth-Century America*. Princeton, NJ: Princeton University Press, 2009.

Carter, Tim. *Oklahoma! The Making of an American Musical*. New Haven, CT: Yale University Press, 2007.

Caton, Steven C. "The Sheik: Instabilities of Race and Gender in Transatlantic Popular Culture of the Early 1920s." In *Noble Dreams, Wicked Pleasures: Orientalism in America, 1870–1930*, edited by Holly Edwards, 99–117. Princeton, NJ: Princeton University Press, 2000.

Chang, David. *The Color of the Land: Race, Nation, and the Politics of Landownership in Oklahoma, 1832–1929*. Chapel Hill: University of North Carolina Press, 2010.

Cohen, Cathy J. "Punks, Bulldaggers, and Welfare Queens: The Radical Potential of Queer Politics?" *GLQ: A Journal of Lesbian and Gay Studies* 3, no. 4 (1997): 437–65.

Conklin, Nancy Faires, and Nora Faires. "'Colored' and Catholic: The Lebanese in Birmingham, Alabama." In Hooglund, *Crossing the Waters*, 69–84.

Cory, Sheila G. "The Women from the Levant: A Study in Cultural Appropriation." MA thesis, California State University, Fresno, 1996.

Craver, Earlene. "On the Boundary of White: The Cartozian Naturalization Case and the Armenians, 1923–1925." *Journal of American Ethnic History* 28, no. 2 (2009): 30–56.

Djebar, Assia. "A Forbidden Glimpse, a Broken Sound (from *Women of Algiers in Their Apartment*)." In *Women and the Family in the Middle East: New Voices of Change*, edited by Elizabeth Warnock Fernea, 337–50. Austin: University of Texas Press, 1985.

Dresbach, Glenn Ward. "The Syrian Peddler." *Poetry* 23, no. 6 (1924): 314–15.

Driskill, Qwo-Li, Chris Finley, Brian Joseph Gilley, and Scott Lauria Morgensen, eds. *Queer Indigenous Studies: Critical Interventions in Theory, Politics, and Literature*. Tucson: University of Arizona Press, 2011.

Dyer, Richard. *White*. New York: Routledge, 1997.

Edwards, Elizabeth, and Janice Hart, eds. *Photographs Objects Histories: On the Materiality of Images*. New York: Routledge, 2004.

El-Rouayheb, Khaled. *Before Homosexuality in the Arab-Islamic World, 1500–1800*. Chicago: University of Chicago Press, 2009.

Eng, David L. "Out Here and Over There: Queerness and Diaspora in Asian American Studies." *Social Text* 52–53 (1997): 31–52.

Fahrenthold, Stacy D. *Between the Ottomans and the Entente: The First World War in the Syrian and Lebanese Diaspora, 1908–1925*. New York: Oxford University Press, 2019.

———. "Ladies Aid as Labor History: Working-Class Formation in the Mahjar." *Journal of Middle East Women's Studies* 17, no. 3 (2021): 326–47.

———. "Transnational Modes and Media: The Syrian Press in the Mahjar and Emigrant Activism during World War I." *Mashriq and Mahjar Journal of Middle East and North African Migration Studies* 1, no. 1 (2013): 34–63.

Fay, Mary Ann. "Old Roots—New Soil." In Zogby, *Taking Root, Bearing Fruit*, 17–23.

Ferguson, Roderick A. *Aberrations in Black: Toward a Queer of Color Critique*. Minneapolis: University of Minnesota Press, 2004.

Fraser, Nancy, and Linda Gordon. "A Genealogy of Dependency: Tracing a Keyword of the U.S. Welfare State." *Signs* 19, no. 2 (1994): 309–36.

"From *Mahatta* to 'Little Assyria': The Beginnings of a Permanent Syrian Presence in La Crosse." *Past, Present, and Future: The Magazine of the La Crosse County Historical Society* 24, no. 3 (June 2002): 5–6.

Furumoto, Kim Benita, and David Theo Goldberg. "Boundaries of the Racial State: Two Faces of Racist Exclusion in United States Law." *Harvard Blackletter Law Journal* 17 (2001): 85–112.

Garber, Marjorie. *Vested Interests: Cross-Dressing and Cultural Anxiety*. New York: Routledge, 1997.

Georgis, Dina. *The Better Story: Queer Affects from the Middle East*. Albany: State University of New York Press, 2013.

Gopinath, Gayatri. *Impossible Desires: Queer Diasporas and South Asian Public Cultures*. Durham, NC: Duke University Press, 2005.

———. *Unruly Visions: The Aesthetic Practices of Queer Diaspora*. Durham, NC: Duke University Press, 2018.

Gordon, Avery. *Ghostly Matters: Haunting and the Sociological Imagination*. Minneapolis: University of Minnesota Press, 2008.

Graham-Brown, Sarah. *Images of Women: The Portrayal of Women in Photography of the Middle East, 1860–1950*. New York: Columbia University Press, 1988.

Gualtieri, Sarah M. A. *Arab Routes: Pathways to Syrian California*. Stanford, CA: Stanford University Press, 2019.

———. *Between Arab and White: Race and Ethnicity in the Early Syrian American Diaspora*. Berkeley: University of California Press, 2009.

———. "From Lebanon to Louisiana: 'Afifa Karam and Arab Women's Writing in Diaspora." In *Arab American Women: Representation and Refusal*, edited by Michael W. Suleiman, Suad Jospeh, and Louise Cainkar, 169–88. Syracuse, NY: Syracuse University Press, 2021.

———. "The Syrian of Sleepy Lagoon: Ethnic Coalitions and Archival Silence." *American Quarterly* 71, no. 2 (2019): 425–47.

Habib, Samar, ed. *Islam and Homosexuality*. 2 vols. Santa Barbara, CA: Praeger, 2009–10.

Haddad, 'Abd al-Masih. "Timthal al-Hurriya." In *Hikayat Al-Mahjar*, 178–82. New York: al-Matba'ah al-Tijerina al-Amrikiyah, 1921.

Haddad, Safia F. "The Woman's Role in the Socialization of Syrian-Americans in Chicago." In *The Arab Americans: Studies in Assimilation*, edited by Elaine Hagopian and Ann Paden. Wilmette, IL: Median University Press International, 1969.

Hagopian, Elaine Catherine. "The Institutional Development of the Arab-American Community of Boston: A Sketch." In *The Arab Americans: Studies in Assimilation*, edited by Elaine Hagopian and Ann Paden. Wilmette, IL: Medina University Press International, 1969.

Hakim, Randa, Marilyn Drath, Marjorie Stevens, and Claire Kempa. "Annie Abdo: A Peddler . . . a Tulsa Woman." Khayrallah Center for Lebanese Diaspora Studies News, Moise A. Khayrallah Center for Lebanese Diaspora Studies, October, 10, 2018. https://lebane sestudies.news.chass.ncsu.edu/2018/10/10/annie-abdo-a-peddler-a-tulsa-woman/.

Halberstam, Jack. "Queer Faces: Photography and Subcultural Lives." In *The Visual Culture Reader*, 3rd ed., edited by Nicholas Mirzoeff. New York: Routledge, 2013.

Halaby, Raouf J. "Dr. Michael Shadid and the Debate over Identity in 'The Syrian World.'" In Hooglund, *Crossing the Waters*, 55–65.

Haney López, Ian. *White by Law: The Legal Construction of Race*. New York: New York University Press, 1997.

Harris, Cheryl I. "Whiteness as Property." *Harvard Law Review* (1993): 1707–1791.

Hartman, Saidiya. "Venus in Two Acts." *Small Axe: A Caribbean Journal of Criticism* 12, no. 2 (2008): 1–14.

———. *Wayward Lives, Beautiful Experiments: Intimate Histories of Social Upheaval*. New York: W. W. Norton, 2020.

Hassoun, Rosina "Class and Color among Arab Americans: The Truly Invisible Arab Americans." Paper presented at the Arab American Studies Association Conference, Dearborn, MI, April 2014.

Hirsch, Julia. *Family Photographs: Content, Meaning, and Effect*. New York: Oxford University Press, 1981.

Hitti, Philip K. *The Syrians in America*. New York: George H. Doran Company, 1924.

Hoganson, Kristin L. *Consumers' Imperium: The Global Production of American Domesticity, 1865–1920*. Chapel Hill: University of North Carolina Press, 2007.

Holland, Patricia. "Introduction: History, Memory, and the Family Album." In *Family Snaps: The Meaning of Domestic Photography*, edited by Jo Spence and Patricia Holland, 1–14. London: Virago, 1991.

Hooglund, Eric J., ed. *Taking Root*. Volume 2: *Arab-American Community Studies*. Arab-American Anti-Discrimination Committee, 1985.

———, ed. *Crossing the Waters: Arabic-Speaking Immigrants to the United States before 1940*. Washington, DC: Smithsonian Institution Press, 1987.

hooks, bell. "In Our Glory: Photography and Black Life." In *The Photography Reader*, edited by Liz Wells, 378–94. New York: Routledge, 2003.

Hourani, Guita. "'Aqlah Brice Al Shidyaq: A Woman Peddler from Northern Lebanon." *Al-Raida* 24 (2007): 116–17.

Howard, John. *Men Like That: A Southern Queer History*. Chicago: University of Chicago Press, 2001.

Howell, Sally. "Picturing Women, Class, and Community in Arab Detroit: The Strange Case of Eva Habib." *Visual Anthropology* 10, nos. 2–4 (January 1998): 209–25.

Ibson, John. *Picturing Men: A Century of Male Relationships in Everyday American Photography*. Chicago: University of Chicago Press, 2006.

"In Memoriam: Alixa Naff (1919–2013)." *Arab Studies Quarterly* 35, no. 4 (Fall 2013): 340–42.

Jacob, Wilson Chacko. "The Middle East: Global, Postcolonial, Regional, and Queer." *International Journal of Middle East Studies* 45, no. 2 (2013): 347–49.

Jacobs, Linda K. *Strangers in the West: The Syrian Colony of New York City, 1880–1900*. New York: Kalimah Press, 2015.

———. *Strangers No More: Syrians in the United States, 1880–1900*. New York: Kalimah Press, 2019.

Jacobsen, Matthew Frye. *Whiteness of a Different Color: European Immigrants and the Alchemy of Race*. Cambridge, MA: Harvard University Press, 1998.

Jarmakani, Amira. *Imagining Arab Womanhood: The Cultural Mythology of Veils, Harems, and Belly Dancers in the U.S.* New York: Palgrave Macmillan, 2008.

———. *An Imperialist Love Story: Desert Romances and the War on Terror*. New York: New York University Press, 2015.

Joseph, Suad. "Introduction: Family in the Arab Region; State of Scholarship." In *Arab Family Studies: Critical Reviews*, edited by Suad Joseph, 1–14. Syracuse, NY: Syracuse University Press, 2018.

———. "Introduction: Theories and Dynamics of Gender, Self, and Identity in Arab Families." In *Intimate Selving in Arab Families: Gender, Self, and Identity*, edited by Suad Joseph, 1–17. Syracuse, NY: Syracuse University Press, 1999.

John, Sarah E. "Arabic-Speaking Immigration to the El Paso Area, 1900–1935." In Hooglund, *Crossing the Waters*, 105–17.

Kadi, Joe, ed. *Food for Our Grandmothers: Writings by Arab-American and Arab-Canadian Feminists*. Boston: South End Press, 1994.

Al-Kassim, Dina. "Psychoanalysis and the Postcolonial Genealogy of Queer Theory." *International Journal of Middle East Studies* 45, no. 2 (2013): 343–46.

Katibah, H. I., and Farhat Jacob Ziadeh. *Arabic-Speaking Americans*. New York: Institute of Arab American Affairs, 1946.

Karem Albrecht, Charlotte. "An Archive of Difference: Syrian Women, the Peddling Economy, and US Social Welfare, 1880–1935." *Gender and History* 28, no. 1 (2016): 134–35.

———. "Narrating Arab American History: The Peddling Thesis." *Arab Studies Quarterly* 37, no. 1 (2015): 100–117, https://doi.org/10.13169/arabstudquar.37.1.0100.

———. "Why Arab American History Needs Queer of Color Critique." *Journal of American Ethnic History* 37, no. 3 (2018): 84–92.

Kayal, Philip M., and Joseph M. Kayal. *The Syrian-Lebanese in America: A Study in Religion and Assimilation*. New York: Twayne, 1975.

Keeling, Kara. "Looking for M—: Queer Temporality, Black Political Possibility, and Poetry from the Future." *GLQ: A Journal of Lesbian and Gay Studies* 15, no. 4 (2009): 565–82.

Khater, Akram. *Inventing Home: Emigration, Gender, and the Middle Class in Lebanon, 1870–1920*. Berkeley: University of California Press, 2001.

———. "Like Pure Gold: Sexuality and Honour amongst Lebanese Emigrants, 1890–1920." In *Sexuality in the Arab World*, edited by Samir Khalaf and John H. Gagnon. London: Saqi Books, 2006.

Kirle, Bruce. "Reconciliation, Resolution, and the Political Role of *Oklahoma!* in American Consciousness." *Theatre Journal* (2003): 251–74.

Kollin, Susan. *Captivating Westerns: The Middle East in the American West.* Lincoln: University of Nebraska Press, 2019.

Kozol, Wendy. "Relocating Citizenship in Photographs of Japanese Americans during World War II." In *Haunting Violations: Feminist Criticism and the Crisis of the "Real,"* edited by Wendy S. Hesford and Wendy Kozol. Urbana: University of Illinois Press, 2001.

Kunzel, Regina G. *Fallen Women, Problem Girls: Unmarried Mothers and the Professionalization of Social Work, 1890–1945.* New Haven, CT: Yale University Press, 1993.

———. "The Power of Queer History." *American Historical Review* 123, no. 5 (2018): 1560–82.

Lorde, Audre. "Uses of the Erotic: The Erotic as Power." In *Sister Outsider.* Berkeley, CA: Crossing Press, 1984.

Lowe, Lisa. "History Hesitant." *Social Text* 33, no. 4 (2015): 85–107.

———. *The Intimacies of Four Continents.* Durham, NC: Duke University Press, 2015.

Luibhéid, Eithne. *Entry Denied: Controlling Sexuality at the Border.* Minneapolis: University of Minnesota Press, 2002.

Macharia, Keguro. "belated: interruption." *GLQ: A Journal of Lesbian and Gay Studies* 26, no. 3 (2020): 561–73.

———. "On Being Area-Studied: A Litany of Complaint." *GLQ: A Journal of Lesbian and Gay Studies* 22, no. 2 (2016): 183–190.

Maghbouleh, Neda. *The Limits of Whiteness: Iranian Americans and the Everyday Politics of Race.* Stanford, CA: Stanford University Press, 2017.

Majaj, Lisa Suheir. "Arab Americans and the Meanings of Race." In *Postcolonial Theory and the United States: Race, Ethnicity, and Literature,* edited by Amritjit Singh and Peter Schmidt. Jackson: University of Mississippi Press, 2000.

Manalansan, Martin F., IV. "Messing Up Sex: The Promises and Possibilities of Queer of Color Critique." *Sexualities* 21, no. 8 (2018): 1287–90.

———. "The 'Stuff' of Archives: Mess, Migration, and Queer Lives." *Radical History Review* 2014, no. 120 (2014): 94–107.

Massad, Joseph Andoni. *Desiring Arabs.* Chicago: University of Chicago Press, 2008.

Mendoza, Victor Román. *Metroimperial Intimacies: Fantasy, Racial-Sexual Governance, and the Philippines in US Imperialism, 1899–1913.* Durham, NC: Duke University Press, 2016.

Mikdashi, Maya, and Jasbir K. Puar. "Queer Theory and Permanent War." *GLQ: A Journal of Lesbian and Gay Studies* 22, no. 2 (2016): 215–22.

Mimura, Glen M. "A Dying West? Reimagining the Frontier in Frank Matsura's Photography, 1903–1913." *American Quarterly* 62, no. 3 (2010): 687–716.

Mink, Gwendolyn. "The Lady and the Tramp: Gender, Race, and the Origins of the American Welfare State." In *Women, the State, and Welfare,* edited by Linda Gordon. Madison: University of Wisconsin Press, 1990.

Miranda, Deborah. "Extermination of the 'Joyas': Gendercide in Spanish California." *GLQ: A Journal of Lesbian and Gay Studies* 16, nos. 1–2 (2010): 253–84.

Mohl, Raymond. "Cultural Pluralism in Immigrant Education: The International Institutes of Boston, Philadelphia, and San Francisco, 1920–1940." *Journal of American Ethnic History* 1, no. 2 (1982): 35–58.

Moloney, Deirdre M. *National Insecurities: Immigrants and U.S. Deportation Policy since 1882.* Chapel Hill: University of North Carolina Press, 2016.

———. "Women, Sexual Morality, and Economic Dependency in Early U.S. Deportation Policy." *Journal of Women's History* 18, no. 2 (2006): 95–122.

Most, Andrea. "We Know We Belong to the Land: The Theatricality of Assimilation in Rodgers and Hammerstein's *Oklahoma!*" *Publications of the Modern Language Association of America* (1998): 77–89.

———. *Making Americans: Jews and the Broadway Musical.* Cambridge, MA: Harvard University Press, 2004.

Munshi, Sherally. "'You Will See My Family Became So American': Toward a Minor Comparativism." *American Journal of Comparative Law* 63, no. 3 (2015): 655–718.

Naber, Nadine. *Arab America: Gender, Cultural Politics, and Activism.* New York: New York University Press, 2012.

Naff, Alixa. *Becoming American: The Early Arab Immigrant Experience.* Carbondale: Southern Illinois University Press, 1985.

———. "The Arabic-Language Press." In *The Ethnic Press in the United States: A Historical Analysis and Handbook,* edited by Sally M. Miller, 1–14. Westport, CT: Greenwood, 1987.

Najmabadi, Afsaneh. *Women with Mustaches and Men without Beards.* Berkeley: University of California Press, 2005.

National Conference of Social Work. *Proceedings: Selected Papers of the Annual Meeting.* Various publishers, 1890–1925.

Olwan, Dana. *Gender Violence and the Transnational Politics of the Honor Crime.* Columbus: Ohio State University Press, 2021.

Ong, Aihwa. *Buddha Is Hiding: Refugees, Citizenship, the New America.* Berkeley: University of California Press, 2003.

Pegler-Gordon, Anna. "Chinese Exclusion, Photography, and the Development of U.S. Immigration Policy." *American Quarterly* 58, no. 1 (2006): 51–77.

———. *In Sight of America: Photography and the Development of U.S. Immigration Policy.* Berkeley: University of California Press, 2009.

Pérez, Emma. *The Decolonial Imaginary: Writing Chicanas into History.* Bloomington: Indiana University Press, 1999.

———. "Queering the Borderlands: The Challenges of Excavating the Invisible and Unheard." *Frontiers: A Journal of Women Studies* 24, no. 2 (2004): 122–31.

Peterson, Jane. "Houston: In the Heart of Texas." In Zogby, *Taking Root, Bearing Fruit,* 61–65.

Phu, Thy. *Picturing Model Citizens: Civility in Asian American Visual Culture.* Philadelphia: Temple University Press, 2012.

Pollack-Pelzner, Daniel. "The Hidden History of 'Oklahoma!'" *Faculty Publications,* Submission 51 (2018). Linfield University. https://digitalcommons.linfield.edu/englfac_pubs/51.

Potter, Claire Bond. "Queer Hoover: Sex, Lies, and Political History." *Journal of the History of Sexuality* 15, no. 3 (2006): 355–81.

Puar, Jasbir K. *Terrorist Assemblages: Homonationalism in Queer Times.* Durham, NC: Duke University Press, 2007.

Rana, Junaid. "The Story of Islamophobia." *Souls* 9, no. 2 (June 6, 2007): 148–61.

Riggs, Lynn. *The Cherokee Night and Other Plays.* Norman: University of Oklahoma Press, 2003.

———. *Knives from Syria.* In *One Act Plays for Stage and Study.* New York: Samuel French, 1927.

Rodgers, Richard, and Oscar Hammerstein II. *Oklahoma! A Musical Play*. London: Williamson Music, 1943.

Rogerson, Stephanie. "Without Words You Spoke: Early Snapshot Photography and Queer Representation." *Afterimage* 36, no. 1 (2008): 10–13.

Said, Edward W. *Orientalism*. New York: Vintage Books, 1979.

Samhan, Helen Hatab. "Politics and Exclusion: The Arab American Experience." *Journal of Palestine Studies* 16, no. 2 (1987): 11–28.

———. "Not Quite White: Race Classification and the Arab-American Experience." In *Arabs in America: Building a New Future*, edited by Michael W. Suleiman, 209–26. Philadelphia: Temple University Press, 1999.

———. "Farewell to the Grande Dame of Arab American Social History." *Arab Studies Quarterly* 37, no. 1 (Winter 2015): 96–99.

Sawaie, Mohammed. "Arabic in the Melting Pot: Will It Survive?" In *The Arabic Language in America*, edited by Aleya Rouchdy, 83–99. Detroit: Wayne State University Press, 1992.

Saylor, Elizabeth Claire. "Subversive Sisterhood." *Journal of Middle East Women's Studies* 15, no. 1 (2019): 3–23.

Schechla, Joseph. "Dabkeh in the Delta." In Hooglund, *Taking Root*, 25–58.

———. "The Mohameds in Mississippi." In Hooglund, *Taking Root*, 59–68.

Schweik, Susan M. *The Ugly Laws: Disability in Public*. New York: New York University Press, 2010.

Sekula, Allan. "The Body and the Archive." In *Contest of Meaning: Critical Histories of Photography*, edited by Richard Bolton. Cambridge, MA: MIT Press, 1992.

Shadid, Michael. *Crusading Doctor: My Fight for Cooperative Medicine*. Boston: Meador, 1956.

———. *Doctors of Today and Tomorrow*. New York: Cooperative League of the U.S.A., 1947.

Shah, Nayan. "Between 'Oriental Depravity' and 'Natural Degenerates': Spatial Borderlands and the Making of Ordinary Americans." *American Quarterly* 57, no. 3 (2005): 703–25.

———. *Contagious Divides: Epidemics and Race in San Francisco's Chinatown*. Berkeley: University of California Press, 2001.

———. "Policing Privacy, Migrants, and the Limits of Freedom." *Social Text* 23, nos. 3–4 (2005): 275–84.

———. "Queer of Color Estrangement and Belonging." In *The Routledge History of Queer America*, edited by Don Romesburg, 262–75. New York: Routledge, 2018.

———. *Stranger Intimacy: Contesting Race, Sexuality, and the Law in the North American West*. Berkeley: University of California Press, 2012.

Shakir, Evelyn. *Bint Arab: Arab and Arab American Women in the United States*. Westport, CT: Praeger, 1997.

Sheehi, Stephen. "A Social History of Early Arab Photography, or a Prolegomenon to an Archaeology of the Lebanese Imago." *International Journal of Middle East Studies* 39, no. 2 (2007): 177–208.

Al Shidyaq, Edward Brice. "Sitta ʿAqlah: A Woman of Faith, Strength, and Dignity. From Blawza to Wheeling, West Virginia." *Journal of Maronite Studies* 1, no. 3 (1997): 3.

Shohat, Ella. "Dislocated Identities: Reflections of an Arab Jew." In *On the Arab-Jew, Palestine, and Other Displacements*, 77–82. London: Pluto Press, 2017.

Shomali, Mejdulene B. *Between Banat: Queer Arab Critique and Transnational Arab Archives*. Durham, NC: Duke University Press, forthcoming.

———. "Dancing Queens: Queer Desire in Golden Era Egyptian Cinema." *Journal of Middle East Women's Studies* 15, no. 2 (2019): 135–56.

———. "Scheherazade and the Limits of Inclusive Politics in Arab American Literature." *MELUS* 43, no. 1 (2018): 65–90.

Simpson, Leanne Betasamosake. *As We Have Always Done: Indigenous Freedom through Radical Resistance*. Minneapolis, University of Minnesota Press, 2017.

Smith, Shawn Michelle. *American Archives: Gender, Race, and Class in Visual Culture*. Princeton, NJ: Princeton University Press, 1999.

Somerville, Siobhan B. "Notes toward a Queer History of Naturalization." *American Quarterly* 57, no. 3 (2005): 659–75.

———. "Queer." In *Keywords for American Cultural Studies*, 2nd ed., edited by Bruce Burgett and Glenn Handler, 198–202. New York: New York University Press, 2020.

———. *Queering the Color Line: Race and the Invention of Homosexuality in American Culture*. Durham, NC: Duke University Press, 2000.

Spence, Jo, and Patricia Holland, eds. *Family Snaps: The Meaning of Domestic Photography*. London: Virago, 1991.

Spivak, Gayatri Chakravorty. *In Other Worlds: Essays in Cultural Politics*. New York: Routledge, 1988.

Steet, Linda. *Veils and Daggers: A Century of National Geographic's Representation of the Arab World*. Philadelphia: Temple University Press, 2000.

Stiffler, Matthew Jaber. "A Brief History of Arab Immigrant Textile Production in the US." Dearborn, MI: Arab American National Museum, 2010.

Stockton, Ronald. "Ethnic Archetypes and the Arab Image." In *The Development of Arab-American Identity*, edited by Earnest McCarus, 119–153. Ann Arbor: University of Michigan Press, 1994.

Studlar, Gaylyn. "Discourses of Gender and Ethnicity: The Construction and De(con)structionj of Rudolph Valentino as Other." *Film Criticism* 13, no. 2 (1989): 18–35.

Tagg, John. *The Burden of Representation: Essays on Photographies and Histories*. Minneapolis: University of Minnesota Press, 1993.

Tannous, Afif I. "Acculturation of an Arab-Syrian Community in the Deep South." *American Sociological Review* 8, no. 3 (June 1943): 264–71.

Tehranian, John. *Whitewashed: America's Invisible Middle Eastern Minority*. New York: New York University Press, 2010.

Tice, Karen Whitney. *Tales of Wayward Girls and Immoral Women: Case Records and the Professionalization of Social Work*. Urbana: University of Illinois Press, 1998.

Ting, Jennifer. "Bachelor Society: Deviant Heterosexuality and Asian American Historiography." In *Privileging Positions: The Sites of Asian American Studies*, edited by Marilyn Alquizola, Gary Okihiro, Dorothy Fujita Rony, and Wong K. Scott, 271–79. Pullman: Washington State University Press, 1995.

Tinsley, Omise'eke Natasha. *Thiefing Sugar: Eroticism between Women in Caribbean Literature*. Durham, NC: Duke University Press, 2010.

Tompkins, Kyla Wazana. "Intersections of Race, Gender, and Sexuality: Queer of Color Critique." In *The Cambridge Companion to American Gay and Lesbian Literature*, edited by Scott Herring, 173–89. New York: Cambridge University Press, 2015.

———. "'You Make Me Feel Right Quare': Promiscuous Reading, Minoritarian Critique, and White Sovereign Entrepreneurial Terror." *Social Text* 35, no. 4 (2017): 53–86.

Toth, Anthony. "Birmingham: The Politics of Survival." In Zogby, *Taking Root, Bearing Fruit*, 33–39.

———. "Jacksonville: As Salaam Aleikum, Y'all. In Zogby, *Taking Root, Bearing Fruit*, 67–71.

Traub, Valerie. *Thinking Sex with the Early Moderns*. Philadelphia: University of Pennsylvania Press, 2016.

Vicinus, Martha. "Lesbian History: All Theory and No Facts or All Facts and No Theory?" *Radical History Review* 1994, no. 60 (1994): 57–75.

Weaver, Jace. *That the People Might Live: Native American Literatures and Native American Community*. New York: Oxford University Press, 1997.

White, E. F. *Dark Continent of Our Bodies: Black Feminism and the Politics of Respectability*. Mapping Racisms 1. Philadelphia: Temple University Press, 2001.

Womack, Deanna Ferree. "Syrian Christians and Arab-Islamic Identity: Expressions of Belonging in the Ottoman Empire and America." *Studies in World Christianity* 25, no. 1 (2019): 29–49.

Younis, Adele L., and Philip M. Kayal, eds. *The Coming of the Arabic-Speaking People to the United States*. Staten Island: Center for Migration Studies, 1995.

Zaatari, Zeina. "Lebanon." In *Arab Family Studies: Critical Reviews*, edited by Suad Joseph, 190–211. Syracuse, NY: Syracuse University Press.

Zachs, Fruma, and Sharon Halevi. *Gendering Culture in Greater Syria: Intellectuals and Ideology in the Late Ottoman Period*. New York: I. B. Tauris, 2015.

Ze'evi, Dror. *Producing Desire: Changing Sexual Discourse in the Ottoman Middle East, 1500–1900*. Berkeley: University of California Press, 2006.

Zengin, Asli and Sertaç Sehlikoglu. "Everyday Intimacies of the Middle East." *Journal of Middle East Women's Studies* 12, no. 2 (2016): 139–42.

Zirbel, Katherine. "Amulets, Fortune-Telling, and Magic: Arab States (excepting North Africa)." In *Encyclopedia of Women and Islamic Cultures*, Suad Joseph, general ed. http://dx.doi.org.proxy.lib.umich.edu/10.1163/1872-5309_ewic_EWICCOM_0157a.

Zogby, James J., ed. *Taking Root, Bearing Fruit* [Volume 1]: *The Arab-American Experience*. Washington, DC: American-Arab Anti-Discrimination Committee, 1984.

AMERICAN CROSSROADS

Edited by Earl Lewis, George Lipsitz, George Sánchez, Dana Takagi, Laura Briggs, and Nikhil Pal Singh